The Philosopher's "I"

The Philosopher's "I"

Autobiography and the Search for the Self

J. Lenore Wright

State University of New York Press

cover art: Untitled oil painting by Sara D. Cocke. Used by permission of the artist.

Published by
State University of New York Press, Albany

Printed in the United States of America

For information, address State University of New York Press,
194 Washington Avenue, Suite 305, Albany, NY 12210–2384

Production by Michael Haggett
Marketing by Susan M. Petrie

Library of Congress Cataloging-in-Publication Data

Wright, J. Lenore, 1972–
The philosopher's I : autobiography and the search for the self / J. Lenore Wright.
p. cm.
Includes bibliographical references and index.
ISBN-13: 987-0-7914-6913-2 (hardcover : alk. paper)
ISBN-10: 0-7914-6913-1 (hardcover : alk. paper)
ISBN-13: 987-0-7914-6914-9 (pbk. : alk. paper)
ISBN-10: 0-7914-6914-X (pbk. : alk. paper)
1. Philosophers—Biography—History and criticism. 2. Autobiography. I. Title.

B104.W75 2006
920.001—dc22

2005036302

10 9 8 7 6 5 4 3 2 1

For George McFarland Luckey Jr. (Mac),
professor emeritus of philosophy at Morehead State University,
who taught me that philosophy begins with knowing the self.

Contents

Preface

In part V of "Little Gidding," *Four Quartets*, T. S. Eliot writes, "What we call a beginning is often the end/And to make an end is to make a beginning. The end is where we start from." The texts I explicate in this book represent ends and beginnings in various ways. As a collection of philosophical autobiographies, they symbolize the end of life's work, a looking back, a narrative gaze at oneself, a reflective glance at professional achievements. They also represent the burgeoning field of philosophical introspection and self-representation, an analytical scrutinizing of the self and the experience of personhood. As both a literary genre and a mode of exposition, philosophical autobiography exemplifies how beginnings and endings, introductions and conclusions, place boundaries around life, circumscribing the self that one subsequently investigates. Whatever the implications such boundaries occasion, we should remember that the boundaries we posit around us are flexible, that we do not entrench ourselves in solitude by creating beginnings and ends. We are both Inner and Outer beings. People come and go, they move in and out of our lives, they partake in our work, and they help us see what we want to see and what we need to see from inside our fields of vision. This analysis is no different. Many colleagues, professional and personal, have contributed to my understanding of philosophical autobiography, helping me see where I was going and where I needed to go. I am grateful for their assistance and encouragement.

First, I would like to thank three former professors, Carolyn Korsmeyer, Kah-Kyung Cho, and Jorge J. E. Gracia. This project owes much to their scholarly insights and generous spirits. Carolyn's openness to multiple domains of investigation and diverse philosophical analyses strengthens the critical perspective she brings to philosophy. Her own work integrates multiple viewpoints without undermining the rigor of analytic scholarship. Professor Cho's erudition transforms continental philosophy as it is generally understood in the United States into the arduous project characteristic of German universities. It was an honor to study under one of Hans-Georg Gadamer's star students. Jorge's commitment to accuracy appears in his insistence that one must grasp the presuppositions, the structure, and the concepts of philosophical theories if one is to understand them. He devotes himself to such a view of philosophy, laboring over ideas and exhibiting a willingness to consider every perspective with grave seriousness.

I must also express gratitude for the support of two colleagues and mentors, Anne-Marie Bowery and Carl Vaught (1939–2005). I had the pleasure of first interacting with Anne-Marie as a student at Baylor University. Because of her novel interpretations of Plato and her excellent teaching, I was able to understand the narrative and dramatic features of Platonic dialogues in new and exciting ways. Her tenacity is unparalleled, and the eye she brings to philosophy captures the nuances of philosophical ideas, nuances that too often remain unnoticed. Our ongoing conversations and collaboration have improved my written work and expanded my philosophical interests in important ways. I value her friendship and collegiality immensely. Dr. Vaught's approach to philosophy raised the level of philosophical investigation and dialogue to new heights. I had the good fortune to sit in on his Augustine seminar at Baylor University in the fall of 2003. It was a highlight of my recent academic experiences. His singular ability to generate a new lexicon and an analytical schema for concrete reflection engendered philosophy with much of its original meaning and thrust. Carl was a philosopher in the deepest sense of the term. I wondered at his ability to not only bridge the analytic and continental divide but also to transform it. In his hands, philosophy became a method for resolving problems and a means for elucidating human experience. I cannot express how grateful I am for his belief in my abilities and his many intellectual contributions to this book. His death has left a void in my life.

I must thank several individuals who contributed in different ways to this book. Amy Antoninka, Christi Hemati, and Sarah Weeks read and edited the manuscript. Amy's training in psychology added much to the psychosocial dimensions contained herein. She has left an indelible impression upon this manuscript. Christi's interpretative abilities helped me refine and clarify many of the analyses within this text. Sarah's reflections on popular culture and autobiography shaped my thinking in significant ways. Amy, Christi, and Sarah are excellent, budding philosophers. I look forward to watching their philosophical growth over the years to come. Also, I would like to thank Sara D. Cocke for permission to use her painting on the cover of this book.

Henry W. Wright, my colleague and husband, has given me years of unconditional support and encouragement. His incessant faith in me has made me who I am today. In addition, his philosophical insights bear upon my analysis in numerous ways. I cannot express my appreciation for his multiple readings and reviews of this book. I would not have completed this project without his support and feedback.

Finally, I must go back to one more beginning and thank my parents, Betty Mullins Womack and Carl Edward Womack Sr., for their support, encouragement, understanding, patience, and love. They were the first to teach me the meaning of commitment, the value of hard work, and the duties to oneself.

Introduction

Like Agathon, the vibrant poet of Plato's *Symposium*, we enact Socratic practices to catch a bit of wisdom.[1] Unlike Agathon, we must bind our search for truth to Plato. His dialogues contain the ideas and allegories that typify foundational metaphysics: the Forms, the Allegory of the Cave, the Divided Line, the Myth of Er. They convey poetical truth as well, such as the mythic view of love recited by the comic symposiast, Aristophanes: a tale of two split-aparts who long for reunion and wholeness. Finally, they elucidate key sociopolitical events and ideas of ancient history. References to military conflicts, historical persons, and celebrated gods abound. Together these threads of philosophy, myth, and history reveal the richness of Plato's insights, a richness expressed most poignantly in his teacher, Socrates.

Socrates never wrote down his philosophical ideas. This simple observation is integral to Plato's characterization of his teacher. As such, it acquires enormous yet ambiguous significance. On the one hand, Socrates' partial illiteracy is unimportant. Within the context of a shared public life—the *agora*, schools of sophistry, religious festivals, performance-driven poetry—Socrates had the requisite audience to advance his philosophical critiques. So he argued. He posed metaphysical questions to his students. He pressed public officials for reasoned beliefs. He sought truth. On the other hand, Socrates' partial illiteracy is paradoxical. He *could* write, and he formed important relationships with writers throughout his lifetime. He scripts poetry prior to the death scene in the *Phaedo*. He offers clear but conflicting views of writing throughout the dialogues. In the *Phaedrus,* for example, he elevates speech above writing by arguing that dependence on the written word weakens memory and dulls thought. Despite his objections, many of his famous students, such as Aristophanes, are writers. And Socrates acknowledges the value of written work in the *Symposium.*[2] Perhaps most importantly, Socrates' star pupil Plato grounds philosophy in the written word, thereby reconciling *mythos* and *logos* within the confines of truth seeking.

A playwright who aspired to the stature of Sophocles and Euripides, Plato spent his early life writing tragedies. Biographers of Classical Athens tell us that upon meeting Socrates, Plato burned his plays and pursued truth. Yet his love of wisdom and of Socrates did not spurn his love of writing. He continued to compose dialogues and letters. He wrote about Socrates and his disciples. And he may have written *for* Socrates. After all, Plato teaches us the Socratic Method. He describes the ever-barefoot and often unbathed Socrates. He depicts the snub-nosed teacher who breaks the hearts of young men. Plato preserves much of the life and work of the Western world's first great philosophy teacher. In his skilled hands, Socrates' death becomes a monumental triumph: Socrates died so that philosophy may live. For all of these reasons, the simple fact that Socrates did not write philosophical texts has deep and abiding significance.

Though he cannot save Socrates, Plato helps save Socratic philosophy. He recognizes the risks and limitations of his teacher's methods. Specifically, he foresees that philosophy too may die a tragic death if it remains bound to the Homeric epic, sophistic rhetoric, or Socratic orality. To guard against the demise of wisdom and our pursuit thereof, Plato puts thought to papyrus. His dialogues and letters shift the philosophical paradigm from the oral to the written arena, elevating dialectic as the primary mode of philosophical inquiry. His academy institutionalizes philosophy as a discipline in its own right, a discipline defined by its discursive narrative form. This shift from Socratic orality to written discourse transforms would-be philosophers into philosophers in the richest possible sense of the term.[3] As beneficiaries of the Socratic tradition, we owe a heavy debt to Plato.

Thanks in part to the legacy of Plato, we philosophers write. We write to clarify our ideas and to add precision to our arguments. We write to explain concepts that define and frame reality. We write to persuade fellow humans with propositions, analyses, and ideas. In striving to clarify, explain, and justify human existence, we endeavor to express our ideas interpersonally, inviting our audience to listen in and learn like Plato's students in the Academia more than 2,000 years ago.

There is a fourth kind of writing and reflection that is perhaps more compelling than all of the above: autobiographical writing. What I have in mind here is not autobiography per se, a genre whose proliferation in the past decade has overwhelmed even the most active readers. Rather, I speak of autobiographies written by philosophers; individuals such as St. Augustine, René Descartes, Michel Montaigne, Jean-Jacques Rousseau, Friedrich Nietzsche, and Jean-Paul Sartre who chose a life of unyielding self-examination. I do not intend to imply that autobiographies produced by nonphilosophers have nothing to teach us. Nor do I wish to imply that autobiography is necessarily philosophical. Some forms of self-narration raise questions that fall squarely within the domain of philosophy. But the recording of those narratives raises literary, psychological, and social queries as well.

What I am suggesting is that the form and content of some autobiographies lend themselves to an explicitly philosophical classification. Some writers incorporate philosophical concepts and language into the recounting of the self and/or their lives. Others write from within the tradition of philosophy; that is, they write as individuals who teach and write philosophy. Their public status as philosophers classifies their autobiographies (along with all written work they produce) as philosophical, even if we rarely acknowledge their self-narrational work as such. I contend that the term *philosophical auto-biography* applies to both kinds of autobiography.[4]

Rather than turning the mind's eye only to the reality beyond them, beneath them, over and above them, autobiographical philosophers consciously and mindfully focus their attention inward and unleash their analytical rigor upon themselves. They explicate the meaning of existence in existential, psychological, moral, aesthetical, and spiritual terms. They investigate personal thought and action as if they are words that carry meaning and texts that import wisdom. They pursue the riddle of the self as vigorously as other philosophical quandaries. For these philosophers, the unexamined self is not worth knowing.

Extending the analysis of Alexander Nehamas in *The Art of Living*, I argue that autobiographical philosophers form a collective of *uncommon*, *idiosyncratic*, and *artful* thinkers who use self-narration as a method of self-examination. Their philosophical *techné* makes them both remarkable and memorable.[5] Each narrator conveys self-knowledge in distinct ways and under different circumstances, presenting varying and vying methods for self-disclosure within their autobiographical accounts. Despite the significant philosophical and stylistic differences that emerge in their writing, a shared commitment to self-examination via self-ascription guides their work. For each, autobiography is more than an act of personal revelation; it is a mode of philosophical exposition. The act of recording life events and expounding upon the meaning of those events is a philosophical exercise: a process of revelation in which a particular image of oneself emerges *as a result of* one's ontological views of the self and *in response to* the rhetorical forces shaping self-representation.

Because of its dual function, philosophical autobiography necessitates a philosophical analysis (not merely a literary or historical reading). Philosophical autobiographers make implicit use of (and explicit reference to) metaphysical and epistemological positions as they formulate self-representations. The lenses through which they examine themselves—lenses that are shaped by philosophical accounts of the self—reflect distinct philosophical commitments. These commitments are not always apparent in nonphilosophical autobiography. To understand the richness of self-reflection and self-representation within philosophical autobiography, we must identify and evaluate the philosophical implications of first-person accounts of the self. We must unveil the self.

One way in which autobiographical philosophers exemplify the richness of human experience is by writing from the dual position of subject and object. As the *subject* of first-person writing, autobiographers extract and convey the meaning of individuated existence through the uniqueness of their lives. As the *object* of written inquiry, authors present records of their experiences and beliefs apart from the emotional and psychological nuances of their lives. Another way that self-disclosure via autobiography occurs is through the sometimes tacit appropriation of ontological views of the self and rhetorical dimensions of self-identity. Philosophers cannot make unexamined assumptions about representational relations that other autobiographers might be led to make, not if they wish to succeed at living an *artful* or self-examined life. Their personal beliefs about self-identity and their views about the relationship between objects and artifacts shape their written texts in profound ways. Their closeness to the questions raised by self-disclosure in a literary medium adds an additional layer of complexity to the study of autobiography. Hence, autobiographies by philosophers form a unique case study of self-disclosure and identity.

Though my view of the self does not correspond exactly to the constructivist view put forward by Nehamas, my understanding of the autobiographical process is consistent with his perspective on self-individuation, which appears early in the introduction to *The Art of Living*:

> The sort of self one constructs as a result of adopting certain theories is not simply a biographical matter. It is, much more importantly, a literary and philosophical accomplishment. . . . It is a philosophical accomplishment because the content and the nature of the self I describe . . . depends on holding views on issues that have traditionally been considered philosophical and not on anything one pleases. It is literary because the connection between those philosophical views is not only a matter of systematic logical interrelations, but also, more centrally, a matter of style. It is a question of putting those views together so that, even when the connections between them are not strictly logical, it makes psychological and interpretative sense to attribute them to a single, coherent character.[6]

Appropriating Nehamas's claim that self-construction is both a literary and philosophical accomplishment, I argue that the kinds of self-mapping that occur within autobiography occur on both ontological and rhetorical levels.

The endeavor to understand what I call *the autobiographing self* initiates a rhetorical and an ontological inquiry: an inquiry into the *subject*, the source of one's identity, and an inquiry into the *self*, the locus of one's experiences. True to its form, philosophical autobiography includes both a first-person literary perspective that maps the subject and a philosophically informed account that maps the self. First-person autobiography is the only form of self-inquiry that discloses the dual nature of the self—self qua self-examiner and self qua self-examinee. Ontologically, the self refers to a writer-self; rhetorically, the self represents an author-subject.

The interplay between the rhetorical and the ontological levels of self-representation within autobiography clarifies two features of the human experience: one's relationship to one's self and one's relationship to others. How is this interplay represented in autobiographical texts? The process of first-person mapping generates a distinct authorial voice, one that distances the writer from his or her life experiences, creating a rhetorical space within which a writer may stand and from which he or she may speak. The rhetorical space forms an authorial presence or a *persona* that narrates the text we read. Put differently, first-person autobiographical writing elevates the writer into an author who stands apart from his or her life, and must do so, in order to analyze that life, record it, comment upon it, and ultimately narrate it. Yet the author is only one of two figures in his or her story. Within the writer resides the being who lived the life, who endured the pain and joy of every moment, and the one who has been formed in character and behavior by the lived moments and experiences now appearing in print. Thinking and writing as both objective author and subjective source bifurcates the self into two distinct philosophical presences within the text: a rhetorical self and an ontological self. This bifurcation generates a unique bilateral perspective on the self—an external (Outer) perspective of the self as the referent of particular statements and actions, and an internal (Inner) perspective of the self as the active creator of one's statements and actions.[7]

Though the use of the Inner and Outer self as a framework to explain first-person self-narration is unique to my analysis, it is not the only dualistic framework that can be culled from (or applied to) philosophical autobiography. In *Ecce Homo*, Friedrich Nietzsche returns to the work he began in *The Birth of Tragedy*, depicting a transformed Apollo, the god of reason, and Dionysus, the god of passion, at battle within human society. René Descartes' mind-body dualism figures prominently in *The Meditations on First Philosophy*, a first-person account of Descartes' pseudoscientific philosophical system. In *Being and Nothingness*, Jean-Paul Sartre deconstructs the conception of humans as *Dasein* taught to him by his teacher, Martin Heidegger, that is, beings thrust into the world and defined by the contingencies to be encountered therein. Instead, Sartre argues that humans comport themselves toward the world in two ways: the *être-en-soi* (being-in-oneself) and the *être-pour-soi* (being-for-oneself). In *Confessions*, Augustine of Hippo speaks metaphorically of himself in the midst of his spiritual struggle as a house divided against itself.

Outside of first-person writing, our contemporary understanding of human sexuality (man/woman), our view of gender (male/female), and the characteristics associated with gender (masculine/feminine) typify our dependence on dualistic systems and binary distinctions. Dualistic modes of thinking circumscribe human experience. But they are misleading. Rather than defying our dualistic tendencies and embracing the complexity of humankind, we succumb to the seductive simplicity of modal opposition and cease investigating the layers of our existence—temporal, psychosocial, spiritual, historical, and metaphysical. Over time, we see ourselves as constructed, rhetorical beings only, rather than as deeply ontological and spiritual creatures. Soon we ignore the uniqueness of each individual's situation within his or her complex culture, choosing to describe human action according to one of several oppositional modes of behavior: good/bad, right/wrong, strong/weak.

With the aim of overcoming dualistic thinking, Carl G. Vaught argues that we must move beyond abstractions of the self. In *The Quest for Wholeness*, Vaught writes, "The quest for wholeness involves a delicate interplay between the individuality we express and the communities in which we participate, and it is the harmonious interconnection between individuation and participation that those who undertake it (the quest for wholeness) must attempt to achieve."[8] My analysis of the rhetorical self and the ontological self is consistent with Vaught's analysis. The ontological self that attempts to understand the nature and identity of its being in the world stands apart from the rhetorical self whose nature has been autobiographed. The truth about the self is that it is neither Inner nor Outer, neither given nor constructed, but something in between. Like a photographic negative, which when placed in the appropriate chemicals produces a positive image, self-representation divides the self, creating positive and negative images that tell *a* story, but not every story, about one's self. The self is neither the photographer nor the photograph; the self is the process in which the photographic elements converge to form an image. Philosophically informed autobiography challenges us to move beyond dualistic thinking and to theorize about the self anew.

To elucidate the relationship between the self qua rhetorical force and self qua ontological entity, I survey the first-person texts of five philosophers: Augustine of Hippo's *Confessions* (ca. 400 C. E.), René Descartes' *Meditations on First Philosophy* (1641), Jean-Jacques Rousseau's *The Confessions* (1782), Friedrich Nietzsche's *Ecce Homo* (w. 1888; pub. 1908), and Hazel Barnes's *The Story I Tell Myself* (1997). Spanning roughly 1,500 years, these rich and complex autobiographical accounts describe both an Inner and an Outer self. I aim to show that the first three privilege the Inner self, while the last two privilege the Outer self. Yet I also contend that in different ways these accounts attempt to unify the bifurcated self by locating a sense of self *between* the Inner and the Outer self and by affirming the subject's identity in the world. Comprehensive analyses of these texts as self-representational entities are conspicuously absent from the canon of philosophy. As we move further into a postmodern period of autobiography and memoir, the need for philosophical critiques of self-narration is greater than ever.

Recent scholarship surrounding philosophical autobiography helps fill this lamentable gap. In *The Self Imagined: Philosophical Reflections on the Social Character of Psyche* (1986), Karen Hanson correlates self-imagination and self-representation as she articulates a thoroughly modern conception of the self.[9] More recently, Michael Mateas and Phoebe Sengers juxtapose everything from Internet writing to personal memoirs to understand how narrative elements of contemporary culture shape intelligence (*Narrative Intelligence*, 2003). George Yancy entitles his recently edited anthology of essays by professional philosophers *The Philosophical I: Personal Reflections on Life in Philosophy* (2004). His collection includes practical advice to students and laypeople about how to live an examined life. And Shlomit C. Schuster's *The Philosopher's Autobiography: A Qualitative* Study (2003) provides an extensive and excellent introduction to philosophical autobiography. An esteemed scholar of philosophy and psychoanalysis, Schuster offers a systematic account of the subgenres of philosophical autobiography. She ends with a set of reflections on "the likelihood for persons to attain different selves through combining philosophical psychoanalysis with narrative writing."[10] Though my own analysis of philosophical autobiography differs significantly from Schuster's, I am both indebted to her work and immensely grateful for it.

In contrast to the aforementioned texts, my analysis shows how the embodiment of the ontological self bears upon the rhetorical subject. This analysis serves four important functions. First, it generates a *genealogy of the self*—an analysis of the self and its development over time. Viewed from the perspective of philosophy, this genealogy provides much-needed continuity to the disparate views of the self within philosophical autobiography. Second, it creates a framework in which to compare self-representations that are historically distant and literarily distinct. Third, it demonstrates different methods for providing continuity to life narratives and unity to the self. Fourth, it fosters an evaluation of self-representation from both an Inner and Outer (ontological and rhetorical) perspective. Previous analyses avoid questions of gender and race associated with contemporary critical theory on self-identity. They fail to offer an account of how gendered individuals who belong to specific classes and races of people with varying degrees of social power experience the world. Nor do they explain how those experiences bear upon metaphysical commitments as well as literary practices. Though I embrace only mitigated constructivist views of the self, I affirm the contemporary literary and philosophical claim that the embodiment of the writer bears significantly upon his or her work. To illustrate this thesis, I reflect upon the connections among theories of identity, the process of self-narration, and the practice of self-reflection.

Literary subtleties and rhetorical complexities emerge out of the autobiographical accounts that I examine herein. For instance, in teaching Augustine's *Confessions*, Carl Vaught suggests that two Augustines emerge out of the text: "The Augustine who authors the first nine books of the *Confessions* is not the Augustine of the tenth and remaining books of the text. Ten years have passed between the events recorded in the writing of the two parts of the text."[11] Yet despite this great divide within his work, Augustine appears to be a "coherent character." Anne-Marie Bowery explains the coherence of Augustine's character this way: the divide created by the temporal gap, and the changes that Augustine undergoes during those ten years, does not mean that there is no relation between the early and late Augustine. Rather, the self-examination that Augustine undertakes in books one through nine enables him to transcend the initially narrow view of the self and see the self in memory, time, eternity, and creation in the latter portions of the text. Vaught and Bowery identify the necessity of delineating the two authorial presences within *Confessions* (and the implications for the self they yield) as we exegete Augustine's view of the self.

Descartes offers a different set of philosophical challenges. In trying to articulate his view of nature as a physical system, Descartes negates the self at the physical but not mental level. Yet he remains ambiguous about the view he presents, creating a smoke screen to cloud whatever truths appear to emerge naturally.[12] Nietzsche goes further than Descartes, adorning contradictory masks that elude his readers rather than merely disorienting them. Who stands behind the mask? Is the man behind the mask the ontological self, a Cartesian "thing that thinks" and not the rhetorical self—the *he* or identity-bearing individual who writes?

The purpose of my analysis is threefold. First, by identifying and analyzing methods of self-examination in first-person philosophical texts, I clarify the role that the first-person plays in self-examination, an examination that bifurcates the self into an Inner and Outer self. Second, in surveying the process of self-examination in written texts, I trace the genealogy of the self—the changing perspective and thrust of the first-person within the genre of autobiography—to shed light on the philosophical assumptions and beliefs absorbed by Inner and Outer views of the self. I expose the influence of such views upon the development of the concepts of the 'self' and 'personal identity' in Western thought. Third, by looking closely at the concept of the 'self' within philosophy, I demonstrate the degree to which human existence is a bifurcated existence, and I offer both historical and contemporary responses to this phenomenon.[13]

My use of the term *self* in this book refers to the Inner, ontological self, the conditions necessary and sufficient to satisfy human existence. I argue that to understand the self we must begin but not end with an understanding of the metaphysics of individuated human existence. The features that track an individual's existence as a particular individual (facial characteristics, voice and speech patterns, handwriting) coupled with the continuity of experience (memory, self-awareness, coherent narrative accounts) raise metaphysical questions that make a study of identity in autobiography compelling. In addition, autobiographical accounts raise literary, psychological, and social questions that reveal the power of writing to shape subjects and selves. As authors seek individuation through the act of writing, particularly while constructing coherent narratives and unified characters, writing becomes the project of organizing distinct events and actions over time, and thereby arriving at the subject—the *he* or *she*—who is the source of one's identity in the world. Hence, my use of the term *subject* in this book refers to an Outer, rhetorical self, the literary, social, and/or psychological ego represented in texts as the source of one's identity.

The chasm between the rhetorical and ontological selves never collapses completely. Contemporary artists are exploiting the space between these senses of self, harnessing the ambiguity within and using it as a source of creativity and self-exploration.[14] We see this process exemplified in the construction of contemporary art objects, objects that combine traditional art forms, such as still life, with digitized imagery: "Art is out of the box. In the process, it now demands our attention, provokes an individual response and inspires us all to think."[15] We experience it in music, where young singer/songwriters such as Beth Orton cross musical genres to create genres of their own. Orton's unique blend of blues, country, folk, and rock music yields "old-timey songs in a late-night futuristic sound scape."[16] And we see it in the literature of contemporary writers such as Allegra Goodman, A. M. Homes, David Sedaris, and Alicia Erian—writers who "gaze unflinchingly at both the grotesque and the banal in an effort to unearth the truth about the human condition in an increasingly complicated world."[17]

I divide this book into four chapters: Chapter 1, "Writing the Self"; Chapter 2, "Bifurcating the Self"; Chapter 3, "Masking the Self"; and Chapter 4, "Transforming the Self." I speak to the issues surrounding autobiography as a philosopher. At times, I direct my comments to other philosophers, those with whom I share a common language. I adopt this rhetorical stance not out of a sense of privilege or feelings of hubris. Rather, I do so out of humility. The lexicon of philosophy, however useful, is limited. My intention in confessing the foundational perspective with which I approach this text is twofold. First, I hope that by revealing the lens through which I view autobiography, readers with varied interests and perspectives will bring their views to bear upon this text in a highly conscious way. As a result, I hope their understanding of autobiography grows and deepens in useful ways. Second, I recognize that examinations of autobiography, regardless of foci, must be cross-disciplinary. The genre is by nature philosophical, literary, and historical. These aspects of autobiographical texts, aspects held in tension within the text, should be valued and weighed within academic studies. My perspective is only one among many that seeks to elucidate the meaning and significance of autobiography.

Though my focus in this book is on the conception and representation of the self within philosophical autobiography, I begin by laying out the groundwork for a study of philosophical autobiography. First I offer an analysis of why people write autobiographies. My conclusions are fourfold: autobiographical writers seek to acquire self-knowledge; to order and unify experiences; to communicate one's identity to others (e.g., to defend or justify specific actions); and to explore the relationship between writing and understanding (though this fourth reason is explanatory only of recent autobiographies that move away from the Inner-self perspective almost entirely). Next I explain the function of the first-person singular in autobiographical writing. I indicate how first-person perspectives—perspectives in which the author may be simultaneously the source of a narrative perspective and the narrative perspective itself—affect philosophical conceptions of the written subject. Lastly I introduce the concept of 'historical figure,' the figure whose identity emerges out of a number of historical documents rather than one's own autobiography: military records, diaries, journals, biographies, and so on.

In Chapter 2 I describe the processes by which self-examination occurs. I begin by examining the methods of self-examination utilized by philosophers within the aforementioned autobiographical texts. I then examine these first-person texts with an eye toward the concepts that grant each text shape and substance: concepts of the Inner and the Outer self, philosophical views of the self, the features of the rhetorical self, and the function of the first-person. As I analyze each text, I identify and interpret the process of self-examination that defines each thinker's philosophical life. I then distinguish between the Inner self and the Outer self, the bifurcated self of autobiographical writing.

Expressed as an Inner self, the self is an ego, a soul, a mind, or an animating spirit, a prediscursive, transparent originator of meaning and actions. Philosophers often characterize the Inner self as an empirical or a transcendental essence. Central to this conception of the self is the belief that the self individuates itself from other selves through acts of introspection, disengagement, and objectification. In order to "know thyself" one must reflect on the conceived nature of himself or herself, distance himself or herself from that reflection, and scrutinize the object of reflection, the self, to which one is attending. The mind, then, interprets itself and gives rise to various degrees of self-awareness. Augustine, Descartes, and Rousseau model their self-presentations upon this view of the self.

The Outer self is a social or psychological self—a product of language and various discriminating acts and thoughts. Many accounts of the Outer self regard the self as an authorially constructed subject, the 'I' of our autobiographical texts, rather than the locus of our minds, souls, spirits, or bodies. This view emerges late in the nineteenth century wherein the subject of texts, the referent of the literary 'I,' takes the form of an outwardly socialized, gendered subject. Nietzsche and Barnes both articulate versions of this view.

Next, I describe the features of autobiographical writing central to this investigation, and I offer an interpretation of each of the five autobiographical accounts named earlier. Augustine, Descartes, and Rousseau appeal to God to enforce the authenticity of their accounts. This literary device raises the question of how one's milieu affects one's working concepts and autobiographical choices. If one writes responsively to one's present circumstances and past traditions, as many writers do, it is no surprise that modern and postmodern writers flout early autobiographical techniques to explain or justify their lives. Other shifts in autobiographical techniques include the altered use of gender in self-assessment. Early female writers adopt male pseudonyms, assume alter egos, and appropriate other conventional literary devices to avoid the stigma they might otherwise experience as female writers. Today, women not only write under their own names they also examine themselves in terms of gender, that is, they assess themselves in terms of gender stereotypes and expectations and in terms of the differences they exhibit as they appropriate particular gender roles. I discuss the differences between male and female autobiography in detail in Chapter 4.

In addition to describing the literary features of autobiographical writing, I introduce and analyze the purposes autobiographies serve—confessing, complaining, bragging, accusing, apologizing, explaining, and evaluating. Some autobiographers are confessional insofar as they disclose their actions, thoughts, and emotions in order to purge themselves of a guilty conscience. Others offer the 'I' as a personal perspective on truth. I argue that the literary features of many autobiographies challenge an ontology that presents autobiographies as factual, historical accounts. The claim that autobiographies are factual, historical accounts does not, however, commit one to the view that autobiographies are mimetic accounts of one's life. In Chapter 4 I outline additional challenges to the view that autobiographies are mimetic representations of one's life.

In Chapter 3 I focus upon the threats to self-identity posed by the bifurcation of the self within writing: deception and concealment. I focus direct attention upon self-deception as a problem that autobiography raises but does not always resolve. I define self-deception as the act of prejudicing or paying selective attention to (or the failure to attend to) certain aspects of oneself.[18] Because autobiographical accounts invoke authorial perspectives—perspectives inextricably tied to the texts in which they emerge—our employment of language and literary techniques often leads us to portray ourselves as larger than life. This literary exaggeration can lead to self-deception. In this section, I outline two forms of deception—*intentional* and *nonintentional*—and explain the conditions from which each arises. Ontologically speaking, self-deception is a relation between a person and a set of false beliefs. Rhetorically speaking, self-deception is a socially construed phenomenon that invokes and places responsibility with others as much as with oneself. It often appears as a consequence of rather than an ignorance about one's situation or life. Nehamas describes and provides several examples of this form of self-deception, including as an example the character Hans Castrop in Thomas Mann's *Magic Mountain*:

> As we observe Hans formulate and manipulate his feelings about his neighbors, as we see him first deny and then excuse their behavior on account of their illness, we miss—we should miss, I think, as Hans himself misses—a number of indications of his own state of health, which is a subject of much greater importance to the novel as a whole. . . . [Nehamas continues this analysis on the following page]. We remain deceived about this character who, because our point of view is so close to his, becomes for a long time our own second self. His errors are also errors of our own. And they are not only errors about Hans. They are errors about ourselves as well.[19]

I offer an alternative conception of deception in keeping with the phenomenological notion of *self-concealment*. To elucidate the enigmatic nature of autobiographical writing further, I argue that autobiography falls within the domain of both historical and literary genres. Because of its dual function and status, autobiography must satisfy different and sometimes conflicting criteria for justification. Categories of "fiction" and "fact" shape the ontological status and the literary identity of texts significantly. For instance, although autobiographies present themselves as authentic, factual accounts of one's life, the author's sense of style, literary conventions, and poetic license push the limits of autobiographies closer to the genre of novels and thus of fiction.

I also describe the challenges of authentic self-presentation and the interpretation of autobiographical texts. The problems raised by the 'I' of autobiographical texts include self-deception, self-protection, and literary manipulation. By exposing the problems inherent within autobiographical projects, I attempt to show the status and meaning of the 'I' in both the Inner and Outer accounts. For example, an author's autobiography may contradict or leave out the facts of his or her life, a choice that begs the question of truth and thwarts our attempt to distinguish truth from falsity. I argue that philosophers can avoid such difficulties by distinguishing the author from the writer wherein the author is the literary construct, the persona, pervading the text, and the writer is the ontological being who writes the text. Plato provides a useful illustration of this distinction.

In Chapter 4 I argue that reading autobiography generates a hermeneutic encounter between a text and a reader. By the term *hermeneutic* I mean a dialectical exercise or methodology of inquiry: a process of asking questions and juxtaposing answers that gives rise to a synthesis of ideas encountered in a text (and realized in response to a text). Like the dialectical encounter that occurs between the writer-self and the author-subject via self-narration, the encounter between the text and the reader is dialectical in nature. The reader identifies and enters into the ambiguity of discursive self-examination—the rich ontological and rhetorical space between the writer-self and the author-subject. He or she then uses this ambiguity as a means for greater understanding. By locating self-understanding between the ontological and rhetorical dimensions of the self, interpretative practices create new possibilities for artful self-understanding.

By interpreting authors, texts, and readers within a hermeneutic framework, we avoid misunderstanding authors *solely* as writers, texts *solely* as artifacts, and readers *solely* as investigators. As Hans-Georg Gadamer argues in *Truth and Method*, the past and present are intertwined in the horizons of texts, authors, and readers. His concept of a fusion of authorial horizons is especially relevant for a study of autobiography. Within the mingling of autobiographical identities, the line between fiction and fact is open to interpretation and understanding. History is not a collection of facts. Conceived this way, hermeneutics is an interpretative act that yields understanding through and because of particular *prejudices* where *prejudices* are *prejudgments* or preconditions that make possible understanding or agreement through discourse. It follows that self-understanding emerges through the interplay between the writer-self and the author-subject, an interplay that is fused in the narrative expression of human experiences. Understood in these terms, hermeneutics is not "filling in the gaps" with information; rather, it is the unfolding of meaning within a tradition. Autobiographies written by philosophers can help us recognize and reject misleading views of the self and reevaluate the meaning of self-examination.

Autobiography creates nuanced meanings of the self by reconceptualizing our relationships to others. Even our responses to the question of identity vary according to the context in which we ask "Who am I?" Indeed, the question itself changes by becoming epistemologically and ethically driven rather than existentially directed. It elicits metaphysical responses rather than psychological reflections. And yet the experience of knowing oneself is both an Inner and Outer experience, both rhetorical and ontological in nature, internal and external to the author who scrutinizes himself or herself. This is why autobiography provides a rich context for identity exploration, a context for reunifying oneself.

At the same time, writing autobiographically constrains our personal identity in important ways. In choosing how we appear to others, we must acknowledge who we are for ourselves. Hence, our self-identity varies according to our philosophical conception of 'self' and political conception of 'person.' Women's autobiographies provide several excellent examples of this point. Though society has always described women's work with socially and politically charged terms—housewife, nanny, nurse—women writers either delineate and prioritize or synthesize these identity markers as they individuate themselves. They must do so. Otherwise they run the risk of having one particular identity-denoting term dominate their entire biographical landscape. Moreover, the conventions by which women tell their stories differ from male conventions. For instance, women's autobiographies do not typify the model of autobiographical writing as confession, the model used by Augustine and Rousseau. Nor are the motivations that inspire women to write shared by men. Carolyn Heilbrun argues that women write to create a rhetorical self, a subject of their experiences; men write to demonstrate their ontological and rhetorical status. Although autobiographical writing introduces the vexing question "Who am I?," a single autobiographical model cannot satisfy that question. With this larger discussion of gender serving as a backdrop, I offer additional analyses of Hazel Barnes's autobiography in the final section of Chapter 4.

Philosophical autobiography jettisons philosophical views that disguise the subject behind the self. We see this exemplified in the work of Friedrich Nietzsche. His deconstruction of the writer-self generates an explicit (albeit masked) author-subject. His exploitation of the author/writer distinction also challenges the traditionally conceived I/You relationship between the author and reader. By contrast, Nietzsche conceives of the author as both I and you, self and other: "What we get hold of is no longer anything questionable. . . . I am the first to hold in my hands the measure for 'truths'; I am the first who is *able* to decide. Just as if a second consciousness had grown in me; just as if 'the will' had kindled a light for itself in me so that it might see the inclined plane, the askew path on which it went down so far."[20] Nietzsche's reconfiguration of the I/You relationship thrusts the reader into the text as a member of the "we" to which the "I" and the "you" belong.

Nietzsche aims to discredit autobiographical perspectives that presuppose the Inner self by cloaking self-identity in paradox. The masks he uses for this purpose recall and invert autobiographical representations of the Inner self. Nietzsche concludes *Ecce Homo* with an aphoristic allusion to his self-representational method of masking, "Have I been understood?—Dionysus versus the Crucified—."[21]

My analysis of autobiography ends with the following conclusions: (1) The interplay between the Inner and Outer self occurs on both rhetorical and ontological levels. This interplay creates a multifaceted context in which we come to understand varied first-person perspectives of the self. (2) The author-subject of autobiographical texts is a self-conscious, social, gendered individual, not an isolated soul or a will trapped within a mechanistic body. (3) Problems associated with self-knowledge (problems of self-deception and questions of truth and knowledge) emerge in tandem with both Inner and Outer views of the self, demonstrating that deception is connected not only to acts of understanding but also to acts of interpretation. To understand fully the relationship between the ontological and rhetorical self—to understand the relationship between self-disclosure and self-identity—we must establish hermeneutic grounds for adjudicating intentional self-deception and genuine masking, a hermeneutics that is responsive to literary conventions.

This examination of the interplay between the Inner and Outer self within autobiography advances the study of the self in two ways. First, it shows how the tension between the ontological self and the rhetorical subject within autobiography provides room for new theories of the self to emerge. Second, it shows that the potential conflict between the ontological ground of being and the rhetorical understanding of that ground prompts a vigorous path toward self-understanding, a path that enables scholars to raise nondualistic questions about identity, questions that elevate the existentiality of the human experience.

The search for the self is a search with ancient origins as exemplified by the artful philosopher, Socrates, at the beginning of the *Phaedrus*. Refusing to indulge the story of Boreas, Socrates says to his young interlocutor, "I don't bother about such things . . . (I) direct my inquiries rather to myself, to discover whether I really am a more complex creature and more puffed up with pride than Typhon, or a simpler, gentler being whom heaven has blessed with a quiet, un-Typhonic nature."[22] Though Socrates practiced the art of self-examination orally, we contemporary philosophers follow Plato and sustain ourselves in word.

Chapter 1

Writing the Self

> I have a duty against which my habits, even more the pride of my instincts, revolt at bottom, namely, to say: Hear me! For I am such and such a person. Above all, do not mistake me for someone else.
>
> —Friedrich Nietzsche[1]

GROUNDWORK FOR A STUDY OF AUTOBIOGRAPHY

Several recurring questions drive contemporary discussions of self-identity. Why do we utter 'I'? Why do we speak about ourselves in the first-person? Who or what does the 'I' of our utterances represent? What purposes do first-person utterances serve? What does the increasing usage of 'I' statements in current parlance (scholarly and popular) suggest about the contemporary human condition?

These questions may seem either so obvious or so arcane as not to be worth raising. But it is important to consider them for two related reasons. First, these questions conceal fundamental presuppositions that underlie autobiographical writing (presuppositions about the nature of the self and presuppositions about the nature of writing). To subscribe to the habits of artful living that philosophical autobiography exemplifies, we must acknowledge the conceptions of self-narration that shape both the story told and the life lived.[2] Second, these questions provide a useful context for examining autobiographical writing. As such, they mitigate the temptation to consider questions of essence and identity in isolation from human experience and expression. They also mediate the urge to collapse the distinction between the author and the writer. I strive to resist both temptations throughout this book.

Speech act theorists H. P. Grice and J. L. Austin offer partial answers to these questions.[3] According to their descriptive account of first-person utterance, we speak in the first-person for five reasons. First, we aim to know ourselves. Second, we wish to both individuate and unify ourselves (i.e., to reinforce our unique existence among other 'I's). Third, we hope to distinguish our privately conceived life from the lives others believe that we lead—to communicate the self to others. Fourth, we strive to give continuity to our lives; that is, we seek to discern our own variegated experiences and to realize how these experiences culminate in a single, albeit syncretic, life. Fifth, we struggle to make our existence and identity transparent both to ourselves and to others (i.e., to explore the relation between the self and the subject). For all of these reasons, we subconsciously or consciously instantiate a single referent to which all of our individual perspectives point. We become an 'I.'

Implicit within Grice's and Austin's work is the philosophical belief that the 'I' is both an ontological and a logical (grammatical) placeholder. Used as a referent of individual experiences, the term *I* implies wholeness of being (i.e., a coherent set of practices, roles, and beliefs converging within the unique life of each person for which it stands, a coherency that is expressed by our names, our familial roles, our social security numbers, our distinctive physical appearance, and other identity-bearing features of our lives). Used as a referent of indicative statements, the 'I' is the subject of sentences one writes about himself or herself. Taken together, the 'I' has both a universal quality and an existential quality. Consider the following statement: "I am limited in my reasoning ability." Here the proposition may refer to an individual limitation (I, the person making this statement, may lack a keen analytical ability, or I may have a particular learning disability that obviates my formal reasoning capacities). In this sense, the 'I' functions as an existential quantifier. The 'I' may also refer to a general limitation (all humans qua humans are limited in their reasoning capacities). In this instance, the 'I' functions as a universal quantifier.

Logic is helpful in clarifying the meaning of 'I' statements as such, but it cannot explain our philosophically rooted desire to live authentic lives, to give expression to our lived experiences, and to extrapolate knowledge about who we are and what we are from these expressions. From a contemporary standpoint, the increasing usage of 'I' statements reflects the deeply modern sensibilities of human agents living today. 'I' statements convey our commitment to individual rights as well as individual accountability. In this sense, the 'I' carries with it the residue of our political and legal history. The 'I' evokes the questions of identity and essence raised first by Descartes and later reformulated by the social, political, and legal philosophers of the modern period. And the 'I' reflects the prevailing influence of modern philosophical conceptions upon our understanding of the ego and the individual, conceptions that inform everything from our political rights and legal contracts to theological beliefs and medical practices.[4]

The seemingly simple conclusion that we might draw from Grice's and Austin's work is that humans seek to know themselves and to be known by others. We use 'I' in a logical sense, a sociopolitical sense, and a poetical sense. We invoke it to circumscribe self-knowledge: to individuate experiences, to acknowledge a particular social and political placement in the world, and to "become who we are," as Nietzsche exhorts. This rich usage, however, creates a paradox. If the human condition is both limited, as modern thinkers suggest, and fragmented, as postmodern thinkers claim, then the 'I' that stands in for ourselves belies the degree to which the human condition is bifurcated. Put another way, 'I' statements disguise the fragmentation of the human encounter with reality; they imply coherency of experience where there is none (or none that is obvious). Even if we acknowledge the fragmentation of human experience, we have no adequate language, no real lexicon, with which to express it. Even if we follow Nietzsche's lead and affirm our fragmentation, using it to deepen our bifurcated identities and to create meaning and identity where there is none, we are cut off from the discourse of the community around us. Even if we attempt integration, following Augustine who transcends his fragmented existence, first confronting and then displacing absolute nothingness with God, exchanging a temporal understanding of reality for a spiritual one, we are bereft of a language to articulate our existential situation.

Kierkegaard points to this limitation in *Fear and Trembling*.[5] He argues that when Abraham stands face-to-face with God, prepared to kill his son to obey God's will, his actions fall outside the scope of moral judgment. In hearing the commanding voice of God, Abraham transcends the ethics that guide human behavior. Abraham's actions, then, are inexplicable to his fellow humankind. Wittgenstein speaks aphoristically of a similar limitation in the *Philosophical Investigations*: "If a lion could speak, we could not understand it."[6] The rules of the language games we play constrain what we know by limiting what we can express and what we can understand to that which falls within the scope of the particular language games we play and within the complicated form of life we live. The limitations of morality and language also constrain the self-knowledge we seek. In both examples, fragmentation of the psyche leads either to silence or paradox, or both.[7] Must we remain agents with obscured identities and inexplicable essences? Or can the act of writing and speaking in the first-person loosen the barriers of speech and yield bits of self-knowledge otherwise off limits to human knowers? Is this why we write autobiographically—to achieve self-knowledge? Why we self-narrate on paper—to self-know?

According to Schuster, Susan Sontag suggests that these questions and concerns drive the philosophical exposition of the self in narration: "One of the responses to the breakdown of the philosophical system-making of the nineteenth century was 'a new of kind of philosophizing: personal (even autobiographical), aphoristic, lyrical, anti-systematic. Its foremost exemplars: Kierkegaard, Nietzsche, and Wittgenstein.'"[8] Historically the desire to know thyself has motivated the adoption of first-person perspectives in discourse. Coupled with the political and legal nuances of the 'I' described earlier, first-person narration connotes ownership of our actions and identity in the world. Yet both a commitment to self-knowledge and a vestment in individual rights fail to explain fully why we pen in the first-person. Furthermore, neither a need for self-knowledge nor a belief in individual rights explains why individuals autobiograph themselves, affixing views of themselves that arise from introspective impressions in written form, presenting and preserving their utterances and actions for others. Nor do these motives explain why we create a deliberate and sometimes carefully constructed self-presentation when we are engaged in self-writing. How, then, do philosophers explain the choice to self-narrate in word rather than in speech?

Recall the lessons of Plato's dialogues. Writing is an act performed for the sake of a temporally and spatially absent reader. Plato learns this lesson from his teacher, Socrates, who shows us that truth does not necessarily yield philosophical knowledge or self-transformation. Changing lovers of shadows into lovers of Forms requires a fragmenting encounter with the self, one that results in a heightened sense of self-awareness. Plato illustrates this change in the *Symposium*: lovers of wisdom must move away from material goods and bind themselves to the Good forever—a bond that necessitates the dialectical model of Socrates and his interlocutors; a bond we attempt to forge today through our written expressions. Yet as Socrates argues in the *Phaedrus*, this bond remains weak. Old men can hand down their traditions in writing, but only they know the truth of their traditions.

Still, written self-narration offers hope. Bound by the conventions of autobiography, written narration occurs through a stylized expression of life that translates ordinary experience into literary form and private thoughts into revealed actions. The distance born out of the writing process—by the invocation of an authorial voice, a distinctive literary form, and a specific narrative structure—enables the writer to engage in a form of self-reflection otherwise closed off to him or her. More importantly, writing autobiographically invites others to see concrete examples of artful living as models they can adopt for themselves.

In the remainder of this chapter and throughout this book, I describe and evaluate the use of the first-person pronoun in five first-person philosophical texts: Augustine's *Confessions*, René Descartes' *Meditations on First Philosophy*, Jean-Jacques Rousseau's *The Confessions*, Friedrich Nietzsche's *Ecce Homo*, and Hazel Barnes's *The Story I Tell Myself*. My aim in giving an account of the 'I' within philosophical autobiography is threefold. First, I aim to clarify "identity" in its varied historical and literary instances. Second, I intend to articulate conceptions of the self and the subject implied by philosophical autobiographies, thereby distinguishing the subject from the self without invoking a formal discussion of "identity" per se. Third, I hope to show which views of the self and the subject best support the artful life. I devote the remainder of this book to these three aims. I pose probing questions along the way to guide the subtextual issues surrounding self-identity and self-knowledge that are part and parcel to this analysis.

Writing the Examined Life

Autobiographical writing is particularly problematic for an inquiry into the self because the writer investigating the agent's life is simultaneously the object and the subject of inquiry. As I have suggested previously in this chapter, the use of the first-person as both an ontological and a logical (grammatical) placeholder imposes specific conditions and constraints upon the philosophical notion of the subject in the world.[9] In addition, the historical and cultural milieu in which one writes shapes the writer's self-conception and defines the angle of critical reflection from which the author speaks. Theories intended to explain the relationship between personal action and thoughts and individual identity develop within discourses that are grounded in ideological commitments and cultural beliefs as well. Philosophical analyses are no exception. If we are to understand the 'I' in philosophical autobiography—a perspective and persona that bear both upon the writer of the text and upon us as readers—then we must investigate the senses of the self and the subject that inform it.

Nietzsche's autobiography offers us a rich preliminary starting point. Completed in 1888, one year before his final and irrevocable collapse, Nietzsche embroiders *Ecce Homo* with Christian imagery and biblical allusions; imagery and allusion he brazenly mocks throughout this corpus. The title of the work is biblical. It is the phrase spoken by Pontius Pilate when he presents Christ to his impromptu jury (John 19:5): "Behold the man." In selecting this line for his title, Nietzsche acknowledges that though we may crucify him, he aims to offer us a redeeming view of humanity. He then appropriates the Christian trinity to describe his own resurrected self: a disciple of Dionysus, a follower of Zarathustra, the Antichrist.[10]

Whereas ancient and modern examples of first-person writing focus sharply upon the nature of the self, Nietzsche dispenses with questions of essence (What am I?) in order to blow open the question of identity (Who am I?). By the time Nietzsche writes *Ecce Homo*, he has rejected essentialist metaphysical accounts of the self and coherence theories of truth altogether. One by one, he deconstructs the "idols" of the Western philosophical tradition. He includes Kant among the world's false gods and thwarts the distinction between the *noumena* (the thing-in-itself) and *phenomena* (things-as-appearing) by embracing and transforming the metaphysical commitment to phenomena into an epistemological perspectivism.

Indeed, Nietzsche self-consciously presents *a* perspective of himself throughout his autobiography.

I cannot overstress the effect of the Nietzschean shift toward perspectivism upon the genre of autobiography. Walter Kaufmann, the great translator and editor of much of Nietzsche's work, aptly acknowledges the contributions and value of Nietzsche's personal insights:

> *Ecce Homo* is one of the treasures of world literature. Written in 1888 and first published in 1908, it has been largely ignored or misunderstood. Yet it is Nietzsche's own interpretation of his development, his works, and his significance; and we should gladly trade the whole vast literature on Nietzsche for this small book. Who would not rather have Shakespeare on Shakespeare, including the poet's own reflections on his plays and poems, than the exegeses and conjectures of thousands of critics and professors?[11]

Nietzsche's efforts to privilege questions of identity over questions of essence offer renewed opportunities for self-examination and self-knowledge. But these opportunities come with challenges as well. For example, Augustine's *Confessions*, Descartes' *Meditations*, and Rousseau's *The Confessions* correlate self-representation with a prediscursive essence either intuited or induced by a writer or thinker. Each then, ipso facto, presupposes degrees of metaphysical determinism wherein the self and thought coalesce, and self-identity either supervenes on or is commensurate with temporal and spatial continuity. By contrast, Nietzsche denies the deterministic claims of his philosophical forbearers for the sake of a constructivist account of the self and a perspectivist account of self-identity. Consequently, Nietzsche undermines the previously privileged writer or thinker who intuits or induces a self; he devalues the act of autobiographical writing as a truth-bearing activity; and he makes explicit the distinction between the rhetorical subject and the ontological self.

Nietzsche's renunciation of essentialist metaphysical claims explains in part why he subtitles his autobiography "How One Becomes What One Is." Indeed, it clarifies why Nietzsche titles the first three chapters of his work "Why I Am So Wise," "Why I Am So Clever," and "Why I Write Such Excellent Books," respectively: to laugh at his own awkward position at the helm of postmodern philosophy, a philosophical movement enamored with ambiguity and illusion. But buried within Nietzsche's provocative claims about his wisdom, cleverness, and literary prowess lie profound questions about the human relationship to oneself, questions about the 'I' or 'who' within our writing, not the 'what' behind our writing.

The genre of autobiography bears witness to fluid philosophical and literary models. Cultures that once embraced the Cartesian cogito as the paradigm of the self now energetically embrace Nietzsche's commitment to constructed and individually perceived selves. American writers in particular are coupling an implicitly Nietzschean self-view with Michel Foucault's claim that power is an ineluctable social fact. According to Foucault, humans create hegemonies to control others, hegemonies that individuals internalize, hegemonies that shape self-identity. As a result of this cross-fertilization between Nietzsche and Foucault, autobiographical writers are adopting a highly personal and heavily social rhetorical stance. For example, when the journalist and *The New Yorker* contributor, Susan Orlean, was interviewed about *The Orchid Thief* (1998), she affirmed the autobiographical edge to her writing and her life as a writer: "The fact is I do not write news that must be reported. I choose to write about whatever captures my curiosity. Simply choosing what you write about is a subjective choice. . . . Sometimes I wonder how it is that I ended up as a writer. . . . Aren't we all inventions of our choices and decisions?"[12] Paradigm shifts that trickle down into culture writ large elucidate the legal, political, and social veneer of the first-person in autobiography.

As inheritors of both a modern political framework and a postmodern mind-set, we acknowledge ownership over the utterances we create by adopting the first-person pronoun (a sign of our commitment to political, social, and legal responsibility). These utterances remind us of the individually weighted positions from which we speak and think. But the generic 'I' that we substitute for our own names casts short shadows on our individual existence, shadows that do not reveal who we are in any important sense. Introspective gazes extend only so far.[13] Nietzsche understood this. He knew, as Stanley Rosen argues, that "the extent to which 'I' am responsible for, or act as an agent of, my world and my life is superficial. The act of will that opens the perspective of my world is also the act by which 'I' as self-conscious ego am created."[14] Nietzsche's perceptiveness and artfulness, combined with his critique of the Western philosophical tradition, render his work a valuable contribution to the study of philosophical autobiography. Yet in displacing a unified, prediscursive, essentialist self with a chaotic abyss of potentiality from which a self is constructed, Nietzsche leaves no room for an integrated account of self-identity.[15] This omission is unfortunate, because self-identity weighs heavily upon contemporary accounts of autobiography.

The corpus of philosophical autobiography generates significant theories about self-identity in several ways. First, the texts that form the subgenre of philosophical autobiography circumscribe views of identity and essence. Second, they provide a unified body of work for the purpose of scholarly comparison and examination. Third, they demonstrate that philosophers cannot make assumptions about representational relations that other autobiographers make, not if they wish to succeed at living an artful life as I argued earlier. Fourth, they demonstrate the degree to which the self is self-ascribing. The provocative corpus of philosophical autobiography invites us to clarify the issues of self-identity, self-narration, and self-knowledge surrounding first-person texts. But the text, with his or her writer and his or her subject, tells only half of the story. Matters are complicated further once scholars introduce the *autobiographer* and the *reader* into the mix.

As the subject and the locus of personal experience, autobiographers assume that they alone are in the position of unerring self-knower. I alone can judge, know, and present myself accurately. I alone can construct a life-story that bears a one-to-one correspondence to the life I have lived. Hence, responses to the questions of identity vary with the particularities of a life and the view of the subject. René Descartes proceeds on markedly different presuppositional grounds than does his fellow Frenchman by birth, Jean-Jacques Rousseau. Likewise, Hazel Barnes's *The Story I Tell Myself*, which appears in print more than 100 years after Nietzsche's *Ecce Homo*, reformulates the questions of identity in existential terms: Who do I take myself to be? What is the source of my phenomenological experiences?

The view of the autobiographer as unerring knower, while attractive, is deeply flawed. As Socrates claims in the *Apology*, "Poets are among the worst interpreters of their own works: they create without understanding, standing on the wings of inspiration; but when they discuss their works they rely on their uninspired reason and falter."[16] Yet inerrancy is an easy presumption to make as an autobiographer. Our experiences and memories are transparent to us because they "coinhere" with sensations that are introspectively accessible. These sensations and introspections shape the texts we produce both in content and in form. But they do not tell the whole story. Despite the immediacy of our sensations and memories, facts that extend beyond our own experiences shape our self-identity in equally profound ways.

For example, in contrast to the autobiographer, a reader shapes a text publicly through the act of ongoing dialogue and politicization of a text. The history of texts and the discourse surrounding subjectivity have been at times isolated to a literate few with privileged access to desirable texts. This predominantly male group is held together by social forces, cultural forces, and political and legal systems, and it manufactures the subject as both an intellectual category into which all subjects fit and as a particular persona from the numerous "facts" assigned to beings in the world.[17] Since listeners and readers often assume that the views expressed in a speech or text are the views, sensibilities, and understanding of the speaker or writer who creates the speech or text in question, they assume also that the subject and speaker or writer are commensurate with one another. Yet the *rhetorical* voice (the Outer self or author-subject), unlike the thinking or speaking subject (the Inner or ontological writer-self), is not a syncretic entity limited by the time period in which he or she is constructed. Rather, the *rhetorical* subject is an open, vulnerable, interpretable persona subject to the men and women who share the capacity to understand linguistic utterances even if they never arrive at truth. Stanley Rosen clarifies this difference by comparing Socrates to Odysseus:

> The least one can say is that the enactment of truth requires the mask of deception and concealment, almost exactly as we learn from the *Odyssey*. The one significant practical difference between Homer and Plato is that Odysseus wishes to return to the tranquil life of city and family, whereas the Socratic eros can be satisfied by neither. But the consequence of this difference is that Odysseus reveals his identity at the end of his adventures. There is, however, no end to the Socratic adventure, and as Nietzsche understood perfectly, the philosopher never relinquishes his masks.[18]

To state this in traditionally analytic terms, the written 'I'—the rhetorical subject or Outer self—signifies rather than refers to a writer; it functions as a sign rather than a reference. Hence, the subject, unlike the writer, is not constrained by theories of truth. By contrast, verbal claims we make about who we are presuppose honesty, relevance, and sincerity, three conditions necessary for successful communication. When we make self-referential utterances within social contexts and conversations, we necessarily do so in undeceiving, intelligible ways.[19]

The writer who transforms the self into a written subject is therefore not subject to the conditions of speech, because written narration is both nonreferential and atemporal. The immediacy of speech elucidates the singular temporal dimension of spoken utterance—its presence (here and now), its necessarily truncated field of vision, its fleeting texture. Writing, however, expands the literary field of vision. As the writer chooses the descriptions, diction, and other components and qualities of the text, the written expressions take on new significance and nuances previously absent from the writer's psyche.

The bifurcation of the self occurs vis-à-vis this intentional, self-conscious literary process. I will introduce the distinction between the rhetorical and the ontological self formally in a moment, but let me describe this process briefly here. The bifurcation of the self within and through writing occurs on both the rhetorical and ontological levels. It occurs rhetorically through the instantiation of an authorial 'I'; it occurs ontologically through an encounter with the self as Other. The latter encounter, which creates a chasm within the psyche, makes possible self-transformation of the Platonic sort and may lead to artful living, both in the writer *and* in the reader. Contra Derrida, I argue that the reading of self-narration leads closer to rather than "paradoxically away from" self-knowledge obtained through self-scrutiny.[20] My thesis is that self-narration implicates the reader in a hermeneutic process of critical reflection, a process that has the potential to transcend in Schuster's terms, "habitual and slavish trends of cognition" and engage the reader dialectically in the ongoing act of self-knowing.[21] I will say more about this process in Chapter 4.

Even writers who seem unaware of the limitations and possibilities that writing occasions exhibit a sense of urgency about their own (literary) mortality. This urgency expresses itself as an ever-pressing need to affirm our existence, to know ourselves, and to show that our lives matter in some nontrivial way. The desire to be remembered runs both deep and wide in Western thought. Diotima, the sophistic stranger invoked by Socrates in Plato's *Symposium*, is one of the first figures in the Western world who articulates the human desire to live forever, at least in word if not in deed.[22] Diotima suggests that our desire for immortality is satisfied through reproduction and/or the production of good works and ideas. Christianity provides additional examples, with its wealth of allusions and references to immortality. For example, Christians receive the sacraments as a sign of Christ's Crucifixion and resurrection, and as a symbol of Christ's continued life through and in his followers. Like reproduction and writing, the past is brought to bear on the present in the taking of the sacraments; the future is promised and consecrated in the past. Writing is an effective strategy for coping with the fear that future generations may forget our existence.[23]

The belief that death encircles and defines life is common among peoples of hierarchical societies. In these societies, social status informs public identity and controls community involvement. Individuals are pressured to conform to codified behaviors appropriate for their status. Yet human beings who adopt predefined ways of engaging the world have little work to do in seeking out the meaning of their lives. One person simply fills the social slot of another upon his or her death. If meaning is given rather than created (or affirmed), then human existence is unchanged by individual choice. Indeed, "choice" is rendered meaningless, and remembrance is futile (this is the bane of essentialist theories of the self). One way human agents mitigate the possibility of forgetfulness is by creating a personal identity through language. Describing our individual lives in language and framing our personal identity by text, we make ourselves into subjects of our histories. Writing autobiographically, then, springs from the psychological and ontological structure of our being, a structure raised to consciousness by language.[24]

The Ontological Self and the Rhetorical Self

Several epistemological queries frame the search for the self within autobiography: Who is recounting the life ascribed to us? Who (and what) is the writer? What is the writer's relationship to the text? What kind of subject is the narrator of the autobiographical account? Is the subject wholly literary, or does he or she gain an ontological status through a connection to the writer? In philosophical autobiography, two distinct views dominate this subgenre, views that I denote the *Inner* self and the *Outer* self. Though I argue that the Inner self and the Outer self emerge naturally through self-narration, philosophers often permit one or the other to dominate their thinking about the self. Moreover, the act of privileging one view of the self shapes the autobiographical account in dramatic ways. Below I describe the Inner self and the Outer self, noting the ontological and the rhetorical dimensions of each.

Speaking ontologically, the Inner self (the writer-self) is a metaphysical entity or prediscursive essence imbedded in the mind or soul of the human being, *or* a soul per se that exists apart from a body (Greek), or a soul comingled with a body (Hebraic). Described differently, the Inner 'I' is a Parmenidean constant, an absolute and unchanging ego of a writer who is unaffected by the vicissitudes of writing and of life. Viewed through a rhetorical lens, the Inner self is an introspectively accessible ego whose identity bears a one-to-one correspondence with the actions, thoughts, and emotions of the writer-self. Hence, those committed to the Inner view of the self believe it is possible to formulate an absolute, objective literary description of one's actions and beliefs that represents who one *in fact* is. Autobiographical writing through the eighteenth century tacitly endorses an Inner orientation toward first-person writing.

By contrast, the Outer self is a rhetorical subject (an author-subject) that can never possess itself completely, because it continuously thrusts itself into the world within a context of social and literary forces. In contrast to the Parmenidean conception of the Inner self, the Outer self is a Heraclitean ego that lingers in a perpetual state of becoming and is always dependent on the shifting contexts, beliefs, and literary aims of a writer for existence. The Outer self "exists," then, only in two senses: (1) as an embodied (gendered, raced) human being, and (2) as a textually embodied authorial identity. Analyzed rhetorically, the writer's self-ascription instantiates him or her as an author. This act of authorial instantiation creates the thoughts and feelings of the author, thoughts and feelings that adherents of the Inner self believe preexist and underlie the text. From the Outer perspective, thought is language; a prediscursive, prelinguistic cogito cannot exist. Events that authors ascribe to themselves in writing ground their existence in the world and sustain their identities as authors.

If the Inner self and the Outer self represent two extreme philosophical positions on the self (one essentialist, one constructivist), then I aim to strike an Aristotelian mean between the two. I contend that both the Inner and Outer self emerge within every autobiographical text, that is, that there is both an ontological self and a rhetorical subject that inform autobiographical texts. This distinction emerges because the subject of the autobiographical inquiry is simultaneously the object of the inquiry. Thus as the subject examines himself or herself through a rhetorical and a literary lens, the self is bifurcated into two entities. This bifurcation is both necessary and good, necessary for the sake of self-examination and self-narration, and good because it initiates the Socratic process of self-transformation and invites a higher form of self-unification to emerge. By juxtaposing the writer-self against the rhetorical-subject in this book, I carve out a rich middle ground in which new philosophical accounts of the self may emerge.

The bifurcation of the self within writing—a chasm between one's life as a writer and one's personal and authorial identities—reveals the difference between our actual and our constructed engagement in the world. We can be both selves and subjects, but the identities of these remain distinct. Self-narrated beliefs, emotions, and sensibilities may denote facts about the writer, the temporal being who decides to engage in the act of writing, and who bears the author's name, but they may also connote the authorial existence and identity of another as well, an identity that is independent of the writer's. The author, then, works between two identities: he is the protagonist in a story and the subject of a textual history that may or may not mimic the writer's own experiences. Despite the famous maxim of the Delphic Oracle, "Know thyself," we cannot grasp ourselves and know ourselves in the way that we grasp a cup and know it. We cannot solve the riddle of who we are with propositional knowledge. Nor can we solve it with any model of knowledge that distinguishes the knower from what is known. As we speak and write about our existence, we implicate ourselves in the epistemic dimensions of existence. Our existence constitutes the world, and, as Paul Ricoeur contends, the world constitutes our existence: "Only a being that is a self is *in* the world. . . . There is no world without a self who finds itself in it and acts in it."[25] Ricoeur captures the fundamental sense in which we are both ontological and rhetorical beings. We assume a first-person perspective *because* we exist in a linguistically structured environment that operates according to grammatically arranged horizons or limits.[26] To be a self, then, is to be a linguistic creature, a point that Ricoeur may have mined from Wittgenstein. Yet the self, conceived as a linguistic creature, does not diminish the ontological ground from which language springs. Indeed, it points to the dual nature that it signifies.

Ricoeur's insights evoke two questions raised at the beginning of this chapter: What does it mean to write about ourselves? And what, if anything, does writing about ourselves reveal? When we speak about ourselves, we invoke an introspective gaze, a retrospective gaze, and what I label an *alterspective gaze*. That is, we gather a sense of ourselves by looking inward, by looking backward, and by looking outward. In hearing the stories of our childhood, the descriptions of our behaviors of youth, we assume the conceptions, beliefs, and preferences that both our perspective and other perspectives constitute. Ricoeur concedes, "The selfhood of oneself implies otherness to such an intimate degree that one cannot be thought of without the other, that instead one passes into the other."[27]

I have noted previously that the formulation of the first-person perspective varies according to the sets of conditions under which a writer finds himself or herself. Autobiography is a special mode of first-person writing that merges these sets of conditions into one expressive literary form, allowing the autobiography to be both a genre of literature and an interpretation of experience. For although we do not and cannot confront ourselves as others do, we do, as Georg Misch maintains, possess ourselves as beings conscious of ourselves and capable of uttering 'I.'[28] We sometimes choose to shed some of the masks that we wear and treat ourselves as an other, a person independent of the being we confront every day. In these instances, the 'I' becomes a 'you,' revealing the I-you characteristic of the self-in-the-world (the linguistic self).[29]

To be sure, literary conventions liberate and constrain first-person philosophical writing. On the one hand, they offer the philosophical writer methods for self-representation ordinarily unavailable to philosophers.[30] On the other, they muddle the view of the self so clearly expressed in philosophical terms, adding ambiguity to texts in which many writers aim for clarity. Accordingly, Misch argues that autobiography and its fluid boundaries "can be defined only by summarizing what the term 'autobiography' implies: the description (*graphia*) of an individual human life (*bios*) by the individual himself (*auto*)."[31] By extension, autobiographical writing imposes no particular style or form upon the writer. It simply conveys the fact that the life circumscribed by the writing is the writer's life *in his or her own words*.[32]

Yet the rhetorical space in which the 'I' appears reshapes our traditional notion of subjectivity.[33] First, by acknowledging one's audience and adopting a rhetorical stance toward that audience, autobiographers give rise to a rhetorical subject.[34] Initially the author's existence is dependent upon the writer's existence (conversely, the writer's existence is not dependent upon the author's existence). But once the author-subject is embodied within a text, he or she will outlive the temporally circumscribed writer in whom the text originated. Moreover, the author-subject may bear little resemblance to the writer herself. Julia Kristeva, Francophone philosopher, psychoanalyst, and feminist, makes this point very simply: "[W]e should remember that the person walking in the street with a driver's license in his pocket is different from the person doing the writing."[35] To complicate matters further, the identity and understanding of the author may vary from reader to reader.

A persona that emerges from the rhetorical stance of a writer, the author-subject takes on new characteristics and meanings in the mediating act of reading. Readers gloss different characteristics of the 'I' as they read texts, thereby drawing different conclusions about authors than do other readers. Hence, while the writer-self is a historical person who exists outside of a text and precedes that text, the author is a figure who exists outside of a text and antecedes it.[36] In "What Is an Author?" Foucault's famous exploitation of the writer/author distinction, the author signifies an ambiguously constrained figure:

> The author is not an indefinite source of signification which fills a work; the author does not precede the works; he is a certain functional principle by which, in our culture, one limits, excludes, and chooses; in short, by which one impeded the free circulation, the free manipulation, the free composition, decomposition, and recomposition of fiction. . . . One can say that the author is an ideological product, since we represent him as the opposite of his historically real function. (When a historically given function is represented in a figure that inverts it, one has an ideological production.) The author is therefore the ideological figure by which one marks the manner in which we fear the proliferation of meaning.[37]

Writing, then, is a public act, a performative and signifying practice, in which the writer-self creates a signifying figure (author-subject) with whom a reader interacts. Thinking through the act of author creation in writing, Foucault notes that writing is "an interplay of signs arranged to the very nature of the signifier. Writing unfolds like a game that invariably goes beyond its own rules and transgresses its limits. Writing . . . is, rather, a question of creating a space into which the writing subject constantly appears."[38] As the subject of a signifying practice, the author-subject exists only within a text; outside of the signifying act of writing, the author-subject vanishes.

Besides creating an author-subject, the act of autobiographical self-narration initiates a hermeneutic event between a reader and a text. I address the issue of interpretation fully in Chapter 4. For now, let me say only that the relationship that the author-subject initiates is significant because it demands direct justification of interpretative acts, thereby forcing the reader to confront the author and himself in the process of arriving at the meaning of a text. By "text," I mean "a group of entities, used as signs, which are selected, arranged, and intended by an author in a certain context to convey some specific meaning to an audience."[39] Texts, then, convey meaning not only because they presuppose readers but also because entities that constitute them are signs within a signifying system. Additional interpretative implications of autobiography run in many directions:

> There is no final, definitive, or incontestable autobiography, but neither are autobiographies undecided, pure text. They speak a subjectivity that is specifically located, yet open to interpretation, dialogue, and

> analysis. . . . In its critical dimension, for reader, writer, and critic, auto/biography works as a form of address.[40]

As Lorraine Code suggests, the identity of the author-subject is mediated by two extra-textual forces: the writer-self, an ontological referent who creates the text, *and* the reader who interprets the text. The meaning of the text is mediated by these same two forces.

Let me restate the three steps that lead to the bifurcation of the self. First, the act of self-narration creates an author-subject (a rhetorical signifier) who stands alongside the writer-self (an ontological referent). Second, self-narration forces the writer-self to examine himself or herself both introspectively and alterspectively: as the ground of being and as an alienated other. And third, by examining opposing perspectives of the 'I,' by yielding to them and submitting to their variations, the writer-self confronts the author-subject, thereby revealing the ontological and rhetorical dimensions of human experience. Hence, as a mode of philosophical exposition, autobiography fosters self-examination through the creation and mediation of an author-subject, a self-creating consciousness. As a genre of literature, autobiography engages readers in an open dialogue about the nature of self-identity and the meaning of texts. To write autobiographically is to embrace both identity and difference in oneself.[41]

The Rationale for Autobiographical Writing

At the beginning of this chapter, I posed a set of questions about the nature and function of self-utterance and self-narration. In response to these questions, I cited the work of Grice and Austin, who argue that humans utter 'I' for five distinct reasons: (1) to make ourselves known and our beliefs understood, (2) to individuate ourselves, that is, to reinforce our unique existence among other 'I's, (3) to distinguish our privately conceived life from the lives others believe that we lead, (4) to discern our own variegated experiences and to realize how these experiences culminate in a single, albeit syncretic, life and, (5) to make our existence transparent both to ourselves and to others.

When we apply the analysis of Grice and Austin to self-narration, we find that autobiographers self-narrate for five reasons: (1) to achieve self-knowledge, (2) to unify the self; (3) to communicate the self to others; (4) to give continuity to their lives; and (5) to explore the relation between the self and the subject. In this section, I evaluate these motivations in the context of philosophical autobiography. I begin with self-knowledge.

In *Patterns and Meaning in History*, Wilhelm Dilthey produces one of the most comprehensive sets of reflections about autobiography to date. Beginning with the claim that autobiographers aim to acquire self-knowledge,

Dilthey argues that we *must* write about ourselves if we are to achieve self-knowledge because knowledge, even of ourselves, depends on the ways knowledge is expressed. Treating self-knowledge as a phenomenological product, Dilthey grounds self-knowledge in a conception of history that informs the arena of human investigation (sometimes by way of autobiography itself):

> The root from which everything grows is the tendency, natural to man, to meditate on the past and future, on his joys and sorrows, successes and failures. . . . With some it becomes a chief concern, they inquire systematically into the meaning of their own lives, and often give literary expression to what they find. The result is autobiography.[42]

Dilthey suggests that the empirical dimension of knowledge is always present alongside the interpretative framework we utilize to understand human life.[43] Therefore, human life, part existential, part empirical, differs from nature insofar as the meaning of that life is expressed in original terms. The difference between the human and natural sciences is a difference in form rather than content; a difference in *how* rather than *what* the two disciplines investigate.

H. P. Rickman explains Dilthey's thought further: "For Dilthey, human life is not only meaningful; it is also articulate; it expresses its own meaning which we can understand. In this lies the difference between the studies of man and the natural sciences."[44] Expression, then, is essential to self-knowledge, since it is only through overt expression that our views of ourselves acquire clarity, stability, or depth. Because an individual's existence is the primary phenomenon of history, autobiography is the greatest form of self-expression. It is also the most profound and deliberate path toward self-knowledge. Indeed, in Dilthey's words, autobiography is "the highest and most instructive form in which the understanding of life confronts us."[45]

Jerome Bruner, Mary Warnock, and other contemporary scholars of autobiography borrow heavily from Dilthey's view. For example, after accepting Dilthey's claim that autobiography is manifest history, Bruner argues for a direct and an explicit link between self-knowledge and truth within autobiography. To know oneself, he argues, one must grasp one's true self, the self that corresponds to the subject of one's interpersonal search, particularly in the case of an autobiographical search.[46] Similarly, Rebecca Goldstein identifies and articulates the historical intuitions about essence and identity that coalesce with philosophical conceptions of the self and subject. On the one hand, we believe in an ideal representation of ourselves, a nexus of fact and true narration, a representation that we may never know entirely. On the other, we believe in a concrete representation of ourselves, fragmenting and conflicting descriptions that taken together approximate who we are. Though we may know this representation entirely, Goldstein wonders whether it is right to conclude that this representation is an accurate representation of ourselves.[47]

I submit that both the ideal and the concrete representations of ourselves are partially accurate and wholly incomplete. To know oneself in the fullest possible sense of the phrase, we must set these representations in dialectical opposition, moving from one to the other until a synthesis of selves emerges. Unfortunately, most autobiographers allow one of these intuitions to dominate their writing and to insidiously shape the presentation of the self that he or she produces. Indeed, some writers who regard the self as an "ideal ego" adopt the rhetorical stance of a transcendent, impartial narrator who uncovers an authentic self to which their being-in-the-world refers. Others who regard the self as a "shattered ego" write from the position of an affected, limited narrator, a narrator who constructs a successive story from bits of information that he or she and others tell about himself or herself.[48]

Though both intuitions are problematic, they pinpoint the difficulties that suffuse the autobiographical process: the uncanny relationship we have with ourselves as we seek self-knowledge and pursue self-knowing, the product and process of artful living.[49] Self-knowledge requires self-narration (a mediating process) as well as an encounter with the ontological and rhetorical modes of our existence. Self-knowing requires an active and intentional encounter with the self as other. Contrary to Dilthey and company, I contend that three modes of reflection, when enacted, make possible self-knowledge and self-knowing: introspection, retrospection, and alterspection. *Introspection* is psychological. It is a turning inward to the memories, experiences, emotions, beliefs, and desires embedded in the psyche. *Retrospection* is temporal. It is a turning backward to the events and encounters that converge to form the life and history we call our own. *Alterspection* is existential. It is a turning away from the psyche and a life history to the alienating author-subject—an ego who emerges through the act of self-narration and constrains the identity of the embodied writer-self.

The enactment of these three modes of reflection (psychological, temporal, and existential) blows open a psychic space in which we stand face-to-face with the ontological and rhetorical dimensions of our being-in-the-world. The reflexive encounter with these dimensions (self-knowing) and the concrete outcomes of this encounter (self-knowledge) generate a literary space in which we reconcile the ontological and rhetorical dimensions of the self. Even if the self-identity we narrate accrues new meaning and significance as readers reflect, look, and interpret the self, the dialectical reconciliation between the writer-self and the rhetorical-subject yields a rich middle ground in which new philosophical theories of the self, self-narration, self-knowledge, and artful living can emerge.

Autobiography as Confession

Written between 397–400 C. E., Augustine's *Confessions* is the earliest extant autobiography in the Western canon. Augustine models his mesmeric life story after the *pro-Romana* writings of Virgil and Cicero, the Christian letters of Paul, and the Hebrew narratives of the Bible. This rhetorical practice is consistent with the intercultural and intertextual landscape of first-century Rome.[50] Though I reserve a comprehensive account of his autobiography for Chapter 2, I mention *Confessions* in this context because it exemplifies the first two reasons philosophers write autobiographically: to know the self and to order experiences.

The search for self-knowledge drives Augustine's encounter with himself: "O Lord, you were turning me around to look at myself . . . and in this way you brought me face-to-face with myself once more, forcing me upon my own sight so that I should see my wickedness."[51] Perpetually thinking, doubting, and suffering as his incompatible desires divide him against himself, Augustine grounds his Socratic search in God. The method by which he seeks self-knowledge is confession. As Genevieve Lloyd remarks, "'Confessing' is not really . . . to make himself [Augustine] known to others," but rather, to make it possible for him to know himself and ultimately for others to know themselves.[52] To this end, he juxtaposes his youthful, concupiscent self against the shamed and humbled self of middle age. These two faces of Augustine's rhetorical self signify the dyadic nature of sin—acts against God that produce both pleasure and pain and split asunder the self, separating humans from God. But the author-subject is not the only self that Augustine confronts in making his confession. Seeking to dispel doubts about the authenticity of his conversion, Augustine qua writer-self confesses not to a temporally and spatially absent audience but rather to a present audience that sees him (and that may judge him) as a man.

Even after his conversion, Augustine remains concerned about "the danger of self-forgetfulness and the corrupting influence of other people who may deflect from the task of self-appropriation."[53] To obviate this danger, Augustine grounds the self in the sacredness of God. Steven Glazer describes divine sacredness as a revelation of unity that supersedes the dualism of self and world that we experience daily:

> Sacredness . . . grows out of two basic qualities of our experience: awareness and wholeness. Awareness is a natural, self-manifesting quality: it is our ability to perceive, experience, and know. . . . Wholeness is the inherent, seamless, interdependent quality of the world. . . . Wholeness, however, can be cultivated within us by experiencing this nondual quality of the world. Through experiences of awareness and wholeness, we begin to establish the view of the sacred.[54]

Carl Vaught's teleology of wholeness suggests that the quest for the sacred drives us beyond mere awareness of our self-knowable qualities, yet Vaught argues that the quest for wholeness remains unfulfilled because we exist between fragmentation and wholeness. In other words, we may have an intuition or awareness about wholeness (as Glazer describes it), but our experience of wholeness is neither concrete nor permanent. The sacred and the spiritual move us vertically toward wholeness, though we remain partially fragmented.[55] Augustine bears out this teleological perspective by continuing the movement from fragmentation toward wholeness throughout *Confessions*. In striving for the sacred dimensions of being, Augustine assumes the rhetorical stance of the Inner self.

The Inner self serves many purposes. First, the Inner self represents the self as an undifferentiated spirit or undivided self, a view in keeping with Christian theology. Second, it provides an inherent unity to the self, since it regards the self as a transcendent essence that survives bodily death to rejoin God in the pervasive sacredness of reality. Closely related to this is the third purpose it serves: to place Augustine temporally within the city of Man and ultimately (eternally) within the city of God, creating an identity that transcends both the writer-self and the rhetorical-subject. Fourth, it signifies Christ's call for remembrance, a process made present and complete in the taking of the sacraments, and a completed process of self-discovery, a process exemplified in the stories of Aeneas, the Prodigal Son, the book of Job, and the life of Moses.

Augustine is not alone in his appropriation of the Inner self. Confessional autobiographers must assume the Inner view of the self insofar as they disclose thoughts and actions in order to disclaim them. In these cases, as in Augustine's, writers engage in autobiographical storytelling for themselves, not for their readers. Within their practice of philosophical autobiography as confession, we must confess our lives if we wish to achieve self-knowledge, that is, we must follow this model and reflect introspectively and retrospectively on our actions and beliefs.

In addition to writing for the sake of self-knowledge, Augustine writes autobiographically to know God, and in knowing God, to order and make coherent his experiences according to God's divine plan. This requires some elaboration. The unity of Augustine's writer-self supervenes on the continuity of his experiences, his memories, and his temporal and spatial self-awareness. A similar process of unification applies to rhetorical-subjects as well. Just as self-identity arises from the convergence of psychological, temporal, and existential modes of reflection, writing about oneself is a unification of autobiographical bits of information:

> Autobiography necessarily involves a collection into unity, a retrieval of the self from its dispersion into the world. For the autobiographer's need to make sense out of her life requires her to forge connections and establish a sense of development through the stages of her existence. And this must give rise to the fiction of a continuing self that maintains its identity throughout.[56]

By privileging the Inner self wherein the self is the ontological ground of experience and the coordinator of mental states, Augustine invests his first-person narrative with an atemporal and ahistorical presence. He engenders in his voice self-referential reason, reflection, retrospection, and self-awareness. He speaks to future generations; he speaks through and to God.

The point of this brief overview of Augustine's *Confessions* is to show how philosophical and rhetorical aims inform both the process and product of self-narration, respectively—self-ascribing/self-knowing, autobiography/self-knowledge. *Confessions* is an endless resource for understanding how an autobiographer's view of the self feeds his or her rhetorical stance (Inner/Outer) and controls his or her literary expression (the organization of the narrative, i.e., the narrative frame, the diction, the imagery, and the episodes of the autobiography).[57]

The product of Augustine's dialectical process is threefold: (1) *revelation* of his sins, his mistakes, his weaknesses; (2) *knowledge* of himself, God, the nature of memory, time, and space; (3) *transformation* of himself into a Christian, his readers into believers, and God from an abstract, Platonic ideal into a loving and fragile being, fully divine and fully human. These three outcomes dovetail nicely with the tripartite view of self-knowledge and self-knowing that I posed earlier: introspective/psychological, retrospective/temporal, and alterspective/existential. I will say more about the connections between my view of self-knowing/self-knowledge and self-narration in later chapters. Now I focus on the two remaining motivations for philosophical autobiography.

Conveying the Self to Others

In the previous section I described two philosophical aims that motivate autobiographical prose writing: to know thyself and to organize experience. I described these aims in the context of Augustine's *Confessions*. Now I examine a third objective: *to communicate to others who we are*. I discuss this objective in the context of Jean-Jacques Rousseau's *The Confessions* (1782), a work modeled explicitly upon Augustine's *Confessions*.

Rousseau's autobiography opens with an invocation to the reader. In this invocation he promises to speak nothing but the truth (as long as his memory avails him):

> I have resolved on an enterprise which has no precedent, and which, once complete, will have no imitator. My purpose is to display to my kind a portrait in every way true to nature, and the man I shall portray will be myself. . . . Let the last trumpet sound when it will. I shall come forward with this work in my hand, to present myself before my Sovereign Judge, and proclaim aloud: "Here is what I have done, and

> if by chance I have used some immaterial embellishment it has been only to fill a void due to a defect of memory. I may have taken for fact what was no more than probability, but I have never put down as true what I knew to be false. I have displayed myself as I was, vile and despicable when my behavior was such, as good, generous, and noble when I was so. I have bared my secret soul as Thou thyself has seen it, Eternal Being! So let the numberless legion of my fellow men gather round me, and hear my confessions."[58]

Rousseau's professed commitment to the tradition of confession requires that he follow the literary standards of confession created in part, but not wholly, by Augustine. He must express sincerity in his writing, even if his expression is ironic. He must appeal to God and man, both of whom are in positions to recognize his sincerity. He must exploit the rhetorical subject and present the writer-self in clear and certain ways. Finally, he must present a linear account of his life. In meeting this fourth convention, he must divulge the secrets and scandals of his life no matter how ludicrous or distasteful they appear. Moreover, this divulgence must appear in the proper chronological order (verisimilitude is a necessary condition of truth). Hence, in the context of the eighteenth century, Rousseau's writing must mirror the events of his life to be deemed accurate and therefore truthful. Otherwise, the veracity of his claims remains questionable.

With the hubris that typifies his life, Rousseau takes pen in hand and proceeds to assume the conventions of confessional autobiography and to meet the conditions of truth endorsed by his contemporaries. He begs for forgiveness, apparently pained by his own words, as he asks the "Sovereign Judge" to hear his confessions. He traces his life from his first memories to six years before his death, leaving no stone unturned. But how successful is Rousseau in answering the questions of identity and essence that beleaguer him? Who (and what) emerges from his autobiography?

Many scholars, including Dilthey, resist grand pronouncements about the success of Rousseau's work, claiming instead that he succeeds in his effort to show his life *as his audience required.* Though Rousseau presents himself in socially prescribed ways, some praise him for his candor in light of constraining standards. H. P. Rickman even goes so far as to express pity for this outcast whose destiny for greatness (he believes) was cut short by fate:

> . . . whatever he had done and suffered and whatever was corrupt within him, he felt, and this was, after all, the ideal of his age, that he was a noble, generous soul who felt for humanity. This he wanted to show the world; he wanted to justify his spiritual existence by showing it exactly as it was . . . Rousseau wanted, above all, to justify his individual existence.[59]

But pity may be a hasty emotion. It becomes increasingly clear throughout *The Confessions* that Rousseau's efforts to confess his life within the standard criteria of confessional writing are done mostly as lip service. His self-portrait—a literary exercise in self-flagellation—serves to justify his own bloated view of himself. Any incredulity detected in the writing belongs to the author alone who undermines his project by incessantly appealing to a God in whom he has no faith.

Rousseau's portrait of himself as a fiercely self-reliant human who nevertheless cries out to God creates unshakable skepticism about his text and his self-representation. His expressed desire to show us his true nature becomes sterile before the autobiography ends. In book seven, Rousseau begins to compromise his initial promise. He is forced to admit his failure:

> I have only one faithful guide on which I can count; the succession of feelings which have marked the development of my being, and thereby recall the events that have acted upon it as cause or effect. I easily forget my misfortunes, but I cannot forget my faults, and still less my genuine feelings. The memory of them is too dear ever to be effaced from my heart. I may omit or transpose facts, or make mistakes in dates; but I cannot go wrong about what I have felt, or about what my feelings have led me to do; and these are the chief subjects of my story. The true object of my confessions is to reveal my inner thoughts exactly in all the situations of my life. It is the history of my soul that I have need of no other memories; it is enough if I enter again into my inner self, as I have done till now.[60]

Rousseau's failure is not entirely his fault, nor is it wholly unforgivable. His objectives, like his philosophical commitments, are at odds with the conventions and standards of his time. On the one hand, he must satisfy the literary standards for confessional writing. He therefore assumes the rhetorical stance of the Inner self in his first-person writing. On the other hand, he must accommodate the sensibilities of his readers. Hence, he conflates his view of the self, an "inner" voice of passion, with his motivation for writing: to stir the hearts and sympathy of his readers.

The tensions between his aim and form leave him (and us) in a quandary. For instance, he claims to seek the forgiveness of God. Yet he places his readers in the vicarious position of God, demanding that we see beyond the facts to the feelings that reside in his heart, the seat of his Inner self. But how can we know and/or judge his feelings? By what standards should we evaluate his self-concept? Why study Rousseau's *The Confessions*?

I contend that Rousseau is the first confessional autobiographer to wear the Inner self like a mask. His exploitation of the Inner self, however meager, provides an invaluable bridge between ancient and modern meditations on the self. It does this in three ways. First, his autobiography mediates the Inner and Outer self by creating an implicit dialogue between the writer-self and the author-subject. Second, his work functions as a direct conduit between the first-person narrations of Descartes and Nietzsche. By endorsing ideals that displace thought with feeling, Rousseau shifts the philosophical paradigm away from the speculative reason of rationalism and toward the entrenched individualism of perspectivism. Third, it offers a fruitful critique of the confessional mode of philosophical autobiography. This helps creates a space for new modes of autobiography to emerge. Despite the limitation of his autobiography, Rousseau's *The Confessions* provides an essential link in the chain of philosophical autobiography. By conveying himself to others as a mask-wearing Inner self, Rousseau politicizes the distinction between the ontological and rhetorical self.

The Relationship between Language and Meaning

There is a fourth aim exhibited by first-person self-narration: *to explore the relationship between language and meaning*. The autobiographies of Nietzsche and Barnes provide two exemplary cases in point. Since I have already introduced Nietzsche's *Ecce Homo* in this chapter, and because I want to bracket the discussion of these texts until I can explore the self qua Outer self in detail, I offer only a few preliminary remarks about their work below.

Both deeply influenced by the post-Hegelian preoccupation with the human subject, Nietzsche and Barnes use first-person narration as a mode of philosophical self-exposition. Instead of appropriating the heavily introspective and retrospective model of confession utilized by Augustine, Descartes, and Rousseau, they assume an alterspective mode of philosophical autobiography: a way of seeing oneself as other; a process of *creating* a self to be identified and known in the world. They, like many first-person writers of the nineteenth and twentieth centuries, borrow an existential paradigm to articulate their experiences in the world: "Writers who are fascinated by the blurring of distinction between illusion and reality find an I-narrator a satisfying means of probing the nature and meaning of experience."[61]

In language, we are able to articulate the far-reaching differences between representational and signifying systems. But writing clouds our ability to see the philosophical nuances of literary forms. On what grounds can we distinguish between the writer and author? Text and work? Self and subject? What conceptual framework makes these distinctions clear? In response to these and related concerns, Nietzsche's self-aggrandizing aphorisms and Barnes's phenomenological techniques push the genre of philosophical autobiography in new directions. An analysis of their autobiographies appears in Chapters 2 and Chapter 4, respectively.

Features of Autobiographical Writing

Autobiography is both a genre of literature and an interpretation of experience. It is an act of personal revelation and a form of philosophical exposition. The act of recording the events of one's life—of creating a text that has an ontological status of its own, independent of the writer—and expounding upon the meaning of those events (as a hermeneutic act) is a philosophical exercise. It is a process of revelation. Within this self-revelatory process, a particular self-image emerges *as a result of* one's ontological views of the self and *in response to* the rhetorical forces shaping self-representation.

But autobiography is a peculiar form of philosophical exposition. "Self-fashioning always begins in the middle," Nehamas insists. "It is only after one has become someone or other, once one realizes that one has already had a life consisting of all sorts of events that appear haphazard, disconnected, imitative, and insignificant, that one can begin to try to put them together and to become not just someone or other but oneself."[62] Like most philosophical investigations, autobiography is indeterminate. Its meaning is neither encoded nor absolute. And the form and content of autobiography vary according to the methodologies and presuppositions at play in the process of reflection and writing.

Autobiography is an equally peculiar genre of literature. It serves both historical and artistic purposes, yet it is neither fact nor fiction. Like the self who is always autobiographed from a middle position, autobiography locates itself in the rhetorical space between fact and fiction. In doing so, it offers a direct challenge to the foundational assumptions that feed philosophical distinctions. Confession, eyewitness monologue, and postmodern instantiations of self-narration radically blur the line between truth and falsity. Some even erase the line altogether. This is where my distinction between the writer-self and author-subject proves useful. Even if we deny essentialist accounts of the self, we must nonetheless acknowledge that someone is writing the text before us, and that someone is at least rhetorically different from and temporally and spatially distinct from the author-subject of the text.[63]

How does the milieu in which one lives and writes shape the literary conventions that he or she invokes? How do those conventions shape the view of the self that permeates autobiography itself? The autobiographies of Augustine, Descartes, and Rousseau ground the self and self-knowledge in God. Nietzsche thwarts this convention by urging his readers to become god-like (to become an *Ubermensch*). Barnes avoids God together. This pattern shows the degree to which writing is a contextual activity suffused with intellectual paradigms and social trends and informed by race, class, and gender, as I suggest. For example, many postmodern writers no longer appeal to God or an Inner self to explain or justify their lives. Such concepts appear philosophically bankrupt, from a postmodern viewpoint, and such conventions seem antiquated and naïve from a constructivist perspective. Once the philosophical and religious views that undergird literary conventions appear untenable, their usefulness disappears.

The relation between literary conventions and philosophical concepts is worthy of further inquiry. How do commitments to theories of truth bear upon the narratives we tell? Alasdair MacIntyre and Martha Nussbaum offer helpful responses. Their work on narratives has been generated independently of one another and is argued from different angles. However, MacIntyre and Nussbaum agree that we use narratives, we construct narratives, to unify our lives, that is, to bring coherence to our otherwise dispersing experiences.[64] Hence, the function of narratives is to organize experience (spatially, temporally, thematically, historically). This view suggests that we create narratives to demarcate our personal history—a view that is consistent with Dilthey's view of autobiography—and in the process of demarcating our history, we give rise to a rhetorical subject who acts as the central figure, the hero, of our narrative.

If MacIntyre and Nussbaum are right about the function that narratives serve, then the act of autobiographing our lives replicates an ordering event we engage in every day: the organization of experience in discursive form. The psychological and philosophical texture of experience bears upon the writer's psyche at both the conscious and subconscious levels. Through acts of reflection (introspection, retrospection, and alterspection) and written narration (self-bifurcation), these experiences move from the subconscious to the conscious mind, thereby enabling the writer to organize these experiences into a coherent narrative.

For these reasons, writing a life story is an activity embedded with the organizing narratological structures of our lives. Additional principles ensure that the account we offer is accessible and understandable (a good story should "flow" after all). Mieke Bal and Lorraine Code make a stronger claim that bears upon autobiographical writing in particular. The notion of objective, impersonal knowledge, they argue, itself born out of Cartesian conceptions of knowledge, is circumscribed by narratological notions of third-person narratives. True knowledge, extruded from scientific inquiry, requires the knower to be distinct, unaffected by, and unaffecting of the knowable object. This method, designed to purify knowledge by extracting the subjective experience from the event of inquiry, only succeeds in pushing truth beyond the reach of the human mind.

For Code, the idea of an objective, universal knowledge is masculine insofar as it arises from philosophical systems produced by men in male-dominated domains of study, such as the empirical sciences. The model of "knowledge" produced along scientific lines is one among many narrative conceptions of knowledge:

> Knowledge produced in seemingly objective ways carries an authority that mirrors, reinforces, and probably also derives from masculine authority. Its alleged derivation from detached, pure thought permits it

> to claim superiority over modes of thought infected with emotional involvement and feeling. Out of this conception of the autonomy of scientific knowledge the conviction emerges that "real" knowledge must be autonomous, detached from the subjective idiosyncrasies and circumstances of both "observer" and "observed"; abstract, independent, and depersonalized.[65]

If knowledge is a product of narratological activities, as Code claims, then knowledge does indeed bear some of the prejudices of its creators. Moreover, if knowledge is corrupted by the activity of knowing, then *self-knowledge* achieved via autobiography is also corruptible by the narratological features that our autobiography circumscribes. Hence, the MacIntyre and Nussbaum view of narratives as the organization of events is not a sufficient account of autobiography.

To understand the narratologial features that circumscribe autobiography, we need an account of narratives that outlines the conditions for and the features of narration. Mieke Bal attempts this task in the following way:

> A narrative is an account in any semiotic system of a subjectivized and often entirely or partly fictionalized series of events. It involves a narrator—whether explicitly or implicitly self-referential, always a "first person"—a focalizer—the implied subject who "colors" the story—and a number of actors or agents of the events. Narrative thus conceived is not confined to literary or, indeed, verbal narrative. It is a mode of semiotic behavior rather than a finite set of objects.[66]

Bal implies that knowledge contains subjective thoughts, feelings, and behavior extending beyond the signs of knowledge itself. This offers us a clue about the relation between narration and autobiography. Autobiographers utilize the narrative features that Bal describes above: a first-person perspective, coupled with an account of the intentional states of the 'I' speaking, and action, or a series of movements and events showing how the intentional states of the 'I' lead to, disrupt, or change other events and activities. In doing so, they create a secondary but distinctive feature of autobiographical narrative: a justification (either explicit or implicit) for the self-narrative. Stated simply, autobiographies must contain some exceptional or unique series of events, experiences, or viewpoints to justify the narrative recording of one's life for others to read. One must show that he or she has valid reasons to write his or her autobiography.

Now a third set of difficulties emerges. If autobiographies are first-person narratives as they appear, and if as forms of narrative they are constructed with many of the same elements or features of fictional narratives, then what distinguishes autobiography from fictional works such as novels or short stories? If, as I have argued, autobiography resides in the rhetorical space between fiction and fact, then on what grounds can I justify autobiography as fictionalized nonfiction? What is the causal or logical link between author and truth?

From the Inner perspective on the self, autobiographical narratives are self-referential facts or objective world events organized into a discursive form. Adapting the empiricist claim that knowledge is a collation of sensory experience, the Inner perspective tacitly endorses a causal relationship between the experiences of the writer-self and the identity of the author-subject. Hence, autobiography is largely factual. Alternatively, the Outer perspective on the self defines autobiographical narratives as self-ascribing events organized into a discursive form. The Outer perspective adapts the rationalist belief that knowledge is a product of the mind's eye reflecting upon (innate) ideas and tacitly endorses a nondetermining affinity or resemblance between the experiences of the writer-self and the identity of the author-subject. Hence, autobiography is largely fictional.

As these diverging points of view indicate, the status of autobiographies is determined in part by the criterion of truth brought to bear on them. Despite well-argued and well-supported claims like Jorge Gracia's, that the existence and meaning of categories are determined by the culture in which these categories appear (and are, therefore, subject to history and politics), many philosophers assert that autobiographies are by nature fictional insofar as authors construct autobiography.[67] As Martin Warner argues:

> The author's vision of man and his place in nature, together with his own remembered or ascertainable past, provide crucial controls on the imagery, selection of incidents, and overall organization of the autobiography. However much the author may be convinced that he remembers "how it seemed then," the presentation will always be that of an adult mind remembering.[68]

While it is true that writers make conscious choices about what to include in their autobiographies based upon sometimes tacit principles of economy, relevance, and simplicity, this does not in itself convict them of fictionality. Instead, I argue that autobiography represents a middle path between fiction and fact, a path that aptly captures the intersubjective nature of the self, a self that is both ontological and rhetorical, both Inner and Outer. As a genre of literature, autobiography reflects the shifts in literary styles and conventions over time and throughout various genres, including historical and autobiographical genres. As a mode of philosophical exposition, it reflects the metaphysical and epistemological commitments that hold sway at various moments in the history of philosophy, commitments that shape the views of the self and the narrative representation of the self in dramatic ways.

A concession that the narrative features of autobiography are shared by fictional works and emerge from social trends and intellectual paradigms does not, I think, weaken the argument that autobiographies are factual, historical accounts in an important sense of those terms. Moreover, to view autobiographies as factual, historical accounts does not commit one to the view that autobiographies are mimetic accounts of one's past recorded for the sake of posterity. As neuroscientists continue to show, memory is not always or necessarily organized into coherent patterns or sequences. Rather, memory may be, as Barnes argues, incoherent and episodic: "For just as in a dream, every figure that in bold relief stands as one thing holds nuances that say it is something else, so my recollections come to me in a multicolored cluster rather than in a coherent pattern. . . . No doubt I am not unique in conjuring up this sort of medley."[69]

Insofar as autobiographies take root in the embodied experiences and ontological conditions of a human life, they constitute factual self-narration. Still, the 'I' that both signifies and refers to a particular life casts short shadows on our self-identity. We are both Inner and Outer, ontological and rhetorical, writer-selves and author-subjects. It follows then that autobiography is both subjective and objective, factual and fictional, literary and philosophical. Furthermore, if the self lies between the Inner and the Outer, and if autobiography resides between fact and fiction, then only a dialectical engagement of the ontological and rhetorical self—an engagement necessitated by the bifurcation of the self inherent to autobiography—will blow open a space for an authentic encounter with the self. Autobiography, then, is an instantiation of artful living, living that commits one to self-knowing and self-knowledge.

In summation, two literary activities make possible the creation of autobiography: the causal and/or temporal organization of events into a narrative form and the justification of self-narration according to an implicit or explicit principle of action. As MacIntyre and Nussbaum argue, narratives must embody systematic and coherent story lines, they must conform to commonly recognized patterns of causation and temporality, and they must suggest a context for interpretation that justifies the self-narration in question. Stated differently, writing autobiographically places writers in a context of action and world events that makes them more intelligible, understandable, and engaging. Hence, autobiographers utilize a number of narrative principles, such as causal and temporal organization, to show how a narrative frame surrounds and gives rise to actions that are themselves causally and temporally mediated. Of course, the organization of events causally and temporally *and* the justification of the written account itself established throughout the history of writing force us to continually evaluate the status of autobiography. Eventually thinkers may deconstruct the concept of 'fact' entirely rendering it useless for philosophical or cultural analysis. With this possibility in mind, we cannot make prima facie commitments about autobiographical writing, commitments that attempt to identify autobiography definitively as fact or fiction and aim to characterize autobiographies merely as narratives, novels, or documentaries. Autobiography lies somewhere in between these literary forms.

Conclusions

Autobiographers invoke a number of rhetorical devices to help them self-narrate. Some confess, complain, brag, accuse, and apologize, while others explain, attack, and evaluate. For instance, the autobiographies of Augustine, Descartes, and Rousseau are confessional, explanatory, and apologetic, as the diction, organization, and content of their work reveal. These devices enable these autobiographers to perform a number of functions. Augustine discloses his actions, thoughts, and emotions in order to acknowledge and overcome them. Descartes infers an 'I' witness to distinguish the cogito (the thinking thing) from the rest of the sensory world. Rousseau recites his emotions and life events with a constrained and defensive tone, a tone that places blame for his failures on others.

Perhaps a more interesting function of autobiographies is that of cultural or literary commentary/criticism. Working at the metacritical level, some autobiographers set out to evaluate autobiography as a literary form (to applaud it, to lampoon it, or to renounce it). Nietzsche's *Ecce Homo* is a prime example. By exaggerating an image of himself as a scholar and philosopher, Nietzsche mocks the activities and images we associate with scholars and philosophers writ large—"Why I Write Such Good Books," "Why I Am So Clever," and so on. Hence, his self-aggrandizement is both personal and professional. To bring into sharp focus the process and product of autobiography, Nietzsche crafts a hyperbolic view of the self that aims ironically to deflate our notions of the self:

> Through exaggeration and hyperbole, Nietzsche offers a self-portrait which calls itself into question at the same time as it focuses our attention upon the traditional devices of autobiography.[70]

By engaging in self-ascription that portrays him as arrogant, insolent, and maniacal, Nietzsche's *Ecce Homo* mocks traditional autobiographers for elevating themselves to the status of a god. Instead, Nietzsche asks us to "behold the man!," the new figure of autobiography, nay, the new figure of the postmodern world, "since man cannot become master without disinheriting the previous ruler, the Enlightenment . . . [and] the dream that man shall become a God."[71]

How does autobiography function in the work of Nietzsche? First, his autobiography exposes the false conceptions of (and slave commitments to) the self as victimized, weak, and fallen. Next, it creates a dialogue between the reader and author, a dialogue that exposes our presuppositions about self-identity and self-presentation. And finally, it challenges erroneous beliefs about Nietzsche himself. As Walter Kaufmann notes in the preface to *Ecce Homo*, "We also hear [in the text] the anguished cry of one who sees—foresees—himself mistaken for a writer he is not: for an apostle of military power and empire, a nationalist, a racist."[72] Recall the epigraph with which I began this chapter: "I have a duty against which my habits, even more the pride of my instincts, revolt at bottom, namely, to say: Hear me! For I am such and such a person. Above all, do not mistake me for someone else."[73]

Nietzsche reinforces what I have said about philosophical autobiography thus far. Philosophical autobiography challenges traditional conceptions of the self in several ways. First, autobiographical writing—writing that adopts the dual perspective of object and subject of inquiry—bifurcates the self into an ontological self and a rhetorical self. The ontological self (the writer-self) is an agent who organizes life events into a narrative form. The rhetorical self (the author-subject) functions as the protagonist of the story. Hence, the author and writer of autobiographies exist within psychologically and temporally distinct spheres of existence. The 'I' is sometimes absorbed into the pure noetic activity of autobiography and expressed as the Inner self. In other instances, the 'I' remains divorced from the act of writing, self-consciously creating the perspective that emerges from the literary work. This self is expressed as the Outer self. The bifurcation of the self in autobiography necessitates a reconceptualization of the self and self-representation.

Second, the bifurcation of the self creates a chasm within the psyche that makes possible both *self-knowledge* and *self-knowing*. As I have argued, autobiography is both a genre of literature and a philosophical exercise. Consequently, autobiography is both product and process generative. The product of self-narration is self-knowledge; the process of self-narration is self-knowing. Prior to the intentional and explicit bifurcation of the self within and because of autobiographical writing, only self-knowledge is possible. Autobiography reconceives Socratic self-examination to include both the acquisition of self-knowledge and the practice of self-knowing. The philosophical practice of self-knowing elevates the examined life into what Nehamas calls "the artful life."

Third, autobiography creates both an occasion and a literary space for the unification of the self. The bifurcation of the self makes possible self-knowledge and self-knowing. But self-knowledge and self-knowing require a dialectical encounter between the ontological and rhetorical dimensions of our existence. The reflective acts of introspection, retrospection, and alterspection mediate this encounter. Moreover, the reflexive encounter with these three reflective dimensions of ourselves (self-knowing) and the concrete outcomes of this encounter (self-knowledge) generate a literary space in which we can reconcile the ontological and rhetorical selves. The dialectical reconciliation of the writer-self and the rhetorical-subject necessitates new theories of the self, self-narration, self-knowledge, and artful living. Knowing thyself, however obscure the product and however onerous the process, is tied inextricably to the dialectic of autobiographical writing.

Chapter 2

Bifurcating the Self

> Since I have undertaken to reveal myself absolutely to the public, nothing about me remains hidden or obscure. I must remain incessantly beneath his gaze, so that he (the reader) may follow me in all the extravagances of my heart and into every least corner of my life. . . . I am laying myself sufficiently open to human malice by telling my story, without rendering myself more vulnerable by any silence.
>
> —Jean-Jacques Rousseau[1]

Self-Ascription and Self-Description

Individual identity has tremendous caché in contemporary culture. Analysts from the political Left and Right attribute its rising currency to capitalism, secularism, hedonism, and/or postmodernism. Their assessment is not entirely off the mark. Money, self-aggrandizement, aesthetic pleasure, and the postmodern revaluation of self-narration contribute in varying degrees to the fixation on the self. However, the primacy on individual identity is not merely a cultural phenomenon. Nor is it new. Confucius's *Analects* describes concrete conflicts between society and human nature that predate the sixth century B. C. E. Aristophanes' speech in the *Symposium* characterizes the psyche as ego driven. Socrates follows the oracular dictum "Know thyself." Augustine's sexual impulses drive him deep into depression.

Psychological and philosophical readings of self-representation suggest a different set of possibilities than the modern variations we frequently hear.[2]

Perhaps the unabated interest in the self signifies our inescapably rooted philosophical natures—a recurring desire to know who and what we are. Fascinations with the self may harken back to the ancient myth of Narcissus, who gazes into the water, falls in love with his own beauty, and drowns trying to embrace the image he sees reflected in the pool before him. Beauty is a powerful and an often destructive cultural force. Maybe we have finally and irrevocably embraced the paradox of identity on a personal level.

Whatever the source of our interest in the self, cultural, philosophical, and psychological elements play important roles in the current fascination with the self. The complexity surrounding identity reflects the frenzied nature of human existence. I think we must learn to appreciate this complexity lest we forget the lessons of our ancient predecessors. We cannot cull simple answers from a single culture or body of research and analysis. Rather, the lifeworld of human beings demands a cross-cultural and interdisciplinary examination. Though I cannot indulge such an examination here, I offer a preliminary account of identity later. My hope is that such an account will clarify the relationship between self-narration and self-identity.

Personal Identity

Philosophers working within the Western analytic philosophical tradition define personal identity as a continuing body, mind, personality, and memories (or some combination thereof), making a person at t1 the same person at t2, t3 . . . t*n*, where t*n* represents any time in the future. But how does a person at t*n* know that he or she is the same as the person at t1, t2, and so on? Does the person at t*n* remember the experiences of the person at t1, as Augustine, Descartes, and Rousseau suggest? Must the self by unified through memory? Or can the unity of self be grounded in other psychological and/or literary methods or processes, as Nietzsche and Barnes claim? And who (or what) is the person remembering himself or herself? What is its essence?[3]

Recent research in neuroscience and postmodern critiques of science suggest that identity is constructed rather than remembered (or that memory is constructive rather than mimetic in nature). Identity construction occurs via a set of perspectives that follows from scientific inquiry but also paradoxically presupposes scientific inquiry. Within this paradigm, personal identity arises from a process of selecting, highlighting, and deleting (or repressing) remembered experiences through a set of precognitive or subconscious concepts or ideas—a process of identity encoding in the brain. As long as the paradigm does not overly constrain the process of identity encoding, then the possible outcomes or arrangements of personal identity for any given person are infinite. A philosophical conclusion we might draw from this research is that humans utilize the ambiguity of identity as an endless source of creativity and artful living. But what does this account of identity imply about the essence of the self who is doing the selecting, highlighting, deleting, and writing? At best, it is a thinking thing (ala Descartes), an unknowable force or will. At worst, it is nothing; that is, no force or will supervenes on cognition, and we are material, mechanistic creatures.

The prevailing views of identity exemplified by philosophical autobiography parallel both Inner and Outer views of the self. Inner autobiographers treat autobiography as a discursive act of self-description in which the remembered self becomes the recorded self. Outer autobiographers regard autobiography as an ongoing discursive process of self-ascription in which the constructed self becomes the characterized or ascribed self.[4] For instance, writers who assume an Inner self perspective characterize identity as a unity or cohesion of self-mapping experiences, experiences that are stored in memory and either discovered or realized through introspection and/or retrospection. Moreover, they construe the self and the subject of first-person writing as a coalescing essence (spiritual or mental). Circumscribed by an individuated ego, this essence is expressed as an Inner self, a self that has "privileged access to the content of our minds, epistemological solitude, and final, incorrigible authority over first-person psychological utterances."[5] The task of autobiographical writing is to "recall, recite, and record those inner, private memories, beliefs, etc. that constitute 'you.'"[6] Augustine, Descartes, and Rousseau hold variations of this view.

By contrast, writers such as Nietzsche and Barnes regard identity as constructed (or co-constructed), often alterspectively and atemporally. The constructed ego or subject is best expressed as an Outer self, a self that is embodied (or circumscribed) by a text. A set of shifting literary and cultural contexts constitutes the meaning of the rhetorical subject and the interpretation of the text. Hence, there is no knowable or identifiable self behind the author, and no meaning beyond the text. Many post-nineteenth-century writers express variations of this viewpoint.

Psychosocial views of identity form a middle path between these two extremes. Recent research in psychology and sociology suggests that identity arises from a confluence of sociocultural forces. These theories do not deny that the self is preformed by hormonal and psychological states and, therefore, can be disclosed at an ontological level. But they suggest that the presocial self is merely a thing, a psyche, not an ego (not an I, a he, or a she). As an embodied psyche embedded in a particular set of social and historical conditions, various forces *form* the self that is known and knowable in the world (social, political, familial, and so on). Hence, personal identity accrues out of a process of formation. The psyche or "thing" becomes an ego, a "he" or a "she." Also, the self can be reformed through psychotherapeutic techniques. My own view of identity parallels the psychosocial view in many respects. I will say more about this in Chapter 4.

A lack of adequate or clear definitions (or circumscriptions) of identity should not sway us from the difficult task at hand. We cannot escape the fact that identity constitutes individuals as knowing, knowable, and self-knowing beings, or that the relation between identity and self-knowing makes self-reflection possible. Hence, to understand both who and what we are, we must translate identity into self-narration. But the shifting views of the self hamper our efforts. Charles Taylor aptly describes the vexing nature of identity in *Sources of the Self*:

> There is a question about ourselves—which we roughly gesture at with the term "identity"—which cannot be sufficiently answered with any general doctrine of human nature. The search for identity can be seen as the search for what I essentially am. But this can no longer be sufficiently defined in terms of some universal description of human agency as such, as soul, reason, or will. There still remains a question about me, and that is why I think of myself as a self. This word now circumscribes an area of questioning. It designates the kind of being of which this question of identity can be asked.[7]

Taylor's insights clarify the hermeneutic dimensions of identity in the world. But how might they apply to identity in texts? What kind of being do questions of textual identity suggest? Who is the author-subject who constitutes the identity of the protagonist? Whatever we learn about the author-subject of autobiographical writing, we learn from the author himself or herself, that is, the figure who pervades the text, the 'I' of the text, who is colored by the writer's philosophical commitments and literary choices.[8] Whether this author-self is a factualized ego, a fictional figure, or a mimetic characterization of the writer is an important question and one that requires further consideration.

Can we assume that the Rousseau of *The Social Contract* is identical with the Rousseau of *The Confessions*? What is the relationship between the writer-self of these texts and the authorial personae that emerge out of these texts? The rhetorical stance of Rousseau in *The Confessions,* for example, shares little with the Rousseau of *The Social Contract.* Rousseau's insipid paranoia and ambivalence in *The Confessions* are absent from *The Social Contract.* We draw different conclusions about Rousseau from these texts; we make different inferences about his identity. When considering these texts independently, there appears to be only nominal justification for concluding that the author "Jean-Jacques Rousseau" is the same person.

To resolve this paradox we could appeal to subtextual information and show that Rousseau's identity carries over both texts, thus the author of the text is one and the same. But what problems might arise if we assume that "identity" is commensurate with "author" (rather than person or writer)? What other assumptions must we make to conflate the writer/author distinction? Suppose the author of *The Social Contract* is the same author of *The Confessions*, because the historically known and socially recognized writer did in fact write both texts. Moreover, Rousseau's memory and the continuity of experiences mutually instantiate him as one and the same person over time. But are these assumptions necessary either logically or psychologically? Can we understand the relationship between an author and a text without them?

Unlike other literary genres, autobiographical writing bifurcates the self into an author-subject (the rhetorical persona) and a writer-self (the individual who writes, arranges, edits, interprets, and perhaps reads the text in which he or she appears as the main or sole character). But if texts are atemporal and ahistorical, as I argue in Chapter 1, and if the author-subject of autobiographical text is atemporal and ahistorical, then we need not invoke the criterion of continuity over time (or other criteria of personal identity) to explain authorial identity. Instead we must develop a distinctive set of criteria for determining the identity of the author-subject and articulating his or her relation to the writer-self. To this end, I introduce a conceptual figure in this chapter who bridges the rhetorical and ontological self: *the historical figure*.

The historical figure is a public figure with specific obligations and duties to others based upon the sometimes tacit expectations of others. Unlike the author-self, whose identity is inscribed by the text that the writer-self creates, the identity of the historical figure is inscribed by the social and interpersonal relations to which the writer-self subscribes. His or her identity derives from independent sources of information—biographies, records, documents, and so on—as well as from friends, family members, and other identity-generative relations. We find this figure especially prominent in Rousseau's *The Confessions* and to a lesser degree in Augustine's *Confessions*. I return to the author-subject, the historical figure, and the writer-self throughout this chapter.[9]

My primary aim in this chapter is to survey the philosophical autobiographies and/or first-person philosophical texts of Augustine, Descartes, Rousseau, Nietzsche, and Barnes. I do not recount these texts narratologically. Rather, I outline the view of the self that each articulates in (or implies by) their self-representations. I reserve additional discussions of these texts for Chapter 3 and Chapter 4, where I reevaluate them in the context of self-masking and gender formation, respectively. Specifically I discuss the effect of masked and gendered self-representation on self-narration generally and on these first-person texts. In Chapter 4 I offer a hermeneutical framework in which we might interpret philosophical autobiography. I argue that just as the writing of autobiography creates a dialogical encounter between the writer-self and author-subject, the reading of autobiography invites the reader to consider his or her identity and self-conception. Artful living necessitates reflective engagement with the self, a form of reflective engagement that philosophical autobiographers exemplify. For now I turn to the task at hand: to expose and express the essence and identity of the self embedded in first-person self-narration.

Authorial Identity

Many autobiographers possess philosophical outlooks or interests, but not all of them are considered philosophers as such. To say, then, that I examine the work of philosophers is to say that I examine individuals who contribute to the discipline of philosophy in historically recognizable and discipline-related ways. These include Saint Augustine of Hippo (*Confessions*); René Descartes (*Meditations on First Philosophy*); Jean-Jacques Rousseau (*The Confessions*); Friedrich Nietzsche (*Ecce Homo*); and Hazel Barnes (*The Story I Tell Myself*).

The Western philosophical tradition acknowledges each individual's contributions to metaphysics, epistemology, ontology, political theory, literature, and continental European thought. Yet except for Nietzsche, little mention is made of the style or form in which their ideas appear. This is unfortunate but not surprising. It shows the regrettable fact that Western philosophy tends to privilege content over form. Our philosophical tradition allows ideas and arguments to reign supreme; forget the text, forget the context, forget the subtext, and forget the pretext. Ironically structuralists and deconstructionists such as Lyotard and Derrida argue that there is nothing outside of the text: no ideas, no author, no meaning. Despite a growing antagonism toward analytic philosophy, ideas still have more currency than the texts in which they appear.

I have selected these particular philosophers for three reasons. First, each takes literary form seriously. The great rhetorician Augustine appropriates the models of Cicero, Virgil, and other formative intellectuals throughout his corpus. Descartes articulates his philosophical ideas within a mathematical framework. Rousseau exploits eighteenth-century literary conventions to persuade his audience that his philosophical ideas are true. Nietzsche's commitment to poetry as a medium that captures and distills truth explains his use of aphorism. Even the title of Barnes's autobiography reflects the Sartrean ontology that penetrates her work: *The Story I Tell Myself.*

Second, their stylized use of the first-person and their philosophical views of the self unify form and content into a distinctive genre of autobiography. I argue that unlike other literary genres, autobiographical writing bifurcates the self into an author-subject (the rhetorical persona) and a writer-self (the individual who writes the text). Once bifurcated, the self stands in reflexive relation to itself as other (as author-subject, as alterspective 'I,' as alienated subject). This reflexive relation opens up dialogical possibilities for self-knowing that may unify the self. Stated differently, if self-knowing necessitates self-narration, and if self-narration initiates self-unification, then self-narration instantiates philosophical unity (the 'I' of the text signifies the author-subject and references the writer-self).

Third, these texts disclose a genealogy of the self within Western philosophy, a progressive movement from the Inner to the Outer self. This point is especially significant, because the number of philosophical inquiries into the self has grown in recent years. Given the prominence of postmodern critiques within the discipline and the phenomenological interests in the self within culture, we should expect additional discussions of the self to emerge. Philosophical autobiography offers a concrete point of departure for these discussions. Mapping the self philosophically and historically clarifies the literary and historical nuances of the self within first-person writing.

The Inner Self

St. Augustine of Hippo, 354–430 C.E.

Augustine's *Confessions* is the oldest extant autobiography in the Western tradition. Though the genre of autobiography was not codified until the seventeenth century, *Confessions* is arguably the most ambitious and most beautiful of philosophical autobiographies to date. Only Nietzsche's surfeit of philosophical allusions and authorial personae rivals the "rich mosaic of literary echoes" of *Confessions.*[10] Augustine's use of alliteration and metaphor gives his work a poetical edge that eclipses Nietzsche's most aphoristic, intertextual moments. Both demonstrate an incredible facility with philosophical ideas and a penchant for language, but only Augustine expresses the transformative power of philosophy as a life history. For these reasons, *Confessions* may be the most preeminent philosophical autobiography ever produced.

One can say much about *Confessions*. However, the exceptional analysis by Peter Brown, the biography by Henry Chadwick, and the three-volume exegesis by Carl Vaught leave little unsaid.[11] Rather than present a comprehensive account of Augustine's autobiography as they do, I focus more narrowly upon four concepts that permeate the text: God, Time, Memory, and Knowledge. Because these concepts shape the form and content of philosophical autobiography in significant ways, I analyze each concept within the five autobiographies examined herein. I begin with a few preliminary remarks.

Thanks in part to *Confessions*, we know an incredible amount of information about Augustine's life and work. We know that he begins *Confessions* in 397, one year after he has been ordained bishop of Hippo. Its completion circa 400 heralds a prolific period of writing that continues until 426, just four years shy of his death. Among other texts written during these years, Augustine completes *On the Trinity*, several anti-heresy writings, and *The City of God*. Each reflects the part-apologetic, part-polemical character of his post-conversion work.

Unlike the aforementioned texts, the purpose of *Confessions* is twofold: to praise and to repent. Chadwick argues that his autobiography is "at least as much a self-vindication as an admission of mistakes."[12] As a textual instantiation of prayer and penitence, it "is extraordinary—a prose-poem addressed to God, intended to be overheard by anxious and critical fellow Christians."[13] Whereas the first nine books comprise the autobiography proper, "the last four books were to describe not the past, but the present concerns of his mind. . . . They consist of Neoplatonic analyses of memory, time, creation, and lastly a *tour de force* of subtle exegesis of Genesis 1."[14] Yet even before Augustine discusses time, memory, and creation explicitly, he alludes to these three phenomenological conditions by recounting his life in pseudo-Platonic terms: the recalling of ideas embedded in memory. He directs the imagery of recollection first at himself, then at the community, and finally at God: "So 'I acknowledge you, Lord of heaven and earth' (Matt. 11:25), articulating my praise to you for my beginnings and my infancy which I do not recall. You have also given mankind the capacity to understand oneself by analogy with others."[15] By recalling his personal sins, Augustine invites his audience to recall their own failings, thereby moving them vicariously from a Platonic state of *anamnesis* to a Christian state of confession and forgiveness: "It is from love of your love that I make the act of recollection."[16] The act of recollection brings God into the eternal presence of the soul by locating God in memory. It also supplants a Greek conception of recollection and knowledge with a Christian understanding of remembering and loving. Chadwick writes, "Lying deeper than knowing and willing, memory is the 'stomach of the mind'. . . . To remember God is a conscious act of will, a decision. The love of God is 'no indeterminate feeling, but a certitude of the consciousness.'"[17]

God

At least until after he is thirty, he tells us, Augustine cannot fathom the true nature of Christ.[18] The writings of the Platonists act as a stumbling block for him.[19] They cannot see the forms, or the Ideal, residing in an earthly image, shadow, or copy of the Ideal form. Christ, then, is an anathema for a Platonist—to be both God and human is to be both the ideal *and* its reflection in earthly matter, an idea that the Gnostics, for example, wholly refused to consider. They thought it heretical.

In fact, one of Augustine's major problems with Christianity is its Hebraic nature. That body and soul are interlinked, undistinguishable from one another, is a Hebrew concept. The Greeks, however, saw the soul as a passenger in the body, a passenger who had come from above into an earthly body that was considerably inferior to the soul. The whole concept of the Incarnation, then, presented major problems for Augustine. In resolving these problems he, more than any other of his time, reconciled the Judaic traditions not only with the new traditions of Christianity—which would have been easy enough—but also with the Platonic philosophic ideas that had intellectual pride of place at the time. Though many scholars have claimed that a Platonic framework was necessary for Augustine's understanding of God, it appears that a Judaic framework was essential to his conversion.

Augustine reasons that the soul recollects ideas stored therein. Like unconscious experiences brought to consciousness through focused reflection or psychological regression, a priori ideas are brought to awareness through introspection. Among these is the idea of God, which was impressed on the soul before birth, an idea first encountered through the reflective act of introspection. However, the idea of God is not recapitulated completely in knowledge, for knowledge is representational, not mimetic. Thus we cannot know God with the mind or intellect alone. Following this line of reasoning, Schuster argues that Augustine's conversion is rooted in an "inversion" or inner change: he inverts the Platonic epistemic order in which understanding supercedes belief and allows the latter to guide the former. Hence, the dialectic of understanding begins with the will rather than the intellect: one must understand God *from* within and *as* within, from the heart and within the heart, loving Christ in oneself and in others.

Once Augustine realizes that "God is found . . . in the deepest abyss of the 'memory'" he understands that his existence and essence point to the absolute value of God.[20] E. L. Allen writes, "Augustine's conception of faith and understanding clearly presupposes that the human mind is not thrown entirely on its own resources in its quest for truth, but that it operates *in* a world prepared by God for an encounter between him and men."[21] Yet to encounter God, to apprehend God's true form, the act of understanding (introspection) must align itself with the object of understanding (God), like a telescope that fixes upon a planet or star. Like a planet or star, God is present in the human mind (via memory) and exists outside of the human mind. God is both immanent and transcendent. Since God stands both outside of the soul and in dialectical relation to the soul, the soul must transcend the introspected knowledge of God to contemplate God in God's fullness. Etienne Gilson clarifies this Augustinian realization: "When we arrive at truths, we arrive at something contained within our reason which cannot be explained from the point of view of reason and which compels us to transcend reason and to affirm the existence of the light that illumines it, i.e., subsistent, eternal, and unchangeable Truth, i.e., God."[22] Although our souls are not contained within reason or memory, our experience is subject to reason and memory, for as Chadwick aptly argues, the soul's experience of God as eternal truth is paradoxically conditioned by human existence in space-time:

> The soul is created out of nothing. [But] it is involved from the start in the process of successiveness. . . . In the *Confessions* the analysis of time is set in the context of mysticism as a timeless awareness of the eternal. . . . Successiveness and multiplicity are simply the experience of the soul in the flux of history. Because multiplicity is a mark of inferiority in a Platonic structure, the transience and mortality of our condition must be in one sense painful. Time presupposes change [C xi.9] and "change is a kind of death" [Jo 38.10]. But in its nature time is a dimension of the mind, a psychological condition attaching to being creaturely. . . . But of God we must say that he is unchanging and therefore timeless. He knows past and future, but not as we do in a psychological experience of successiveness.[23]

An encounter with God necessitates an encounter with the self. As I argue later, the latter emerges from the interplay between introspection and retrospection.

Time

In books 10–13, Augustine "shifts the focus from the field of object known to the activity itself of knowing . . . [t]o look towards this activity is to look to the self; to take up a reflexive stance."[24] Since knowledge of God is embedded in the soul, one must look reflexively inward and backward (upon the essence of the self and its identity in the world) to contemplate the telos toward which the soul strives. Indeed, the first nine books of the *Confessions* are retrospective: they look back on Augustine's past deeds. The last four are introspective: they examine the present concerns of his mind. Among his present concerns we find temporality and memory, as well as creation and Genesis 1. Schuster argues that this shift in the text directs our attention away from Augustine's personal history to universal history, "two themes that describe a personal and universal philosophical journey to what he considered ultimate truth."[25] This artful journey presupposes space-time.

The aural and visual metaphors in the text—seeing, looking, sensing; calling, listening, hearing—symbolize the inscription of the self in space. Beseeching God to remake his small, shambled soul, he pleads, "The house of my soul is too small for you to come to it. May it be enlarged by you. It is in ruins: restore it. In your eyes it has offensive features. I admit it, I know it, but who will clean it up?"[26] Sight pulls us outside of our self-experience so that we can examine our selves in the world (as physically immanent beings) and in the community. Sound pulls us toward God so that we may understand ourselves as beings made in God's image (as spiritually transcendent beings). Yet we are also beings conditioned by time: "I confess to you, Lord, that I still do not know what time is, and I further confess to you, Lord, that as I say this I know myself to be conditioned by time."[27] Even as early as books 4 and 5, Augustine ponders the channels through which a human being's mental picture is transmitted to the material world, thus granting us the ability to see and know the external world.[28]

Augustine's interest in the natural world and the nature of human perception compels him to discuss time in both astronomical and phenomenological terms. More specifically, he believes that our physical and epistemic limitations bind us in two specific ways. First, they prevent us from knowing the relationship between time and external events apart from the way time appears to us. The lens through which we experience the world asserts itself here as it does in our eidetic experience of space: "What place is there in me where my God can enter into me?"[29] Second, they reveal in a self-conscious way the restricted capacities of our minds to understand the interaction of forces in time. "Try as they [humans] may to savor the taste of eternity," Augustine writes, "their thoughts still twist and turn upon the ebb and flow of things in past and future time,"[30] like the Manicheans whose philosophy runs just below the surface of book 11.

Human beings are agents in space-time. With respect to our actions in the past, present, or future, we are both rhetorical and ontological creatures: protagonists in a continuing story and loci of events in space-time. Temporal moments identified as "past" track the self we recognize as *X*—the historical figure. Those identified as "future" foreshadow a historically and rhetorically unknown person to come—the Outer self. Yet the spatio-temporal bifurcation of essence and identity, not to mention the autobiographical bifurcation thereafter, abstracts from our concrete experiences in the world, experiences in which our identity and agency coalesce in the Inner self. For this reason, we do not experience time discretely. Augustine proves that space-time conditions our identity and our agency in the world, just as identity conditions the dialectic of self-knowing.

Memory

In what sense, and by what means, do we experience time? Augustine argues that finite beings do not experience time per se. We experience events *in* time. Memory unifies our experience of events in time, as Augustine explains in book 11 of *Confessions*: "[f]or everything which happens leaves an impression on it [the mind], and this impression remains after the thing itself has ceased to be."[31] The mind needs memory to attend to events of the past. But memory alone cannot account for our experiences in time; memory provides no way of knowing or anticipating what kind of lives we may lead in the future. Awareness of the present dimension of experience and memory of the past is not sufficient for the "three times" of which we ordinarily speak. Hence, Augustine concludes, "[I]t can only be that the mind . . . performs three functions," those of expectation, attention, and memory.[32]

Augustine concludes that time is a distention of the mind: "So it is in you, my mind, that I measure periods of time. . . . The impression which passing events make upon you abides when they are gone. That present consciousness is what I am measuring, not the stream of past events which have caused it."[33] To anticipate what may happen, to be attentive to what is happening, and to reflect on what has happened, one must be capable of storing various impressions or images in the mind, that is, one must fix the impressions of events so that one can conceptually manipulate them. This is why some writers, such as Emmet Flood, discuss "memory" rather than the "mind" as the center of experience—the storing of information (which is the means of access to the mind's manipulative capabilities) occurs only after we capture or "save" past events in memory. Thereafter, manipulation of the stored event can occur in various ways. Flood explains, "Through its multiple functions of expectation, consideration (attention), and recollection, memory is the locus, the hinge, in which things future, present, and past are all made present through the action that Augustine's translator calls 'the mental synthesis'."[34]

Memory is a prerequisite not merely for knowledge[35] but also for self-knowledge *and* self-identity, because memory individuates our ontologically embedded encounters in space-time (events in history). Flood continues, "Memory itself is only possible because we are temporal beings . . . [t]hus human memory presupposes time itself."[36] This means that the intentionally unified and externally identified self—a self individuated in space-time (historical figure) and signified in autobiography as 'I' (the Outer self)—exists only insofar as a recurring present mind continues to organize and individuate events in space-time (the Inner self). Hence, the spatial and temporal organization of events in space-time enables us to think, speak, and act in the world as embodied individuals with mental capacities and social identities (the Inner self perpetuates the historical figure and creates the Outer self). If it were not for mind and its continuous attention to, expectation, and remembrance of events in space-time, we could never know who we are and what we are.[37] Knowledge is contingent upon human agency.[38]

Knowledge

Exegesis of *Confessions* leads to two important conclusions about the dialectical process of self-knowledge and autobiography. First, writing engages the mind in the self-reflective acts of introspection and retrospection—looking inward at the present situation of one's life and thoughts, and looking backward at the previous events of one's life and thoughts. Introspection reveals that the self is the locus of memory, space, and time (Inner self). Retrospection reveals the relation among memory, space, and time (historical figure and/or Outer self). Agency and identity coalesce within the process of introspection and retrospection. Second, writing invokes the threefold function of memory to recollect the relation between God, time, self-identity, and truth in an ever-recurring presence.[39] The self functions as an erotic force that pushes Augustine toward a personal encounter with God—an encounter that enriches the interplay between fragmentation and wholeness and offers Augustine deeper and deeper dimensions of self-knowledge.

Preliminary Conclusions

Augustine regards the self as an Inner self—a composite of intellect, will, and memory instantiated in space-time.[40] Autobiography maps the self in space-time, presenting it both as an agent in the world and as a rhetorical subject in writing (an Inner and Outer self). The coalescing of agency and identity in memory indicates that the Inner self experiences a pull toward God yet remains rooted in the space-time conditions in which the self reflects. Indeed, Augustine ends his discussion of time with memory's ascent to God.[41] This view of the self presupposes a teleological system in which life changes represent movement either closer to or further away from God. Genevieve Lloyd writes, "For Augustine, the self's hope of completeness is not seen as an illusion, though its full attainment lies in a state beyond death. The soul's capacity for memory, enacted in autobiography, is seen as both an intimation and an imitation of this desired completeness."[42]

As I argued in Chapter 1, self-narration enables the self to both introspect and retrospect. It bifurcates the self into an Outer self and an Inner self, thereby creating a dialectical encounter with the self that in turn drives the self upward to greater moments of unity and continuity. Schuster offers an explanation of the relation between autobiography and self-knowledge in the context of *Confessions*:

> Autobiographical and universal history are related through the author's self-knowledge. Memory and a faculty that transcends knowledge of the temporary (i.e., "truth that dwells in the innermost house of thought") make known to the self its final, redemptive, and eternal history.[43]

Though Schuster maintains that the self is unified through a psychological form of self-reflection, I argue that self-reflection is richest when undertaken in narration, wherein literary and rhetorical devices drive a wedge between the self qua knower and self qua knowee. This medial wedge creates a liminal space in which the bifurcated self can introspect and retrospect (and sometimes alterspect)—a space in which we can raise questions of identity and essence by reflecting on the self that we deposit in our writing. When all three dimensions of self-reflection coalesce, we move from the past to the present and begin to live not merely examined lives that lead to self-knowledge, but artful lives that lead to self-knowing.

We first learn this lesson from Plato in the *Republic* and the *Symposium*. To know the self is to instantiate *logos* in a discursive form:

> [O]nly by writing do we know what we know; nonetheless our development depends upon our thought and our thought upon our language. But beyond the latter is the action of our illative sense in which, paradoxically, we determine what exists and is knowable before we make it explicit.[44]

Augustine couples this Platonic insight with a Judaic view of the self so that self-identity and self-unity are rooted in both soul and body. Contrary to the view that the self is timeless, Augustine argues that time itself generates self-unity through due influence of the past over the present.[45] Twelve centuries later, René Descartes resurrects and modernizes this view by granting substance to the soul and thus persistence over time.

Descartes, 1596–1650

Anyone familiar with Cartesian thought knows that the *Meditations on First Philosophy* (1641) is not an autobiography.[46] In it Descartes does not recount the events of his life. Nor does he describe self-identity in either personal or philosophical terms. In fact, the autobiographical content of the *Discourse on the Method for Conducting One's Reason Rightly and for Searching for Truth in the Sciences* (1637) fits more neatly with the genre of autobiography. Nonetheless, *Meditations* is an invaluable source for a study of philosophical autobiography, because it contains the first cohesive philosophical account of mental sensations and ideas that we associate with first-person experience. In fact, Descartes is the first to group these ideas and sensations together: "ideas are merely modes of thought; I see no inequality among them."[47] Moreover, *Meditations* is the first text in the history of philosophy to show that "there cannot be such a thing as a thought or a perception or a tickle without a thinker who can experience it as his."[48]

Though it is not an autobiography, strictly speaking, Descartes reveals several interesting facts about his daily habits in *Meditations*. He tells us, for example, that "several years have now passed since I realized how numerous were the false opinions that in my youth I had taken to be true."[49] To correct these errors, he reserves some free time to reconsider his opinions. "I have today suitably freed my mind of all cares, secured for myself a period of leisurely tranquility, and am withdrawing into solitude."[50] He reports that he composes parts of *Meditations* at night in his dressing gown, that he writes on paper and by firelight, and that he writes over a period of days.[51]

We should also observe that Descartes expresses his philosophical claims in a relatively candid and personalized tone. "These arguments," he asserts, "are such that I believe there is no way open to the human mind whereby better ones could be found. For the urgency of this cause, as well as the glory of God . . . compels me here to speak somewhat more freely on my own behalf than is my custom."[52] However modest he appears, these arguments are integral to the Western philosophical conception of the self. I analyze *Meditations* using the same four concepts with which I explicated Augustine's *Confessions*: God, Time, Memory, and Knowledge.

God

Descartes' relationship to and understanding of God are complicated by the rhetorical dimensions of *Meditations*. On the one hand, his ontological proofs for God's existence echo Anselm's and Augustine's who, with the great scholastics, defined the theology of his day. On the other, the placement of these arguments in the text (post-*cogito*) and the nonreligious role that they play make them dubious. Contra Augustine, for example, the mind does not elucidate truth revealed by God; rather, the mind discovers or generates truth on its own. It follows, then, that humans do not need God to know the truth (though Descartes leaves this conclusion unstated). Descartes' prominent placement of God both in the title of the work and in Meditations Three, Four, and Five creates additional ambiguity once we realize that the role of God has little effect on the *cogito*. It becomes difficult to know God's role in the systematic formulation of knowledge (self-knowledge and other). Finally, the lack of extensive information about Descartes' religious practices and beliefs, especially in comparison to Augustine, complicates our efforts to interpret the text. This complexity points back to the deeply rhetorical dimensions of the text.

Descartes assumes a highly personalized rhetorical stance at the outset of *Meditations*: "At last *I* will apply *myself* earnestly and unreservedly to this general demolition of *my* opinions."[53] His tone seems confident and relaxed; the text reads like a philosophical epistolary rather than an essay. Yet he sets up many of his strongest philosophical arguments as hypotheticals or conditionals, most of which he expresses in the first-person. For example: "I realized . . . I had to raze everything to the ground and begin again from the original foundations, if I wanted to establish anything firm and lasting in the sciences. . . . It will suffice for the rejection of all of these opinions, if I find in each of them some reason for doubt."[54] Moreover, the frequency with which he invokes the first-person in the text is dizzying. 'I' appears thirteen times in the first paragraph, an average of two appearances per sentence. This is ironic, given Descartes' reputation for cold, calculated, objectifying philosophizing. Also, Descartes takes great pains to root his arguments in personal introspection and sensation rather than universal human experience. Most surprising of all, Descartes makes no mention of the self proper until Meditation Two, despite the personal flourishes of *Meditations*:

> . . . "I am—I exist" is necessarily true every time I utter it or conceive it in my mind. But I do not yet understand sufficiently what I am—I, who now necessarily exist. And so from this point on, I must be careful lest I unwittingly mistake something else for myself, and thus err in the very item of knowledge that I claim to be the most certain and evident of all.[55]

Descartes' rhetorical stance raises many philosophical and literary questions. Why does he invoke the first-person so regularly (or even at all)? Why does he personalize hypothetical or conditional propositions? What do these carefully formulated first-person claims suggest? What should we make of his delayed examination of essence? Why does the proof of existence precede a discussion of essence? Is this a dramatic foreshadowing of Sartre's famous claim that existence precedes essence? And what does Descartes prove when he argues, "I think therefore I am"? What (and who) is the 'I' that exists? How does God relate to his arguments for the self?

Certainly his hesitancy to argue from the position of objective author is perplexing. On the one hand, we have a set of personal thoughts written in the warmth of a small living room. On the other, we have a rigorous examination of the foundations of knowledge and belief embroidered with caveats and carefully formulated propositions. His complete title promises a demonstration of God's existence, yet Descartes begins with a proof for the self. Several possibilities might explain his rhetorical strategy.

First, Descartes might aim to temper his reflections so that he does not become ensnared by his writing and become forced into believing what he cannot establish with certainty. For example, in Meditation One, he admits, "But it is not enough simply to have realized these things; I must take steps to keep myself mindful of them. For long-standing opinions keep returning, and, almost against my will, they take advantage of my credulity, as if it were bound over to them by long use and claims of intimacy."[56] To further support the sense of threat or risk of his work, he presents himself as a castaway, lost in a stormy sea, trying to get to shore, to safety, to steady himself.[57] At several places in *Meditations* he acknowledges the precarious nature of human existence by contemplating death.[58]

Another possibility, which Stanley Rosen and Robert Miner suggest, is that these Cartesian ambiguities point to an esoteric layer of meaning in the text. By hinting at an embedded meaning in his writing, by introducing disruptive moments to rouse the mind of the reader and to get him or her to look more carefully at his arguments, Descartes employs the Platonic practice of concealment, perhaps for political reasons. We find textual support for this interpretation in remarks such as the following:

> But now, after having to some degree, conducted an initial review of the judgments of men, here I begin once more to treat the same questions about God and the human mind, together with the starting points of the whole of first philosophy, but not in a way that causes me to have any expectation of widespread approval or a large readership. On the contrary, *I do not advise anyone to read these things except those who have both the ability and the desire to meditate seriously with me, and to withdraw well that such people are few and far between.* As to those who do not take the time to grasp the order and linkage of my arguments, but will be eager to fuss over statements taken out of context (as is the custom for many), they will derive little benefit from reading this work. Although perhaps they might find an occasion for quibbling in several places, still they will not find it easy to raise an objection that is either compelling or worthy of response.[59]

Descartes' intentions are further obscured by his dedication and appeal to the "Dean and Doctors of the Faculty of the Sacred Theology of Paris" to take up the defense of his work.[60] Is he attempting to avoid the intellectual and physical harm that his friend, Galileo, suffered? Is he trying to deceive the good doctors by paying homage to them while surreptitiously renouncing their beliefs? How should we understand his relationship to his audience? For example, why does Descartes attempt to sway the reader in favor of his views before they read his six meditations, imploring them "not to form a judgment regarding the *Meditations* until they have deigned to read all these objections and the replies I have made to them."[61] Indeed, he lulls his readers into a feeling of security by doubting *for* us so that we may believe. And we believe, as Augustine and Anselm argue, in order to understand. For "although the utility of so extensive a doubt is not readily apparent, nevertheless its greatest utility lies in freeing us of all prejudices, in preparing the easiest way for us to withdraw the mind from the senses, and finally, in making it impossible for us to doubt any further those things that we later discover to be true."[62]

Yet God, a perfect idea that could not come from imperfect human creatures, appears both necessary and unnecessary. Descartes argues first in Meditation Three and more extensively in Meditation Five that the cause of an idea, such as God, must have at least as much reality as the idea itself. God, then, could not originate in imperfect human minds; God must originate in a source greater than the idea of a perfect Godself. Only an existing God is greater than the idea of God. Hence, God must exist. In this sense, God is logically necessary if one grants that existence is a form of perfection. But is God *epistemologically* necessary? Is Descartes' proof for the existence of God immune from Cartesian doubt? Does a deducing mind *need* God to know reality and distinguish truth from falsity?

Time

Reasoning from the premise in Meditation One that he has been deceived in the past and therefore he must doubt or question many things he once regarded as true, Descartes concludes in Meditation Two that there is one thing that is immune from doubt: thinking. Once thinking has been posited, it follows that there must exist a person doing the thinking, for thought cannot be separated from a thinker. Hence, he arrives at the Cartesian formulation "*cogito, ergo sum*."[63] Descartes concludes this line of inquiry by acknowledging that the certainty of his own existence is self-evident: "'I am, I exist,' is necessarily true every time I utter it or think it."[64]

But who is the subject of the proposition "I am, I exist"? What is its nature? Descartes invokes a series of questions that leads to the proposition that he is a "thinking thing":

> . . . But as to what this soul might be, I either did not think about it, or else I imagined it a rarefied I-know-not-what, like a wind, or a fire, or ether, which had been infused into my coarser parts. . . . But now what am I, when I suppose that there is some supremely powerful and, if I may be permitted to say so, malicious deceiver who deliberately tries to fool me in any way he can? Can I not affirm that I possess at least a small measure of all those things which I have already said belong to the body? I focus my attention on them, I think about them, I review them again, *but nothing comes to mind*. . . . What about thinking? Here I make my discovery: thought exists; it alone cannot be separated from me. I am; I exist—this is certain. . . . I am therefore precisely nothing but a thinking thing; that is, a mind, or intellect, or understanding, or reason—words of whose meanings I was previously ignorant.[65]

As I argued earlier, Descartes' discovery that thought cannot be separated from the thinker thinking the thought leads him to the conclusion that as long as thinking is manifest in the world, the mind from which the thoughts arise exists. He continues, "But what then am I? A thing that thinks. What is it? A thing that doubts, understands, affirms, denies, wills, refuses, and that also imagines and senses."[66]

By conjoining the varied activities and sensations associated with the "thinking thing" under the general rubric of "thought," Descartes implies that the thing that thinks is a logically (or mathematically) circumscribed agent that intuits itself and the corporeal world a priori. Thought is the essence of the Cartesian self. But this conclusion raises a number of additional concerns. For example, if the self is tantamount to thought only or essentially, can the self be said to exist once thinking ceases? Can thought alone create continuity of experience, that is, a unified experience as selves, especially if thought, though varied, reflects present concerns rather than ideas we have had in the past? Or must we combine thought with memory to create unity over time, not merely mathematical unity but metaphysical and psychological unity as well? Bernard Williams argues that Descartes attempts to resolve these concerns and create unity of self in two ways: first by invoking the concept 'substance' and second by invoking God.

Descartes first ascribes substance to the self in Meditation Three:

> . . . I think that a stone is a substance, that is to say, a thing that is suitable for existing in itself; and likewise I think that I too am a substance. Despite the fact that I conceive myself to be a thinking thing and not an extended thing, whereas I conceive of a stone as an extended thing and not a thinking thing, and hence there is the greatest diversity between these two concepts, nevertheless they seem to agree with one another when considered under the rubric of substance. Furthermore, I perceive that I *now exist* and *recall that I have previously existed for some time*. And I have various thoughts and know how many of them there are. It is in doing these things that I acquire the ideas of *duration* and number, which I can then apply to other things.[67]

Descartes' invocation of substance aims to ground the self in time and prove that the self necessarily endures over time. For as I indicated earlier and as Williams rightly notes, the "proof of Descartes' own existence in the cogito was, strictly speaking, only a proof that he existed so long as he was thinking."[68] By making the self into a substance, an "enduring thing," Descartes hopes to overcome this limitation of the cogito. He fails to do so, however, because substance relies upon the idea rather than experience of time. Aware of this failure, Descartes turns immediately to the concept of God: "Thus there remains only the idea of God."[69] He argues that his own existence as an enduring, thinking thing is dependent upon God in whom he experiences an infinite and a permanent being:

> . . . when I turn the mind's eye toward myself, I understand not only that I am something incomplete and dependent upon another, something aspiring indefinitely for greater and greater or better things, but also that being on whom I depend has in himself all those greater things—not merely indefinitely and potentially, but infinitely and actually, and thus that he is God. The whole force of the argument rests on the fact that I recognize that it would be impossible for me to exist, being of such a nature as I am (namely, having in me the idea of God), unless God did in fact exist. From these considerations it is quite obvious that he cannot be a deceiver. [70]

Though the mind can reason without the intervention of God, the mind cannot endure without God. Hence, Williams argues that it is through God that Descartes ushers in the concept of permanence of being (or continuity):

> . . . the proof of the existence of God introduces an idea of permanence hitherto lacking. The proof of Descartes' own existence in the cogito was, strictly speaking, only a proof that he existed so long as he was thinking. . . . The idea of God as a conserving principle may help to overcome this limitation.[71]

This argument generates a number of problems. First, serious inconsistencies appear in the text. Foremost among these is the contradictory bifurcation and unification of the self. Let me clarify. You will recall that through the appropriation of a highly personalized rhetorical stance, Descartes creates an author-subject (an 'I' signifier) who conceals the writer-self. While some scholars argue that he conceals himself for political reasons, others point to the literary effect of his stylization to explain his appeal to God. I do not disagree with these views. But in addition to them, I argue that this example of bifurcation is to some degree inevitable and unavoidable in autobiographical writing where the writer is both the object and subject of inquiry, though Descartes appears to intentionally exploit this distinction more than some writers, certainly more than Augustine. Stated differently, regardless of the reason for his concealment, Descartes bifurcates the self into an author-subject and a writer-self, distancing himself from his own ideas. In the same text, Descartes unifies the various mental activities of the thinking thing into a single, wide-ranging attribute of "thought," thereby equating the soul, the mind, and the 'I' with the thinking thing. Herein lies the paradox: if the 'I' of *Meditations* signifies Descartes qua author-subject as his rhetorical stance suggests, then the self to which the 'I' belongs is a rhetorical subject, that is, a textually inscribed first-person, a protagonist in a story. Yet when Descartes refers to the essence of the self as thought, he does not mean that the essence of the rhetorical subject is thought, or that thought is a textually inscribed activity as Derrida might argue. Rather, he means that the self qua writer-subject—the universal sense of 'I', the self qua human being, the self qua psyche—is a substance that has thought as its essential attribute.

Descartes' equivocal use of the first-person further complicates the view of the self in autobiographical writing. Either one embraces the paradox and explores the mystery of Descartes' rhetorical stance further, or one concurs with Ricoeur that there is no equivocation in the text, because there is no self outside of *Meditations*, that is, there is only a rhetorical subject: "the 'I' who does the doubting and who reflects upon itself in the *cogito* is just as metaphysical and hyperbolic as is doubt itself with respect to all knowledge. It is, in truth, no one."[72]

Second, although Descartes rightly argues that thinking entails a thinker, he fails to consider the fact that thinking becomes manifest in the world through language (through the use of linguistic signs) that also requires use of the body (vocal cords, tongue, mouth, hands, etc.). This too seems paradoxical given the mind-body dualism generated by the text, a dualism that is only seemingly resolved in Meditation Six, where he suggests that there is a union between the mind and body: ". . . nature also teaches . . . that I am most tightly joined, and so to speak, commingled with it [a body], so much so that I and the body constitute one single thing."[73]

Third, Descartes' conclusions presuppose the idea of himself, the idea that he says is "one that displays me to myself (about which there can be no difficulty at this point)."[74] Initially, it appears that we arrive at the self inductively: I think, therefore I am. But Descartes later shows that we must deduce the self from the idea of God, an infinite and enduring being who gives us the idea of ourselves in the first place. God, then, makes possible the unity and enduring reality of the self. Thus God makes possible self-knowledge—a nice Augustinian point. However, by invoking God in arguments for the self, Descartes appears to beg the question of the self. Williams offers a poignant analysis of this problem:

> The idea of God as a conserving principle may help to overcome this limitation [of the cogito existing only when thinking]. Descartes sometimes says that it is only the existence of God that validates memory, and so deduction: a process which, unlike the instantaneous steps of intuition, presupposes the reliability of memory. Since, however, Descartes has already relied on deduction in his somewhat complex proofs of the existence of god, if not in the cogito itself (a much disputed point), there is a strong suspicion of a circular argument here.[75]

Though Descartes dedicates his argument explicitly to the task of embedding the self in time—memory presupposes time—he also seems content to regard the mind as an atemporal, mathematical substratum. In doing so, he is able to generalize from his own thought to universal (clear and distinct) ideas, relying only on the objectifying, detached *cogito* for eternal truth.

Memory

Descartes mentions memory in several places in *Meditations*. Where he does so he appropriates the language of Recollection. For example, following an overtly Augustinian line of thought, he argues that the idea of God resides in the "storehouse of my mind."[76] Yet he also describes the corrupting influence of memory on our judgments.[77] Here again we face a paradox in Cartesian thought.

Descartes' personalized stance drives an intentional wedge between the writer-self and the author-subject. From a philosophical perspective, his stance exemplifies the thesis that knowledge necessitates introspection—a turning of the mind upon itself—so that it may fasten upon absolute certainty and self-evident, a priori truths. To prove his thesis, he argues that the mind is the hub of knowledge with reason as its axis. What appears to the mind when we reflect on true sensations and beliefs are clear and distinct (and atemporal) ideas. Moreover, the existence of the mind—the self or 'I'—is also known clearly and distinctly; one is unable to doubt his or her existence, even if one does not understand the essence of his or her existence. In Descartes' words, ". . . the idea I clearly have of the human mind—insofar as it is a thinking thing . . . is far more distinct than the idea of any corporeal thing."[78] Because the mind engages clear and distinct ideas, the mind is truth generating and truth adjudicating, not merely recollective. That is, once we have established a methodology by which we can distinguish truth from falsity—once we identify clear and distinct ideas—then we can create sets of true propositions heretofore unarticulated.

By suggesting that the mind generates truth rather than simply recollects it, Descartes displaces the Augustinian conception of soul as spiritual ego with a mathematical conception of the soul as scientific ego. Thus Descartes transforms the Platonic understanding of rational soul or mind into a mechanistic, intuiting "thinking thing" or substance (*res cogitans*).[79] Indeed, as I indicated earlier, Descartes does not carefully and explicitly distinguish "things of body and things of the soul until after he moves from the discussion of existence to a consideration of essence in Meditation Two."[80] Passage 26 indicates that one of his aims is to reconceptualize the soul:

> Now it occurred to me first that I had a face, hands, arms, and this entire mechanism of bodily members: the very same as are discerned in a corpse, and which I referred to by the name "body." It next occurred to me that I took in food, that I walked about, and I sensed and thought various things; these actions I used to attribute to the soul. But as to what this soul might be, I either did not think about it or else I imagined it a rarefied I-know-not-what, like a wind, or a fire, or ether, which had been infused into my coarser parts.[81]

He proceeds to distinguish between the soul and the body by objectifying the self. He writes, ". . . the only order I could follow was the one typically used by geometers, which is to lay out everything on which a given proposition depends."[82] The Cartesian objectification of the self requires a disengagement from both the acts of the mind and the objects and people who are represented by the mind. Taylor argues that this form of disengagement—the "disengagement of Modernity"—amounts to a disengagement of the self from the activity in which the self is engaged in order to examine "the self itself." Thus one's conscious awareness of the moment (the present) is set over and above one's awareness of continuity, a conceptual arrangement that characterizes Modernity.

Scientific projects isolate objects in order to prevent environmental substances from tainting the objects themselves. The sterilization of both knowledge and the self arose from this empirical model of investigation, a model that can be recognized as the ultimate form of disengagement—the scientist from the object of study, the object from its surroundings, and the body performing various tests from the mind analyzing test results. "Modern disengagement," Taylor explains, ". . . calls on me to be aware of my activity of thinking, of my processes of habituation, so as to disengage from them and objectify them."[83] Moreover, this self-reflective objectified self ". . . cannot be conceived as just another piece of the natural world. It is hard for us simply to *list* souls or minds *alongside* whatever else there is. . . . This ungrounded 'extra-worldly' status of the objectifying subject accentuates the existing motivation to describe it as a self. . . . The punctual agent seems to be nothing else but a 'self' and 'I.'"[84]

Knowledge

Both Augustine and Descartes formulate questions to guide their search for the essence and identity of the self. Augustine's confessional dialogue is cast in religious and metaphysical terms; Descartes' analytic dialogue is cast in pseudo-empirical terms:

> . . . I believe that nearly all the arguments which have been brought to bear on these questions (God and the human mind) by great men have the force of a demonstration, when they are adequately understood. . . . I was strongly urged to do this (provide demonstrations) by some people who knew that I had developed a method for solving all sorts of problems in the sciences—not a new one, mind you, for nothing is more ancient than the truth, but one they had seen me use with some success in other areas. [He adds in the next section] . . . although the arguments I use here do, in my opinion, equal or even surpass those of geometry in certitude and obviousness, nevertheless I am fearful that many people will not be capable of adequately perceiving them, both because they too are a bit lengthy, with some of them depending on still others, and also because, first and foremost, they demand a mind that is quite free from prejudices and that can easily withdraw itself from association with the senses.[85]

Knowledge—a set of demonstrably clear, distinct, and therefore certain ideas—is by default propositional, because sensory limitations on the body and mind obscure reality. Hence, reality cannot be known directly. Knowledge, then, is a picture or representation of reality, a referential representation and not a mere linguistic signification.

The desire for demonstrative evidence shapes the questions that Descartes raises in *Meditations*. More importantly, Descartes' assumption that the ground of knowledge is doubt rather than belief shapes the philosophical landscape he envisions: an abstract God, a disembodied, rhetorical 'I,' and an unreliable natural order. Ricoeur's impassioned critique of the Cartesian project begins with this diatribe:

> The foundational ambition belonging to the Cartesian cogito can be recognized from the outset in the hyperbolic character of the doubt that opens the area of investigation in the *Meditations*. The radical nature of the project is thus of the same scope as the doubt, which includes within the domain of "opinion" common sense, the sciences—mathematical and physical—and even the philosophical tradition. More precisely, this radicality stems from the nature of a doubt that has no common measure with respect to doubts that might be exercised within the three areas just mentioned. . . . In order to dramatize this doubt, Descartes creates the incredible hypothesis of a great deceiver or an evil genius, an inverted image of a truthful God, itself reduced to the status of mere opinion.[86]

Ricoeur is right to question the sincerity of Cartesian doubt. For example, Descartes writes in Meditation Two, ". . . suppose that everything I see is false. I believe that none of what my deceitful memory represents ever existed. I have no senses whatever. Body, shape, extension, movement, and place are all chimeras. What then will be true? Perhaps just the single fact that nothing is certain."[87] At this point, Descartes has already claimed that at least three things are certain, namely, that God exists, that we exist, and that the material world exists. Why, then, does he posit a doubting subject, a doubting 'I'?

I submit that Descartes' claim that "nothing is certain" is designed to move the reader away from nihilism and toward truth. To that end, Descartes presents the reader with the most dire epistemic possibility—that nothing is certain. From there he demonstrates with mathematical precision that at least one thing is certain—one's own existence. He then argues that God and the corporeal world are equally certain. He even acknowledges the arduousness of this philosophical journey, asserting that he is the captain of the figurative boat that "will attack straightaway those principles which supported everything I once believed."[88] Once Descartes has the reader's sympathetic ear, he raises the epistemological ante by doubting his own doubts: "I have persuaded myself that there is absolutely nothing in the world: no sky, no earth, no minds, no bodies.

Is it then the case that I too do not exist? But doubtless I did exist, if I persuaded myself of something. . . . Thus I will meditate once more on what I once believed myself to be, prior to embarking on these thoughts."[89]

But not all readers are either sympathetic or persuaded (nor is Descartes so guileless). For example, Descartes' view of knowledge as an objective representation of an unchanging reality is suspect to the feminist philosopher, Lorraine Code. She argues that the assertion that knowledge is objective is itself grounded in a form of male subjectivity, that is, a privileging of the male perspective that objectivity, value neutrality, and rational autonomy are the necessary features of knowledge. She argues further that this epistemological view has been used against women to falsely posit that women are not and cannot be objective, value neutral, and autonomous, and thus that women are not and cannot be "knowers."[90]

Code's argument extends beyond the scope of her feminist concerns to a general critique of the Western epistemological tradition. This critique turns on the fact that the history of modern philosophy, the goal of which was to establish the necessary and sufficient conditions of knowledge, is guided by the principle that knowledge is a representation of a permanent, objective, ahistorical framework in which truth generates certain knowledge. As such, mathematics is a system that models the way certainty can solidify one's knowledge of objects in the world. Heidegger too interprets the Cartesian project in light of Descartes' use of physics and mathematics as a model of true knowledge about reality:

> Mathematical knowledge is regarded by Descartes as the one manner of apprehending entities which can always give assurance that their Being has been securely grasped. If anything measures up in its own kind of Being to the Being that is accessible in mathematical knowledge, then it *is* in the authentic sense. Such entities are those *which always are what they are*. Accordingly, that which can be shown to have the character of something that *constantly remains* (as *remanens capax mutationum*), makes up the real Being of those entities of the world which get experienced. That which enduringly remains, really *is*. . . . Thus, the Being of the "world" is, as it were, dictated to it in terms of a definite idea of Being which lies veiled in the concept of substantiality, and in terms of the idea of a knowledge by which such entities within-the-world are cognized. The kind of Being which belongs to entities within-the-world is something which they themselves might have been permitted to present; but Descartes does not let them do so.[91]

Descartes' concealment of the world behind the wall of mathematics implies that the knower of the world, the mathematician himself or herself, is an isolated and autonomous reasoner. This view also implies that all knowers are alike, that introspection is not an intersubjective act, and that knowledge is propositional (the entire point of Kant's transcendental deconstruction is to show that a self without a world is meaningless or at least without content).[92] The propositional form in which knowledge claims are expressed, *"S knows that P,"* bifurcates the knower from the known, the object of knowing from the knower.[93] Code is right to suggest that all strict or rigid distinctions between the object of knowledge and the knower stand contrary to the dialectical process of knowing.

Yet I find myself defending Descartes. Despite the obvious problems with a knower/known distinction, I argue that this distinction creates the possibility of self-knowledge in the richest possible sense. Let me recapitulate my argument on this point. The distinction between the knower and the known is a necessary condition for self-representation. In the case of self-narration, the use of the first-person serves to bifurcate the self into two primary modes of being: the Inner self or writer-self, and the Outer self or author-subject. This bifurcation, which is impermanent and fluid, creates a middle space between the self as knower and the self as knowee. Once bifurcated, the ontological self and the rhetorical self (the knowing self and the known self) stand in dialectical relation to one another, although they are sometimes mediated by the historical figure, a third figure that informs first-person texts. This dialectical configuration is a necessary condition for self-knowledge and thus makes wholeness of self possible. Self-narration instantiates the dialectic of self-knowing.

Like other features of Descartes' *Meditations*, the separation of the knower from the known (though necessary for self-knowledge) is paradoxical. Descartes argues that thought cannot be separated from the thinker. Why, then, does he imply that an autonomous, disembodied knower stands removed from the process of knowing? Is this rhetorical posture meant to drive us to an esoteric level of the text where these apparent contradictions disappear? Scholarly views of Descartes' rhetorical stance vary. Might the recognition and exploration of these paradoxes implicate the reader in a dialectical process of self-knowing? Certainly.

Preliminary Conclusions

As I argue throughout the Introduction and Chapter 1, the Inner self is a transcendent essence that is coincident with the mind, soul, or spirit. Descartes exemplifies this perspective throughout *Meditations* in passages such as the following: "What am I to say about his mind, that is, about myself?"[94] In the context of autobiographical writing, I characterize the Inner self as the writer-self, the ontological being behind the text. The Outer self is a constructed identity that stands in relief to the mind, soul, or spirit. I describe the Outer self in first-person writing as the author-subject. Both Augustine and Descartes adopt variations of the Inner self.

For Augustine, the Inner self is capable of nonrhetorical individuation via the three functions of memory. These functions result in the mutual expression of agency and identity in space-time. The agent (historical figure) and identity-bearing individual (Outer self) are engendered by the ontological conditioning of the self in space-time. Hence, time provides continuity and unity to the self through influence of the past over the present.

Descartes both affirms and then inverts Augustine's insights. He agrees that time provides continuity and unity of the self through the influence of the past over the present, and this is why God is a necessary condition for existence. He also implies that atemporal reflection provides unity and knowledge of the self through the influence of the present over the past. Hence, the Inner self may individuate itself through the various functions of thought, but the individuation of thought into discrete units or actions does not give rise to either a historical figure or an Outer self. Rather, the autobiographical bifurcation of the self through the first-person conceals the individuation of the self in the world (the 'I' of *Meditations*, though clearly rhetorical, parades itself as a universal quantifier). The self becomes subsumed by the activity of the mind and does not supervene on or become recorded by the mind, nor does it become individuated by a psychological or social persona.

The reflective analysis that the dialectic of autobiography occasions (via introspection and retrospection or disengagement and objectification) does not end in self-knowing for Descartes. Rather, as Ricoeur suggests, *Meditations* implicates the reader in a process of self-reflection:

> [T]he question "who?" related first to the question "who doubts?" takes on a new twist when it is connected to the question "who thinks?" and more radically, "who exists?" The utter indetermination of the answer —an indetermination inherited from the initial, hyperbolic nature of doubt—indicates that, in order to flesh out the certainty obtained, Descartes was forced to add to it a new question, namely that of knowing *what* I am. . . . This, so to speak, epistemologizing tendency . . . is tempered by a "phenomenologizing" tendency, expressed in the enumeration that preserves the real internal variety of the act of thinking: "What is [a thing that thinks]? A thing that doubts, understands, affirms, denies, wills, refuses, and which also imagines and senses." . . . This enumeration poses the question of the identity of the subject, but in a sense entirely different from the narrative identity of a concrete person. This can involve nothing but a kind of point like ahistorical identity of the "I" in the diversity of its operations.[95]

Though the text remains deeply paradoxical, its edifying dimensions complicate the search for the self in useful ways. As Vaught argues, every thinker is tilted in specific directions, sometimes strongly. Descartes presents a view of nature that is tilted toward self-negation at the physical but not the mental level. He is not committed to the view he presents; the author-subject is a smoke screen. Political forces seem to drive his arguments.

The bifurcation of the self intentionally abstracts the identity from the essence of the self. Without a clear reference to the writer-self, the 'I' of the text remains detached from concrete experience; the author-subject dissolves into thought itself. Though Descartes' diaphanous view of the self as an ontological entity is essentialist in nature, his implicit view of the writer is rhetorical.

By exploiting the author-subject and writer-self distinction within *Meditations*, Descartes deepens the fissure between the author and the writer. In the context of first-person writing, the author/writer distinction creates a complex middle ground in which the self can be known and understood yet neither determined nor constructed. Descartes leads his readers elliptically to this rich middle ground between the subject and object, the author and writer, the knower and known. By concealing the identity of the text's first-person, he magnifies the ontological and rhetorical dimensions of the self.

Rousseau, 1712–1778

The bombastic "citizen of Geneva" completed *The Confessions of Jean-Jacques Rousseau* in 1770. He died eight years later near Paris, France. Rousseau never took to Paris. Perhaps Paris never took to him. His eccentric behaviors and uncommon sensibilities fostered an isolationist attitude toward the Parisians, and his debilitating paranoia tended on all accounts to get the best of him. He made a habit of disparaging foreign places before he visited them. This tendency skewed his experiences of the places themselves. He confesses, for example, that his introduction to Paris was psychologically devastating:

> I had imagined a city of a most imposing appearance, as beautiful as it was large, where nothing was to be seen but splendid streets and palaces of marble or gold. As I entered through the Faubourg Saint-Marceau, I saw nothing but dirty, stinking little streets, ugly black houses, a general air of squalor and poverty, beggars, carters, menders of clothes, sellers of herb-drinks and old hats. All this so affected me at the outset that all the real magnificence I have since seen in Paris has not been sufficient to efface my first impression, and I have always retained a secret aversion against living in the capital.[96]

Despite Rousseau's disdain for Paris, it seems appropriate that his life should end near the place he hated yet frequented. He thrived on contradictions and dichotomies: reason and emotion; man and God; religion and the state; satire and sincerity.[97] His text exemplifies his philosophical penchant for categorical distinctions. He reports, for example, feeling overwhelmed by a divide between his capacities for reason and emotion:

> In me are united two almost irreconcilable characteristics, though in what way I cannot imagine. I have a passionate temperament and lively and headstrong emotions. Yet my thoughts arise slowly and confusedly, and are never ready till too late. It is as if my heart and brain did not belong to the same person.[98]

Here and elsewhere in *The Confessions,* Rousseau suggests that human failure is the consequence of human weakness. By contrast, human flourishing is the consequence of strong emotion illocuted against the confounding views of reason promulgated by Enlightenment temperaments. Ironically, he links his failures in life to emotion, that is, to the behavior committed out of heart not mind. His autobiography is, as he sees it, "the story of his feelings, and of what they led him to do."[99] Though we are right to interpret this claim as a rhetorical ploy to gain sympathy from his readers, emotion nevertheless plays a pivotal (and less dubious) role in his interpretation of life and his understanding of himself.[100]

Insofar as Rousseau illustrates his nature with his affective responses to nature, his work parallels St. Augustine's. Schuster compares these two confessions in the following ways:

> Rousseau's *Confessions* can be called the eighteenth-century version of Augustine's autobiography. . . . Through his autobiography Rousseau reflects on or attacks the philosophical and theological conflicts of his revolutionary century. Like Augustine, Rousseau aims not only to reveal his own true self, but to reveal human nature as a whole. Whereas Augustine believed himself to be successful in solving the mysteries of the soul in general, including his own, Rousseau claims to understand only his own soul, while the world around him remained a mystery because of a perceived lack of "transparency" in other people.[101]

Another surface similarity between these two texts, and perhaps Descartes' too, is the frequent appeal to God. Though Rousseau converted to Catholicism at the urging of his patron and lover, Madame de Warens, his invocation of God seems more conventional than religious, theological, or logical. Indeed, he seems to satirize the religious dimensions of autobiographies written in the vein of Augustine or Descartes. Several clues point in this direction. First, Voltaire's satire of naïve religiosity inspires Rousseau's critique of collective faith.[102] Second, Rousseau maintains an incessant focus on political accounts of human nature at the expense of religious ones throughout the text. Third, he talks about God but rarely refers directly to God. Indeed, Schuster argues that unlike religious confessions that "try to achieve a reconciliation between the confessor and a deity . . . Rousseau's *Confessions* have as their sole aim a person to person reconciliation."[103] In this respect his text bears a great similarity to Descartes'. Both intentionally conceal the writer-self and exaggerate the author-subject for political reasons as much as philosophical ones.

God

Despite the conventional invocation of God, Rousseau dispenses with God and grounds the self not in God but in human nature. To act in accordance with our true nature, Rousseau argues, we must act according to emotion (an inversion of Cartesian thinking, one that parallels Augustine's ordering of the will over the intellect in the final books of *Confessions*). Rousseau does not mean that we must live life surrounded by the effluvium of feeling. Rather, he argues that a strong conception of emotion is needed to offset rationalistic fetishes so that the emotive self can express itself. He speaks with no regret when he confesses that "throughout the course of my life, as has been seen, my heart has been as transparent as crystal, and incapable of concealing for so much as a moment the least lively feeling which has taken refuge in it."[104]

It is not surprising that Rousseau elevates sentiment over and above reason.[105] He acknowledges the powerful, heartfelt feelings he experiences around the age of five or six while reading sentimental novels and bawdy literature with his father:

> In a short time I acquired by this dangerous method, not only an extreme facility in reading and expressing myself, but a singular insight for my age into the passions. I had no idea of the facts, but I was already familiar with every feeling. I had grasped nothing; I had sensed everything.[106]

Here and elsewhere, Rousseau assumes the distinction between knowing and feeling; he accepts that knowing and feeling are distinct phenomenal acts whose primary natures and secondary characteristics are mutually exclusive. Despite the efforts of first Descartes and later Hume to formulate mental phenomenon as both sensible and intelligible, the eighteenth century bears witness to a growing division between reason and emotion. Within this dualistic framework, emotion defers to reason (though emotion is not deficient in merit). Catholicism, for example, reinforces the importance of confessing one's heart and mind, thereby influencing Rousseau's predilection toward emotive responses and encouraging his conversion at an early age. He confesses, ". . . a continuous need to pour myself out brings my heart at every moment to my lips."[107]

Rousseau's emotional temperament engenders both positive and negative events in his life, events for which he rarely accepts responsibility. He explains his sexual desires, for example, as a natural condition that he can neither thwart nor change. In book nine (1756), he suggests that deep psychic wounds feed his sexual habits:

> The first, the greatest, the strongest, the most inextinguishable of all my needs was entirely one of the heart. It was the need for intimate companionship, for a companionship as intimate as possible, which was the chief reason why I needed a woman rather than a man, a woman friend rather than a man friend. This singular need was such that the most intimate physical union could not fulfill it; only two souls in the same body would have sufficed. Failing that, I always felt a void.[108]

To trace out the relationship between the emotions and the self in personal terms, Rousseau appropriates the model of Augustine's *Confessions* and places his life events into a temporal series. Embedded in the narratological use of the past, present, and future resides a version of the Inner self, a view that the self is a composite of temporally circumscribed experiences. However, Rousseau does not regard this temporally circumscribed self as either an empirical or a mental essence. It is neither a soul nor a mind. Rather, the self is a spiritual ego that is individuated by social forces over time. Thus one's emotional and rational dimensions may shape one's character and one's concrete identity in the world, but society determines who one is.

In his turn toward a socially constituted self, Rousseau moves away from Augustine and Descartes and in the constructivist direction of Nietzsche, who also elevates the question of identity over essence. Yet he walks a middle line between Descartes and Nietzsche by continuing to view the self primarily as a historical figure needing to be laid bare, examined, and understood.[109] In his own words:

> Although in certain respects I have been a man since birth, I was for a long time, and still am, a child in many others. I never promised to present the public with a great personage. I promised to depict myself as I am; and to know me in my latter years it is necessary to have known me well in my youth. . . . I should like in some way to make my soul transparent to the reader's eye, and for that purpose I am trying to present it from all points of view, to show it in all lights, and to contrive that none of its movements shall escape his notice. . . . His [the reader's] task is to assemble these elements and to assess the being who is made up of them. The summing-up must be his.[110]

The historical figure that Rousseau wishes to make clear to his reader is a concatenation of the mental and physical acts that Rousseau engaged in throughout his life—his travels, his writings, his feelings and thoughts, and so on. Rousseau argues, "When I trace my nature back in this way to its earliest manifestations, I find features which may appear incompatible, but which have nevertheless combined to form a strong, simple, and uniform whole," and "If I am to be known I must be known in all situations, good and bad."[111] As exhibited in Descartes' *Meditations*, Rousseau's use of the 'I' is frequent, and his tone is relaxed. To whom does the 'I' refer? To answer the question let us contrast the first-person in Rousseau's and Descartes' work.

The Cartesian 'I' signifies a universal thinker—a person qua first-person—a thinking thing unindividuated. By shrouding the self with paradoxical claims about essence and knowledge, the reader of *Meditations* is placed into the position of the 'I,' a position that forces him or her to think dialectically about the relation between self-narration and self-knowledge. By focusing the reader's attention on the essence of the self, Descartes leaves the important questions of identity open for debate.

Conversely, the Roussean 'I' signifies a socially constituted and identifiable writer-self—Rousseau *as* historical figure—an Outer self, known by the particular nuances of his or her life in history. Rousseau uses the 'I' to make explicit and frequent references to himself and his views, yet he offers no philosophical account of the self. He also makes explicit and frequent references to the reader throughout *The Confessions*. By focusing the reader's attention upon the identity of Rousseau, he leaves open the question of essence. He also shifts the focus from the universality of human experience to the particularities of human life. Indeed, the 'I' appears to function as an existential placeholder for Rousseau. Consider his justification for *The Confessions*:

> My *Confessions* are necessarily linked with the tales of many others; and in everything bearing on myself I record the truth about myself and others with equal frankness, in the belief that I owe no more consideration to other people than I show towards myself, although I should like to show them much more. I want always to be fair and truthful, to say as much good as I can of others, and only to speak of evil when it concerns myself and in so far as I am compelled to do so. My *Confessions* are not intended to appear in my own lifetime, or in the lifetime of the persons concerned. If I were master of my own destiny and that of my book, it would not see the light till long after my death and theirs. But the attempts made by my powerful oppressors, who dread the truth, to destroy every trace of it, compel me to make every effort consonant with the strictest justice and the most scrupulous fairness, in order to preserve them. If my memory were to be

> eclipsed with me, rather than compromise anyone I would uncomplainingly endure an unjust and transitory obloquy. But since my name is fated to live, I must endeavor to transmit with it the memory of that unfortunate man who bore it, as he actually was and not as his unjust enemies unremittingly endeavor to paint him.[112]

This passage illustrates Rousseau's desire to circumvent his enemies' potentially misleading presentations of his life and beliefs by remaking his public image. Of course, the methods by which he does so must conform to the literary standards of his age. He must assume the rhetorical stance of the Inner self in his first-person writing; he must persuade his readers of his wounded and bleeding soul. He must also regard autobiography as a historical genre, presenting each life episode as rigid, historical fact. On the other hand, he must accommodate the sensibilities of his readers and mediate his rejection of self-constraining rationalism. I maintain that Rousseau conflates the writer and the author to resolve the conflict between the Inner and Outer conceptions of the self.

Huck Gutman offers a comparable reading of *The Confessions*. He describes Rousseau's self as a "self as subject," a self grounded in subjective experiences and imagination yet aimed at transforming society: ". . . he [Rousseau] realized that by reason alone he could no longer grasp the conflicting reality of his inner world."[113] Gutman describes the creation of Rousseau's reconstruction of the self as a "technology of self." Hence, he credits Rousseau with the creation of "vital techniques in the constitution of the self as subject."[114] Extending Gutman's argument further, Schuster asserts that "Rousseau's lifelong flight from internal and external conflicts and inconsistencies became an intellectual-mystical reverie, which in turn produced a revolutionary and homogeneous social philosophy."[115]

By wearing the Inner self as an Outer self, Rousseau ameliorates the distinction between the writer and author. Instead he creates a first-person literary construct *who appears to be* an authenticating, ontological self. First, he conflates personal and authorial identity. Then he distinguishes his newly created persona from the society-determining figure I described earlier (the historical figure). He accomplishes this conflation in two ways.

First, contra Augustine, he invokes amnesia to show that memory alone cannot generate personal identity. Hence, in the present act of writing, the act of authorship unifies the self as much as memory. Second, Rousseau invokes a constructivist model of truth wherein the reader co-creates meaning and generates truth. Hence, truth is not confined to the present act of writing or thinking as it is in Descartes' *Meditations*. The reader, who is temporally and spatially absent from the text, is partly responsible for the identity of the writer-author.

How does this prior conflation lead to the distinction between the ontological self and the historical figure? Rousseau implies that the narration and reading of texts unify the self; reflective/reflexive acts presuppose successiveness or temporal order. But these forms of successiveness are instantiated in history and not in time per se. Rousseau suggests, then, that history (which presupposes time) provides continuity and unity of the self through the influence of the past over the present. This does not contradict the Augustinian or Cartesian views, but it does qualify it in an important way. Following Rousseau's logic, our experience of time is not simply an experience of events in time. Rather, when we experience events in time we experience events that are also and always conditioned by history (by a narrative account of events in time). This implies that time is not merely a distention of the mind; it is a distention of a necessarily socialized and/or politicized mind. To know the self, then, is to know the historical self—the historical figure.

Time

At the beginning of book 12, the last book of *The Confessions* (1762), Rousseau claims that public scorn prevents him from understanding the truth about his personal affairs. Rousseau appeals to the reader to help him discern the truth about his life:

> In relating, therefore, the events that concern me, the treatment I have suffered and all that has happened to me, I am in no position to trace them to their prime mover or to assume reasons when I state facts. These first causes are all noted down in the three previous books. . . . But to explain how these various causes combined to bring about the strange events of my life, this I find impossible to do, even conjecturally. If there are any among my readers generous enough to try and probe these mysteries till they discover the truth, let them carefully reread the last three books.[116]

Rousseau moves away from the Augustinian and Cartesian epistemological models where truth emerges through a process of introspection and retrospection (or disengagement and objectification) and moves toward a constructivist model where truth is the dialectical conclusion reached by a reader through an act of engagement with a text. Implicit in the latter model is the view that truth may be propositional, narrative, or logical in form but does not necessarily correspond to a real state of affairs in the world. Rather, truth is a product of analysis (produced simultaneously by a reader and a text) that is itself shaped by the author-subject.

Equating the self with the historical figure, an ontological entity that is individuated by society, commits Rousseau to a mitigated form of essentialism and constructivism—to a view of the self that is both Inner and Outer. For instance, the essence that animates the creature dissipates at death, but the records that individuate the historical figure live on.[117] His appropriation of an

Outer self becomes clearest when he argues that the self we know and experience is a façade of human nature, a façade co-constructed by the recorded events of one's life as interpreted by publicly instantiated and political peoples. The following excerpt from book eight, which sounds quite Nietzschean in tone, expresses his dual thinking about the self:

> I demolished the petty lies of mankind; I dared to strip man's nature naked, to follow the progress of time, and trace the things which have distorted it; and by comparing man as he had made himself with man as he is by nature I showed him in his pretended perfection the true source of his misery. Exalted by these sublime meditations, my soul soared towards the Divinity; and from that height I looked down on my fellow men pursuing the blind path of their prejudices, of their errors, of their misfortunes and their crimes. Then I cried to them in a feeble voice which they could not hear, "Madmen, who ceaselessly complain of Nature, learn that all your misfortunes arise from yourselves!"[118]

If identity is contingent upon the social situation into which the presocial self is born, then what can be said about the presocial (Inner) self? What is the relation between the presocial and postsocial self from Rousseau's viewpoint?

Both nature and society objectify humans in the process of identity formation. Gender, race, and age shape public identity in inescapable ways. This public identity often eclipses our more introspective sense of who we are to the detriment of our spiritual and psychological well-being. We are either compelled to remember who we were in a presocial state, then reflect on who we have become, to perhaps dwell on those memories, and then to resolve to accept them as representations of ourselves. Or, we are compelled to regard those memories as past identities, now overcome by the recreation of identity and the creation of new memories. Rousseau attempts the latter project, rewriting his own memories and recasting his identity in a more pleasing light with the hope that he might change his identity. He hopes to destroy the public conception of himself and recreate the historical figure of Rousseau. He also conceals his actions, feeling, and thoughts from others so that they will not distinguish between personal and authorial identity. In sum, Rousseau obscures the relation between the Inner and Outer self in order to recoup his identity.

Memory

A second technique that Rousseau consistently employs to obscure his identity is amnesia: he claims that he has forgotten the facts of his life. His amnesia both protects him from harsh judgment by the reader who may disapprove of his actions and alleviates the guilt he may otherwise experience were he to confess his deeds and thoughts. So he appeals, with expressed sadness, to the reader for patience while he attempts to recall the particularities of momentous life events:

> In thinking over the details of my life which are lost to my memory, what I most regret is that I did not keep diaries of my travels. Never did I think so much, exist so vividly, and experience so much, never have I been so much myself—if I may use that expression—as in the journeys I have taken alone and on foot.[119]

Conveniently, Rousseau's defining life experiences are neither recorded nor remembered. Again, when Rousseau is ordered to leave Geneva because of the public outrage incited by his *Letters Written from the Mountain,* he writes:

> I have so confused a memory of this whole affair that it is impossible for me to impose any order or connexion on the ideas which come back to me. I can do no more than record them in the scattered and isolated form in which they come to my mind. I remember that there were some sort of negotiations with the clergy, in which Montmollin acted as mediator. He pretended that people were afraid I should disturb the country's peace by my writings, for which the country would be held responsible.[120]

Here Rousseau directs his self-reflections outward to the reader, implying that the reader holds equal responsibility for Rousseau's identity and, therefore, that the reading of *The Confessions* is an act of self-ascription. He becomes the person that we understand him to be through the act of reading, because he himself admits to little and remembers even less. The reader, then, is forced to draw the inferences Rousseau carefully avoids drawing. In so doing, Rousseau is able to justify his identification of the self with the historical figure. Dilthey interprets this as an admission of guilt covered over by a layer of emotional fervor, an attempt on Rousseau's part to "justify his spiritual existence. . . . Rousseau wanted, above all, to justify his individual existence."[121]

Rousseau's attempt to mislead readers in order to elevate our opinion of him is perhaps forgivable if it can be shown that Rousseau's emotional state skews his perception of his life and distorts his memory. Two passages in *The Confessions* appear to support this possibility. The first describes the treatment Rousseau received from friends after he was banned from entering many city gates. Once again, Rousseau sees himself as a victim and interprets the actions of his friends as acts of jealousy outside of his control. They mistreated him:

> . . . whilst I was trampling underfoot the senseless opinions of the vulgar herd of the so-called great and so-called wise, I allowed myself to

> be enslaved and led like a child by so-called friends, who were jealous at seeing me strike out alone down a new road and, whilst appearing to be much concerned for my happiness, in fact used every endeavor to make me look ridiculous. . . . It was not so much my literary celebrity as the change in my character, which dates from this time, which evoked their jealousy; they would perhaps have forgiven me for brilliance in the art of writing; but they could not forgive me for setting up an example by my conduct; this appeared to put them out. *I was born for friendship; my easy and gentle disposition had no difficulty in fostering it.*[122]

Note here that Rousseau does not name names when he censures those he considers former friends. He instead focuses the reader's attention on the harm that his friends' actions have caused him, not the harm they may have caused themselves.

The significance of this quotation arises not from its truth or falsity but from the view of the self that it conveys. Does Rousseau want us to regard him as a victim? Does he see himself as a victim? Can both be true? Reconsider the focus Rousseau places upon himself rather than his friends: the passivity of the 'I' he imposes on the text, the exaggeration with which he characterizes his success, and the amnesia that clouds his thinking. Rousseau makes no distinction between presenting himself as a victim and being a victim: he is what his readers make him, and he writes *The Confessions* solely for them.

The second passage in which Rousseau invokes amnesia appears in book twelve:

> The further I go in my story, the less order and sequence I can put into it. The disturbances of my later life have not left events time to fall into shape in my head. They have been too numerous, too confused, too unpleasant to be capable of straightforward narration. The only strong impression they have left me is that of the horrible mystery enveloping their cause, and of the deplorable state to which they have reduced me. Now my story can only proceed at haphazard, according as the ideas come back into my mind. . . . And even if I had thought otherwise, it is unlikely that I should have been more circumspect, since *by nature I am absolutely incapable of concealing anything that I feel or think.*[123]

Here Rousseau's feigned sincerity is a mere convention. The outrageous claims he makes in this passage, such as "I am absolutely incapable of concealing anything that I feel or think," contradict prior claims that he was mistaken on occasion about his feelings and thoughts.[124] Rousseau's forgetfulness obscures some of the traumatic moments of his life. Belá Szabados aptly notes that the aura of sincerity in Rousseau's writing, alongside the blatant lack and violation of sincerity, leads us to mistrust Rousseau: "As we read on, we begin to mistrust that paragon of honesty and sincerity that is Rousseau's self-portrait."[125] His lack of sincerity, coupled with his appeal to amnesia, obscures more than Rousseau's self-portrait; it obscures the reader as well, whose sole duty, Rousseau insists, is to be just.[126]

Knowledge

By eroding the distinction between the author and writer, Rousseau positions the reader outside of the dialectical process of self-knowing that is initiated by self-narration. What does this rhetorical stance suggest about his own ability to introspect and retrospect on his life? I note in several places that Rousseau's account of the self as a socialized persona moves in the direction of constructivist accounts of the self. Schuster shares this reading, observing that in "Rousseau's . . . notion of the self, which is not identical with the mechanical deterministic and scientific concepts that were fashionable among his fellow philosophers, but based on consciously observing thoughts and feelings . . . [one can] sense in *The Confessions* an early Existentialist conception of life."[127] We see this clearly in his discussions of the reader and the author.

In book nine, Rousseau identifies the author-subject as an independently existing source of creativity tied neither to an extant individual nor to a set of ideas:

> What made me still happier . . . was that the government of France, though it might not look on me with great favour, would make it a point of honour, if not to protect me, at least to leave me undisturbed. . . . By not molesting me they would hold the author as a surety for his works and, what is more, would abolish prejudices firmly established throughout the rest of Europe.[128]

However, in the same book, Rousseau alludes to the tacit distinction between himself as a historical figure and himself as conflated writer-author:

> In the storm that has engulfed me my books have served as a pretext: the attack was against myself. They cared very little about the author, but they wished to destroy Jean-Jacques. . . . I do not know whether this mystery, which remains one to me, will be cleared up in my readers' eyes. I only know that if my declared principles really brought down on me the treatment I suffered, it would not have been so long before I was its victim.[129]

Though Rousseau makes a last-minute attempt to salvage the distinction between the author and writer (primarily to avoid persecution in the form of personal diatribes), the conflation of the author-subject and writer-self is too far gone. With his appeal to the reader as a textual force and his use of amnesia, Rousseau lays the foundation for a constructivist obliteration of the writer-self. He wonders whether an author who writes multiple texts, who arises from the pen of a single writer, who is called by the same name within all texts, can be the same author. Or does each text invest the same-name author with a unique set of characteristics so that each text has its own individual author? Answering on the side of the individual, Rousseau responds rhetorically, "Could the writer of *Perpetual Peace* be a spreader of discord, the creator of the Savoyard Vicar be an infidel, the author of the *New Héloise* a wolf, and that of *Émile* a madman! What should I have been then, in heaven's name, if I had written *The Spirit of the Laws,* or something of that kind?"[130]

Preliminary Conclusions

Jean-Jacques Rousseau is an essentialist with constructivist tendencies. He implies that the self is a composite of intellect and emotion unified in history through the influence of the past over the present. He relies on history to provide continuity and unity to the self, a self that is incidentally embedded in time. Yet Rousseau maintains that the self's identity is determined by the social forces in which the self is situated, because time is historicized. Rousseau also believes that through writing, our identities can be altered, our narratives challenged, and our selves bracketed, allowing the author of texts to merge with the writer of texts so that the distinction between the rhetorical and ontological dimensions of existence remains usefully ambiguous. This explains why Ann Hartle characterizes *The Confessions* as "imaginative construction." Extending Hartle's argument, Schuster claims that "Rousseau's real object in his autobiography is neither to write fiction nor to create a narrative of data that can be judged factually, but to compose a truthful narrative of himself by himself: 'to contribute to an accurate knowledge of my inner being in all the different situations of my life.'"[131] In engaging in imaginative construction, Rousseau anticipates the artful work of Nietzsche and Barnes who strive to destroy the self and reproduce many authors. We see his essentialist and constructivist tendencies clearly in the following passage from *The Confessions*:

> The sight of the countryside, the succession of pleasant views, open air, a sound appetite, and the good health I gain by walking, the easy atmosphere of an inn, the absence of everything that makes me feel my dependence, of everything that recalls me to my situation—all these serve to free my spirit, to lend a greater boldness to my thinking, to throw me, so to speak, into the vastness of things, so that I can combine them, select them, and make them mine as I will, without fear or restraint. I dispose of all Nature as its master.[132]

Before moving on to the Outer self and its role in the autobiographies of Nietzsche and Barnes, let me summarize my argument thus far. I argue that Rousseau is the first confessional autobiographer to wear the Inner self like a mask. His appropriation of the Inner self, however meager, provides an invaluable bridge between ancient and modern meditations on the self.

First, his autobiography mediates the Inner and Outer self by conflating the writer-self and author-subject into one historical figure. Second, his work functions as a conduit between the first-person narrations of Descartes and Nietzsche—from universal to existential instantiations of the self. By endorsing ideals that displace thought with feeling, Rousseau shifts the philosophical paradigm away from the speculative reason of rationalism and toward the entrenched individualism of perspectivism. Third, he offers a fruitful critique of the confessional mode of philosophical autobiography. This in turn creates a space for new modes of autobiography to emerge. Rousseau, then, offers a middle perspective between the Inner self and the Outer self. For Augustine and Descartes, the self is a thinking substance unified and conditioned by time but capable of reflecting atemporally and knowing eternal truths. As I will argue in the following two sections, Nietzsche and Barnes regard the self as a fictional concept or mask that disguises human potentiality and the construction of meaning. Because they regard humans as beings situated in time, conditioned by time, but *not determined by time*, they maintain that only narration and reflection can unify the creative potentiality we call the "self." Despite the limitations of his autobiography, Rousseau's *The Confessions* provides an essential link in the chain of philosophical autobiography from essentialism to constructivism. By conveying himself to others as a mask-wearing Inner self, Rousseau erodes the distinction between the Inner self and the Outer self.

The Outer Self

Nietzsche, 1844–1900

Nietzsche advances an unrelenting attack on the traditional philosophical conception of the self as an Inner self. *The Birth of Tragedy* (1872), *Thus Spoke Zarathustra* (1885), *Beyond Good and Evil* (1886), *On the Genealogy of Morals* (1887), *Twilight of the Idols* (1888), and *Ecce Homo* (1889) all characterize the idea of an enduring, prediscursive self as illusory, dangerous, and life denying. "I do not refute ideals," he writes in *Ecce Homo*, "I merely put on gloves before them."[133] Though his diatribe stresses the paucity of a temporally and an ontologically defined (or a circumscribed) self, the quest for identity does not elude him. Thus the preface to *Ecce Homo* directs our attention to self-identity: "Seeing that before long I must confront humanity with the most difficult demand ever made of it, it seems indispensable to me to say who I am."[134]

Ecce Homo is a unique example of philosophical autobiography. For one thing, it intentionally recapitulates many of the ideas that comprise Nietzsche's philosophy. He quotes extensively from *Thus Spoke Zarathustra* throughout. And he writes more aphoristically here than in previous publications (and certainly more than other autobiographers). This adds to the rhetorical beauty and mystique of the text, but it complicates the analysis of the self. Since my task in this chapter is to elucidate the development of the self in five philosophical autobiographies, I include additional accounts of Nietzsche's view of the self. For example, to explain what Nietzsche regards as the false positing of a 'self,' he articulates a penetrating genealogy of the self in *On the Genealogy of Morals*: ". . . When he [man] found himself finally enclosed within the walls of society and peace . . ." he became an 'individual' born into 'consciousness' and weighed down by 'morality.'[135] Because the genealogy elucidates Nietzsche's view of the self in significant ways, I restate it in abbreviated form below.

Nietzsche begins his genealogy by arguing that "consciousness is only a net of communication between human beings," not the locus of the psyche, the essence of existence, or the center of the "self."[136] But history tells a different tale. Consciousness came to typify the self when the desire to express private and often tragic feelings or insights (a Dionysian impulse) was compromised by a secondary desire for simple and clear (propositional) knowledge (an Apollinian impulse).[137] The subsequent translation of impulses and ideas into logical claims, coupled with the cultural embracing of an Apollinian temperament, led to the increasingly complex compartmentalization of ideas and emotions. Eventually discrete and categorized thought, "S knows that P," evolved into a distinct "consciousness," a mind that can think those clear and distinct thoughts, as Descartes argues. He explains, ". . . they [humans] no longer possessed their former guides, their regulating, unconscious, and infallible drives; they were reduced to thinking, inferring, reckoning, coordinating cause and effect, these unfortunate creatures; they were reduced to their 'consciousness,' their weakest and most fallible organ."[138]

The genealogical reduction of reflective human activity to consciousness resulted in compartmentalized and independent thinking. This in turn generated the epistemological belief that human beings are unique individuals or mechanistic thinkers (alá Descartes), which isolated human beings and set them in competition with one another (an idea Nietzsche undermines in an overtly anti-Cartesian essay, "Untimely Meditations"). Nietzsche argues that the coalignment of consciousness and individualism blinds human beings to the universality of experience, that is, to the chaotic, Dionysian abyss from which all human experience originates and all meaning emerges. Humans then internalize the Apollinian desire for simplicity of thought and feeling over and against the contemplation of complex reality in flux. This internalization process gives rise to defense mechanisms that protect humans from destructive impulses. Hence, whenever human experience or expression threatens our thickly veiled sense of individuality and order, we begin to blame others for our random or inexplicable experiences. Nietzsche continues:

> All instincts that do not discharge themselves outwardly turn inward—this is what I call the internalization of man: thus it was that man first developed what was later called his 'soul.' The entire inner world, originally as thin as if it were stretched between two membranes, expanded and extended itself, acquired depth, breadth, and height, in the same measure as outward discharge was inhibited.[139]

Nietzsche famously describes this reaction to chaos as a herd mentality or a slave morality. "My idea is, as you see, that consciousness does not really belong to man's individual existence but rather to his social or herd nature."[140] Humans express a "herd mentality"[141] whenever they assume the unquestioned dogmas (religious, psychological, and so on) that suppress their will to power, that is, the most basic human drive to become creators rather than creatures.[142] Humans seek to dominate others, which is their only remaining means to power, by deeming others' thoughts and actions inferior to their own. Nietzsche argues further that the dogmas of society overpower the weak herd and mask the universal dimensions of consciousness, a consciousness in which all human experience and understanding originates:

> [A]ll our actions are altogether incomparably personal, unique, and infinitely individual . . . [b]ut as soon as we translate them into consciousness they no longer seem to be. This is the essence of phenomenalism and perspectivism as I understand them: the world of which we become conscious is a surface and sign world, a world made common and meaner. Whatever becomes conscious becomes by the same token shallow, thin, relatively stupid, general, herd signal; all becoming conscious involves a great and thorough corruption.[143]

He concludes that the way to stall or even reverse the disintegration of the individual into consciousness is to overcome the feelings of psychic comfort that a belief in consciousness—a belief in a self—evokes. Hence, Nietzsche bids us to reascribe the meaning of humankind, human activity, and human knowledge, to look into the Dionysian abyss and recover life-affirming practices therein. The first step toward becoming what we are is to stop sublimating and extirpating our desires, a practice that leads thematically, and perhaps genealogically, to Nietzsche's anti-Christian polemics and the death of God.

God

In *Thus Spoke Zarathustra*, the protagonist descends from the mountain and announces that God is dead and that we have killed him.[144] The death of God theme, which Nietzsche repeats in *Twilight of the Idols*, is a mocking appropriation of Christian beliefs, a polemic against traditional metaphysics, and a strident rejection of herd mentality. It also sets the stage for a reascription of the self, in two ways. First, the "death of God" signifies the annihilation of absolute values and ideas. When applied to metaphysical conceptions of the mind, the death of God simultaneously destroys all false ideals that identify the self with consciousness, ego, or will and frees the self to express its fundamental will to power. Second, the death of God translates "man back into nature."[145] Nietzsche recoups the individual from the ancient and modern philosophers and reinserts the will to power as the source of human identity.[146] The *will to power*, the human instinct to create, drives humans to overcome morality and suffering. It alone is the life-affirming solution to herd resentment. If one can say meaningfully that there is an essence to the self, and it is unclear whether Nietzsche thinks one can, then the will to power is it—a primordial urge to flourish and create:

> . . . life itself has been defined as a more and more efficient inner adaptation to external conditions. . . . Thus, the essence of life, its will to power is ignored; one overlooks the essential priority of the spontaneous, aggressive, expansive, form-giving forces that give new interpretations and directions.[147]

Nietzsche's view of the self as a matrix of instinctual desires or "will to power" does not contradict ontological views of the self entirely. Clearly, Nietzsche regards the will to power as a universal characterization of nature and life. However, Nietzsche uses the phrase "will to power" in different senses in different places. For example, though all people exhibit the will to power, many subconsciously and in unhealthy ways, only some acknowledge and affirm the will to power—that is, only a few say *yes* to the will to power and thus transform the will to power into a will to life (e.g., immoralists, the *Ubermensch*, et al.) Hence, the will to power is like a sliding scale of kinetic and potential energy. It suffuses all of life, but it is intentionally embraced and affirmed by some rather than all individuals. In the latter sense, Nietzsche's will to power represents a refinement of the Inner self, a displacement of individuated consciousness or transcendent spirit with subconscious will or desire. Activity and instinct eclipse stasis and substance.

Nietzsche's identification of himself as "a disciple of the philosopher Dionysus" in contrast to a saint or prophet illustrates this shift in thinking about the self. The former creates and intoxicates; the latter perverts and infects: "Here no 'prophet' is speaking, none of those gruesome hybrids of sickness and will to power whom people call founders of religions."[148] Indeed, the Dionysian impulse toward irrationality is the creative condition for the will to life and human animal to emerge. Moreover, because the will to power describes *what* one is, that is, one's essence, then all manifestations or expressions of that creative power, all creative products, circumscribe *who* one is. I *am* my creations: this is the "anguished cry of one who sees—foresees—himself mistaken for a writer he is not: for an apostle of military power and empire, a nationalist, and even a racist."[149]

Nietzsche's autobiography exemplifies the process by which the Inner self is reformed and strengthened through the creative construction of an ambiguous Outer self. This process stands in opposition to the Apollinian sublimation of creative potential. Kaufmann explains:

> *Ecce Homo* does not fit any ordinary conception of philosophers. It is not only remote from the word of professional or donnish philosophy, from tomes and articles, from footnotes and jargon—in brief from the modern image. It is equally far from the popular notion of the wise man: serene, past passion, temperate, and Apollinian. But this is plainly part of Nietzsche's point: to offer a new image—a philosopher who is not an Alexandrian academician, nor an Apollinian sage, but Dionysian.[150]

Throughout his writings Nietzsche exhorts us to remember that the reduction of humanity to metaphysical, linguistic, and logical terms renders impossible the authentic experience of life. He implies that rationality breeds misery: "Man has evolved that queasy stomach and coated tongue through which not only the joy but the innocence of the animal life itself has become repugnant to him."[151]

By recovering the will to power, we exercise our life-affirming desire to reconstruct values. Nietzsche writes, "It, [the human will] needs a goal—and it would rather will nothingness than not will."[152] Yet by directing the will to power toward a will to life, humans generate a psychic tension between power and reason, the spontaneous impulse to become a creator versus the guilt-ridden belief that we are mere creatures. I contend that this tension opens up a space between the Inner self and the Outer self—between disorderly Dionysian and orderly Apollinian impulses, between the herd and master mentality (or morality), between the created and the creator—a space in which the will to power and individual identity finally and ultimately coalesce. Kaufmann observes that Nietzsche advocated the juxtaposition of such opposing forces even as late as *Twilight of the Idols*: "Nietzsche leaves no doubt that, although he far prefers a master morality . . . he calls attention to its inhuman aspects; and in the final analysis he finds both types of morality 'entirely worthy of each other.'"[153]

Nietzsche transfigures Augustine's, Descartes', and Rousseau's views of the Inner self by privileging the self-creating acts of the will over the self-reflective acts of consciousness. We see an illustration of this reordering in Nietzsche's rejection of the confessional models of autobiography, models exemplified by Augustine and Rousseau in which the 'I' confesses and apologizes for past deeds, regrets lost opportunities, and laments bad choices.[154] Instead, Nietzsche adopts a poetical model of autobiography and affirms the past in the present, exemplifying the poetic overcoming of resentment that the herd promulgates, a triumph he represents elsewhere as the *Ubermensch* or overperson. Kaufmann concurs and suggests further that Nietzsche's use of autobiography is self-edifying: "There is no 'if only' in this autobiography, and there are no excuses. A man who was in physical agony much of his adult life and warned by his doctors not to read or write much, lest he strain his half blind eyes, does not once complain. He is thankful for his illness and tells us how it made his life better."[155]

The death of God foreshadows Nietzsche's figurative murder of the self. Once Nietzsche destroys what he considers to be pernicious metaphysical conceptions of the self—ego, consciousness, will—he frees human beings to will the attainment of oneself and the creation of one's values. Nietzsche argues that the act of willing or creating *is* the affirmation of life, a life grounded in the natural phenomena of human experiences that is present, new, and reconstructed from the past. The will to power is the only truth of existence. And this truth "came more and more for Nietzsche to be a criterion of human greatness."[156]

Time

Through the process of willful domination and control of nature, we construct self-identities without negating the will to power.[157] Nietzsche maintains that the will to power fosters the formation of self-identity by empowering individuals to organize and ascribe meaning to events in time. These events bear out meaning, understanding, and beliefs about the past, the present, and the future, and these events are "consecrated" in the present. Nehamas describes this process in both physiological and psychological terms:

> . . . the body provides the common ground that allows conflicting thoughts, desires, and actions to be grouped together as features of a single subject. . . . Exactly the same is true of their patterns—that is, of our character traits. Dominant habits and traits, as long as they are dominant, assume the role of the subject. . . . It is such traits that speak with the voice of the self when they are manifested in action. Their own coherence and unity allow them to become the subject that, at least for a while, says 'I.' . . . And though, as is often the case with the

> voice of the state, the 'I' seems to refer to the same thing, the content to which it refers and interests for which it speaks do not remain the same. It is constantly in the process of changing.[158]

As a result of this self-creating process, we remain grounded in a recognizable history. Yet our identity as meaning-ascribing creators requires that we affirm events in time *as if they transcend time*—as if they might recur eternally. Nietzsche's account of the Eternal Return (or Eternal Recurrence) appears most prominently in *Thus Spoke Zarathustra*, *The Gay Science*, and *The Will to Power*. Consider this passage from *Thus Spoke Zarathustra*:

> "Behold," I continued, "this moment! From this gateway, Moment, a long, eternal lane leads backward: behind us lies an eternity. Must not whatever can walk have walked on this lane before? Must not whatever can happen have happened, have been done, have passed by before? And if everything has been there before—what do you think, dwarf, of this moment? Must not this gateway too have been there before? And are not all things knotted together so firmly that this moment draws after it all that is to come? Therefore—itself too? For whatever can walk—in this long lane out there too, it must walk once more . . . must we not eternally return?"[159]

Read metaphysically, this passage is a polemic against the Platonic idea of an absolute, unchanging realm of Forms. Nietzsche suggests that everything in life, every finite moment, every finite event, is caught in an infinite Heraclitean vortex of flux. The past, present, and future bend or fold together to form one singular ever-recurring present; a moment of infinite and eternal return. Viewed this way, every moment is as significant as the next. Neither the present nor the future eclipses the past, neither the past nor the present overshadows the future.

Read psychologically, the Eternal Return is a meditation on the endless cycle of tragedy that life generates, tragedy that, if affirmed, can produce irrevocable joy. Expressed as a pregnant psychic possibility, the idea of the Eternal Return is the idea that our life in every minute detail will recur unchanged. Whoever faces such an idea with courage and joy, affirming even the "sternest of problems," will crush the debilitating "illusion of chronology" and live an all-too-human life. Nietzsche writes:

> What if some day or night a demon were to steal after you into your loneliest loneliness and say to you: "This life as you now live it and have lived it, you will have to live once more and innumerable times more; and there will be nothing new in it, but every pain and every joy and

> every thought and sigh and everything unutterably small or great in your live will have to return to you, all in the same succession and sequence—even this spider and this moonlight between the trees, and even this moment and I myself. The eternal hourglass of existence is turned upside down again and again, and you with it, speck of dust!" Would you not throw yourself down and gnash your teeth and curse the demon who spoke thus? Or have you once experienced a tremendous moment when you would have answered him: "You are a god and never have I heard anything more divine." If this thought gained possession of you, it would change, you as you are or perhaps crush you.[160]

On both readings the Eternal Return becomes an ideal that affirms rather than rejects life: "[The Eternal Return] becomes a perspective on life that asks us, even forces us, to recognize life for what it is, and within that recognition, to embrace it, stripping away from life the masks we have placed over it. Nietzsche's doctrine of absolute affirmation is the 'absolute YES!' to all possibilities. Absolute affirmation means that all possible events are actual, and no impossible combinations of events become actual. In other words, every possible world is actual right now!"[161] Nietzsche expresses this idea in the following two passages from *The Will to Power*:

> Duration "in vain" without end or aim is the most paralyzing idea.[162]

> To endure the idea of the recurrence one needs: freedom from morality; new means against the fact of pain (pain conceived as a tool, as the father of pleasure; there is no cumulative consciousness of displeasure); the enjoyment of all kinds of uncertainty, experimentalism, as a counterweight to this extreme fatalism; abolition of the concept of necessity; abolition of the "will"; abolition of "knowledge-in-itself."[163]

In contrast to Augustine, Descartes, and Rousseau, Nietzsche implies that neither time nor history—"mere duration"—provides continuity or unity to the self. In lieu of an introspecting and retrospecting self, a self that looks inward and backward, a self conditioned by psychology and temporality, Nietzsche proposes what I refer to as an *alterspecting* self: a self that looks outside of the alienating dimensions of the psyche and time and instead conflates the past, present, and future into a single psychic moment. Once embedded in this creative, noetic moment, the self wills and uses this noetic force to create identity and affirm life. Together life affirmation and self-narration provide unity to the self through the reflective act of alterspection. The *Ubermensch* symbolizes the penultimate manifestations of the alterspecting self—the "alter self."

Memory

Nietzsche implies that the herd ascribes to the self an enduring, unchanging entity. This unity of self is temporally and historically situated and ontologically individuated via memory. Hence, the herd creates the historical figure from which false or masked self-identity emerges. In addition, the herd creates the Inner self from which self-knowledge is brought to consciousness through the mental functions of memory, awareness, and expectation (introspection and retrospection). By contrast, Nietzsche argues that the *Ubermensch*, an *alterspective* self, must learn to practice "active forgetfulness":

> To close the doors and windows of consciousness for a time; to remain undisturbed by the noise and struggle of our underworld of utility organs working with and against one another; a little quietness, a little tabula rasa of the consciousness, to make room for new things, above all the nobler functions and functionaries, for regulation, foresight, premeditation . . . that is the purpose of active forgetfulness, which is like a doorkeeper, a preserver of psychic order, repose, and etiquette: so that it will be immediately obvious how there could be no happiness, no cheerfulness, no hope, no pride, no *present*, without forgetfulness.[164]

He then argues that memory is a construct: it is necessary for the fulfillment of contractual promises. Memory was created for the human animal because of its economic value; it is nothing more than a "terror" that attends all promises and pledges: "Man could never do without blood, torture, and sacrifices when he felt a need to create a memory for himself."[165] The actively forgetful human being who wills himself or herself artfully and eternally will begin by forgetting the ego.

The self qua Outer self or author-subject exhibits a multiplicity of character traits and alienating appearances. The self is both Apollinian and Dionysian, both subconscious and conscious, both rational and emotional. In this regard, Nietzsche's view of the self appropriates both the Cartesian cogito, which unifies mental activity, and the Rousseauean figure, which embodies "heartfelt feelings." Nietzsche proclaims, "[T]o renounce belief in one's ego, to deny one's own 'reality'—what a triumph!"[166]

The triumph for Nietzsche occurs on two levels: (1) It shows the look into the true nature of things, the Dionysian abyss; and (2) It instantiates the will to power. When one legislates reality, when one overcomes the self, one eradicates the individual and neutralizes the herd mentality. Moreover, the overcoming of the self elevates the self-creating consciousness to the position of bird of prey and strengthens creative power and desires. Nietzsche suggests that the noetic force must come from a Dionysian encounter with reality. Hence, the power of self-creation arises from the authentic experience of life, not from the philosophical views one adopts. His objection to philosophical accounts of the self becomes clear in the following extended passage from *Beyond Good and Evil*:

> If one listens to the footsteps of an anchorite, one can always hear something of an echo of desolation, something of the whisper and the fearful vigilance of solitude. In his strongest words, in his shriek even, there resounds a new, more dangerous type of silence, of silent concealment. Whoever has sat alone with his soul year-in and year-out, day and night, in confidential discord and discourse, whoever became a cave-bear or a treasure seeker or a treasure guardian, a dragon, in his lair (which might be a labyrinth or a gold-mine)—in the end his very concepts will take on a unique twilight-color, an odor of depth as well as of mold, something incommunicative and repulsive that blows cold on anyone who passes by. The anchorite does not believe that any philosopher (assuming that all philosophers were once anchorites) ever expressed his essential and ultimate opinions in a book. On the contrary, one writes books in order to conceal what is concealed in one. He will doubt, in fact, that a philosopher can ever have an "ultimate and essential" opinion. He will suspect behind each cave a deeper cave, a more extensive, more exotic, richer world beyond the surface of a bottomless abyss, a bottomless abyss beyond every bottom, beneath every "foundation." Every philosophy is a fore-ground philosophy: this is an anchorite's judgment. There is something arbitrary in the fact that the philosopher stopped *here*, that he looked back and looked around, that *here* he refrained from digging deeper, that he laid aside his spade. There is, in fact, something that arouses suspicion! Each philosophy also conceals a philosophy; each opinion is also a hiding place; each word is also a mask.[167]

Because he regards the self as something to be achieved rather than discovered, Nietzsche aims to achieve himself, to become himself, by first becoming an anchorite, one who lives in philosophical seclusion by renouncing the herd mentality.[168] He is an overman; he is no "self" in either the philosophical, historical, or literary sense. He is Dionysus, Zarathustra, sage, overman, philosopher, musician, and poet simultaneously—the subject of multiplicity.[169] He refuses to circumscribe identity with a literary label or a metaphysical concept. The authors of his texts, as I argued in Chapter 1, cannot be identified with the historical figure or writer-self. He resists these arbitrary classifications, as we see in *Ecce Homo,* "Why I Am So Clever," section 4:

> [A]nd damn it, my dear critics! Suppose I had published my Zarathustra under another name—for example, that of Richard Wagner—the

> acuteness of two thousand years would not have been sufficient for anyone to guess that the author of *Human, All Too Human* is the visionary of Zarathustra.[170]

Nietzsche self-narrates to eradicate the essentialist self that the tradition of philosophical thinking perpetuates: "Henceforth, my dear philosophers, let us be on guard against the dangerous old conceptual fiction that posited a 'pure, will-less, painless, timeless knowing subject'."[171] Personal and philosophical truths are identical for Nietzsche.[172]

Knowledge

After he deconstructs essentialist views of the self, Nietzsche turns his attention to the process and product of self-representation—self-knowing and self-knowledge. He remarks in book three of *On the Genealogy of Morals*, "There is only a perspective seeing, only a perspective 'knowing'; and the affects we allow to speak about one thing, our 'objectivity' be." What we call objectivity is perspectivity. What we call "self" is always a self-representing will. Nietzsche reminds us in this passage that our desire to communicate gives rise to consciousness, which gives rise to the ego or individual. Once we see ourselves as communicative individuals who articulate personal experiences, we falsely understand and represent ourselves as private selves or egos. John Atwell describes Nietzsche's point in causal terms:

> For Nietzsche, the so-called being of a thing is only its "effects," its actions, its properties, all of which are . . . networks of relationships. There are no agents apart from the actions, no egos or selves apart from their thoughts, and no things apart from their properties or qualities.[173]

Nietzsche's point is that representations of the self, either self-generated or other generated, are not coincident with the self. He insists that he is neither a biologically determined nor socially defined individual. And his insistence means that the self is neither Inner nor Outer, neither philosophical nor historical, though philosophers and societal forces attempt to equate the self with representations of the self. In this and only this sense is there no self for Nietzsche. The represented self is always many rather than one. To exemplify this point clearly, Nietzsche represents himself as many selves with many identities, many "faces," none of which are coincident with each other or the will to power.

By distinguishing the self and the self-represented, Nietzsche invokes the distinction between the author and the writer. Yet like Rousseau, he redefines the meaning of both terms. The *author* connotes a textually inscribed identity written from a first-person perspective. If the textually inscribed identity is created by a perspective other than a first-person perspective, then the identity remains textually inscribed, but it is not authorial. For example, Nietzsche distinguishes between the Jesus of the Gospels, whose identity is inscribed by the Gospel writers and the *historical figure* of Jesus, the public and religious figure whose identity is circumscribed by religious worship and theological belief and so on.[174] The *writer*, on the other hand, is a self-inscribing creator who narrates the facets of his or her existence by first engaging in the authenticating act of alterspection. Hence, self-knowledge falls outside of this discursive procedure. I say more about Nietzsche's view of autobiographically relevant concepts in Chapter 4.

Preliminary Conclusions

Nietzsche's renouncement of the ego, the consciousness, and the will exemplifies his rejection of a metaphysics that privileges the Apollinian expression of reality over the Dionysian experience of reality. Nietzsche extirpates a wholly formed, preexistent self for the will to power, the will to create. Understanding "who one is" means becoming who one is, instantiating the representation of the self one creates. By reducing the self to the properties of objects, Nietzsche eschews epistemological theories that define truth as correspondence between a thing and its syntactical representation. Nimrod Aloni regards this as Nietzsche's repudiation of the existence of any kind of world "in-itself."[175] Instead, existence is pure activity: "There is no 'being' behind doing, effecting, becoming; 'the doer' is merely a fiction added to the deed—the deed is everything." Likewise, there is no being, no doer, no agent in Nietzsche's philosophy—no metaphysically or epistemologically inscribed ego. However, it does not follow that there is no psyche, no Dionysian gazer, no creative force in the world. On the contrary, Nietzsche exploits his concept of the "will to power" to redefine *what* we are (creators) and *who* we are (whatever we create ourselves to be). Like the Gay Scientist, he gives style to his character.[176]

Nietzsche assumes the distinction between the writer and the author to reascribe himself throughout his work. He deconstructs the claim that time, memory, or history unify one's self or one's identity. From his point of view, "who one actually is" is not "who one actually is all the time." As Richard Rorty argues, Nietzsche attaches a new meaning to the phrase "I am." One is "whom one turned oneself into in the course of creating the taste by which one ended up judging oneself."[177] Nothing is more life affirming for Nietzsche than self-ascription.

Hazel Barnes, 1915–

Hazel Barnes's autobiography—*The Story I Tell Myself* (1997)—distinguishes itself from the four previously discussed autobiographies in a number of ways. For instance, Barnes is a woman, a lesbian philosopher, the first in this group to comment directly and personally upon issues of gender and sexuality. Her scholarly reputation reflects her efforts to appropriate and disseminate the views of Jean-Paul Sartre rather than create a unique perspective or philosophy of her own. She has dedicated her life to the American academy, both by teaching philosophy and by serving on committees, becoming politically active, and shaping the model of education that the University of Colorado at Boulder endorses. To honor this significant portion of her life she entitles Chapter 7 of her autobiography, "Teaching for a Living." Finally, Barnes's work—the only one in this study written in English—is familiar and accessible, exemplifying the late twentieth-century and early twenty-first-century narrative style that we have come to appreciate and expect in America. The full title of her work, *The Story I Tell Myself: A Venture in Existential Autobiography*, is appropriately contemporary, philosophical, and personal.

In keeping with the four philosophical autobiographies already discussed, *The Story I Tell Myself* advances a philosophical view of the self. Borrowing from Sartre's conception of consciousness and ego, Barnes claims that the self is "enclosed within the horizon of consciousness."[178] This means that our "consciousness creates a personalized self [an ego] as it reflects upon the material world and others. Creating a self is the unavoidable task for a consciousness that must make itself be."[179] In this respect, her conception of consciousness bears some similarity to Nietzsche's will to power. Both negate and recreate the meaning of the world, and both retain the power to determine who and what one is. Neither memory, nor time, nor history unifies the self. Rather, as beings free from the apparently deterministic claims of history and memory, conscious self-reflection gives unity to the self—a self that changes in part and parcel to our ongoing reflection and creative recollection.

Barnes's description of autobiography denotes her view of the self: "Autobiography is an extension of what we do inwardly each day of our lives; that is, we construct an ego/self that is an object for others as well as for ourselves in our every encounter. An autobiography is a visual map of what has been our network of ends and means."[180] Whereas Nietzsche advocates a creative will animating all of human activity and therefore resists the tendency to ascribe this activity to an ego, Barnes affirms a structure of being beneath the activity of self-reflection and therefore embraces the idea of a constructed but changing ego.[181] Hence, for Nietzsche, the act of self-narration *creates* a self; it posits a textually inscribed ego. For Barnes, self-narration simply *maps* a self that is already circumscribed by consciousness. Her provocative claim that *The Story I Tell Myself* is "the arranged truth" elucidates this important difference.

God

Surprisingly, Barnes does not model her autobiography on the two autobiographies she admires most: Sartre's *Words* and Simone de Beauvoir's four-volume autobiography, *Memoirs*.[182] As writers who combine fiction and philosophy, Sartre and de Beauvoir are especially attentive to the relationship between the self and consciousness and the nuanced meanings that "author," "narrator," "protagonist," and "writer" express. Barnes, however, prefers to focus the inquiry into the self directly upon her life experiences, obliquely connecting her venture in existential autobiography to psychoanalysis. Her autobiography is no less radical than these two famous French philosophers'.

Barnes begins by describing her childhood experiences in the Free Methodist Tradition. Though she does not deny the existence of God until college, even as a child she questioned the apparent contradictions between the church's theology and her family's practices, especially her father's devotion to the church. An avid reader of William James, her father encouraged Hazel and her sister Jean to "memorize and recite each day sections from the venerated philosopher's work."[183] Ironically, she became an atheist after reading James's *On the Varieties of Religious Experiences*, which convinced her that "there are no claims to absolute truth."[184] Thereafter, she studied existentialist ideas and themes, not because of her atheism, but because of her interest in the relation between individual freedom and human values that she found articulated in existentialist philosophy.

In the midst of her self-exploration, Barnes discovers the work of Sartre, a fellow atheist who gave voice to her beliefs and conviction, especially her view of the self: "Like Sartre, Barnes never perceived a self that could be discovered by digging it up as if it were a buried treasure."[185] But Sartre's atheism differs from hers to a significant, ultimately influential, degree. Whereas Barnes's early atheism signifies a lack of absolute ideals or values (cf. Nietzsche) and therefore the impossibility of absolute truth, Sartre's admission that there is no God is an admission that there is no absolute authority.[186] This means that the individual is radically free not merely to create his or her own individual ethics but to create him*self* or her*self*. Indeed, Sartre confesses in *Being and Nothingness* that he aims to become God.[187] Like Sartre, Barnes realizes that writing is the creative means by which one assumes the position and power of God. Schuster observes:

> . . . Jean-Paul probably felt he had been destined for a supreme purpose, something like a divine calling. When by mistake he missed the call of God, Sartre appropriated the divine mission his family seems to approve of: the profession of writer. As an alternative revelation Sartre experienced a "fundamental illusion": writing made him powerful; "all things would humbly beg for a name; to name the things was both to create and take it."[188]

At times, Sartre "blames the absence of God and the meaninglessness of life for his writing neurosis."[189] But the godlike activity of self-creation appeals to

Barnes's "individualism and self-determinism" and fosters in her a political orientation toward the world.[190] She embraces feminist thinking, for example, which she regards as a logical extension of existentialist ideals, and she becomes involved in the push for women's rights in America. She rejects the patriarchic model of "dominance and submission" that informed the family life and social structure of her upbringing.[191] Sartre's influence upon her understanding of power and self-creation alters her view of writing dramatically. She maintains that writing fictionalizes our experiences and our representations of our selves:

> It is not only that, as has so often been pointed out, words distort even as they reveal, that what is lived can never be the same as what is told. Questions of sincerity, the reliability of memory, and concern for others' feelings turn out to be far more complex than I had imagined. The problem of selectivity, which in other contexts may be purely literary, becomes more urgent; to single out these factors as most important in shaping a self is to mold the self presented. The most I can claim, and this I do affirm, is that the fictional character portrayed here is, at least in my eyes, a true reflection of what I reflectively see.[192]

Writing captures and reflects back to us the relationship between what Sartre calls the *être-en-soi* (being-in-oneself) and the *être-pour-soi* (being-for-oneself). Being-for-oneself is consciousness; being-in-oneself is everything else, including the body and the ego, both of which are objects for the freely constructing activity of consciousness. The bifurcation of the self into these two modes of being generates the problem of freedom within human existence. I will explore the similarities and differences between Sartre's view and my own view of the bifurcation of the Inner self and the Outer self in Chapter 3.

One way that Barnes narrows the gap between the bifurcated self and first-person narration is by fictionalizing the 'I' that her conscious writing creates. She succeeds in bringing her personal story to life by interweaving her philosophical perspectives with descriptions of relevant, personal problems. Her erudition, tempered by honesty, is refreshing: she says to us, one can be both knowledgeable and human, one can love philosophy and people, one can understand X yet experience Y:

> I had always felt that I carried with me a self-structure that was a burden without being a recourse. It was liberating to me to think of consciousness as distanced from its own creation, capable of assuming a new point of view on it and altering it. Sartre's concept of the self made sense to me. It had never seemed to me that self-realization was a matter of discovering and fostering a true self that lay buried inside, like the oak in the acorn.[193]

Time

Sartre and Barnes share Nietzsche's intuition that we are beings situated in time, conditioned by time, but not determined by time. Humans may transcend their historical consciousnesses by either freely reconstructing their *being-in-oneself* or by overcoming their herd mentality via the creative channeling of the will to power. Through these acts we transcend time. We respond freely to our historical situations and choose our reactions to temporally imbued and conditioned events, including the ascription of meaning to historical situations and temporal events. Kearney writes, "We can choose either to abandon ourselves to the status of a mere object among objects. Or we can choose to transcend what is given by projecting ourselves authentically towards a new horizon of possibility. Either way, we are always choosing what we are and never able not to choose."[194]

The influence of Sartre's understanding of the human relation to time on Barnes's conception of the self is especially evident in her political orientation toward the world. For example, Barnes observes the skill with which her Aunt Ruth juggled conflicting gender roles, stating, "Her [Aunt Ruth's] example suggested that it was best to move between two worlds rather than to forsake one wholly for the other, or to attempt to remodel the old one."[195] Sartre offers a similar response to shifting worlds and identities in *Words*. Schuster explains: "He [Sartre] envisions himself as reborn time and again. He rises from ashes, not out of his past, but out of nothingness: he subordinates the past to the present, the present to the future.... He tries to totalize himself in the moment."[196] Both Barnes and Sartre present themselves as Outer selves.

The liberating experience of freely coordinating self-identity is especially relevant for women who must adapt themselves to sometimes conflicting roles: partner, employee, daughter, mother, and so on. Barnes argues that one can engender and regender oneself by remaking the gender roles recognized and tacitly endorsed by society. One can, for example, either resist the gender roles that one is asked to assume, or one can change oneself in order to step into a different gender category. Barnes notes that one could even undergo a sex change operation and thereby become either a woman or a man in the eyes of the outside world—the ultimate exemplification of Sartrean self-making.[197]

Barnes recognizes a similar movement between fictional worlds in writing, one described by Sartre in *A Plea for Intellectuals*. The writer does not simply recapitulate events in the world through a set of symbols. He or she goes beyond language, endowing writing with a conceptual truth that communicates its truth through the writer's use of ambiguous phrases and creative, stylistic choices. These ambiguous phrases and stylistic choices result in a new, nonsignifying mental event, an original mode of communication—Nietzschean aphorisms, for example—inscribed in words. The message of the new, nonsignifying mental event is communicated when the message attaches to ordinary language and transmits the truthful expression and ideas of the writer to the reader.[198] Thus the reader understands the newly created literary work when his or her consciousness transcends ordinary language but preserves the meaning of that understanding in common expressions. This does not mean that autobiography has no relation to the life one lives, but rather that the written account always conveys more and means more than the experiences themselves. From this perspective, we become an authentic 'I' when we express our ideas in new forms of communication, rejecting the language of the world as defunct, corrupted, and nauseating. Richard White aptly shows that for both Sartre and Barnes, this is true of the self as well: ". . . true selfhood is not an enduring unity but rather a movement away from any fixed determination of the self towards openness and empowerment."[199] This implies that the most authentic form of self-reflection is self-narration, for writing encourages original methods and modes of self-expression. It also implies that self-reflection unifies the self in good faith—in the face of freedom—whereas history and memory deceive the self by conditioning the self to embrace the faulty structures of continuity accepted in childhood. Barnes writes:

> In turning my lived history into a written autobiography, I have tried to connect the dots in such a way that the shape of the story that emerges is a faithful copy of the 'I' that my consciousness has formed. As Gerald Edelman has pointed out, memory is a re-creation, not a playback. We know that the borderline between remembering and imagining is sometimes blurred. But just as there are degrees of certainty . . . so what is intended as an objective eyewitness account is different from a fairy tale. At the very least, the picture of what my life is and has been is what I take to be the truth of myself; it is the reality I live with. . . . But even if my own judgment on my life is to be given no privilege, the way I look at and feel about it is part of the story.[200]

The authentic individual, like the *Ubermensch* or alter self, is the one who recognizes his or her power to will or create the self in opposition to received notions of essence and identity. The authentic individual is a *hyper-alterspective self*: a self that does not merely look outside of itself but also *negates* the alienating dimensions of consciousness and history and conflates the past, present, and future into a single, ego-instantiating moment. Hence, the authentic individual satisfies two conditions of freedom: he or she accepts the gratuitous nature of reality, and he or she avoids self-deception or bad faith.[201] Authentic existence means living apart from humankind while existing amid humankind, a life that I have described as artful. Moreover, living authentically means accepting the two Sartrean truths of our being-in-the-world: "First, the universe has no purpose or meaning beyond what humans put into it. Second, consciousness itself is nothing substantial—only the pure activity of assuming a point of view on something, that is, it is consciousness of objects and simultaneously self-consciousness."[202] In Sartre's words:

> Without the human race, mankind, there is no truth; that is certain. There would remain only an irrational and contingent swarming of individual choices to which no law could be assigned. If some sort of truth exists capable of unifying the individual choices, it is the human race which can furnish this truth for us. But if the race is the truth of the individual, it cannot be a given in the individual without profound contradiction. . . . The for-itself, in order to choose itself as a person effects the existence of an internal organization which the for-itself surpasses toward itself, and this internal technical organization is in it the national or the human.[201]

Memory

Recall that Augustine and Descartes regard the self as a thinking, enduring substance unified by memory but capable of reflecting atemporally (an Inner self). Rousseau contends that history provides continuity and unity to the self, a self that is ipso facto embedded in time. Yet for Rousseau, the self's *identity* is determined by the social forces in which the self is situated. Through *writing*, our identities can be altered, our narratives challenged, and our selves bracketed, allowing the author of texts to merge with the writer of texts (a medial Inner-Outer self). Nietzsche and Barnes regard the self as a creative will or ego that liberates human beings through the authenticating construction of meaning (Outer self). Because they regard humans as beings situated in time, conditioned by time, *but not determined by time*, only narration and reflection can unify the creative potentiality we call the self. From the perspective of the Outer self, memory should be used as a means for overcoming one's past, for resisting bad faith, but it should never become a resting place or unifying force in itself. Memory castrates the creative power of the self.

Barnes resists the reduction of the self to a single essence while simultaneously affirming the existence of an active, consciousness-created ego. "The ego," Barnes reminds us, "is never part of consciousness but separated from it as a book is separate from its author."[204] The encounter between consciousness and the alienating dimensions of people and things in the world—the bifurcation of the self into a being-in-oneself and a being-for-oneself—creates an existential conflict between freedom for ourselves and freedom for others, "each one trying to 'nihilate' the other in order to preserve its own sovereign autonomy."[205] For the reasons I stated earlier, the bifurcation is resolved through reflection in writing, not through the reflective acts of memory. Schuster points out that Sartre describes how reflected thought unifies the self in *Words*.[206] The tension generated by this bifurcation, like the bifurcation between the Inner self and the

Outer self, creates the possibility of authentic, artful living. Moreover, the bifurcation of the self is essential to contemporary accounts of identity formation, because it explains the emergence of many selves from the multiple projects in which individuals are engaged in the world. Barnes continues, "[W]hatever image best describes it, my ego has become by now my personality, my character, the accumulated patterns of conduct, preference, and attitudes that I carry with me as the ground for every new encounter."[207] In constructing the ego, the consciousness chooses freely the characteristics of the 'I' it instantiates (like Nietzsche's Gay Scientist). Hence, our literary projects do not objectify us into a distinct entity to be known; rather, the construction of who we are is our project.[208]

Knowledge

Although Barnes insists that we must accept or reject the ego, and in doing so fall into self-deception or persist in good faith, we are free to choose our own personalities and pathways from a host of available characteristics, traits, and modes of being that give meaning to our existence. Barnes appeals to Sartre's view of freedom in justifying her analysis of bad faith. According to Sartre, "I do not choose to be for the Other what I am, but I can try to be for myself what I am for the Other, by choosing myself such as I appear to the Other. . . . Although I have at my disposal an infinity of ways of assuming my being-for-others, *I am not able not to assume it*."[209] This means that a host of possible arrangements of imposed and created facets of our being is present to others, an image that Nietzsche captures in his concept the "Eternal Return." However, we are never able to stand in the sight of others completely unaware of who or what we are, empty of all characteristics and perspectives. Character traits, willfully chosen or constructed, attach themselves to us; they *are* who we are, whether we acknowledge them or not. Sartre writes:

> As soon as a freedom other than mine arises confronting me, I begin to exist in a new dimension of being. . . . It is I myself who sees a meaning conferred upon me, and I do not have the recourse of accepting the responsibility . . . since it cannot be given to me except in the form of an empty indication.[210]

This relationship runs in two directions, for while we are what we have not chosen to be, we are not what we have chosen to be. To put it more simply, the self-presentations we create for others, the aspects of our being we knowingly present to others, are not who we are finally or authentically, for they are neither enduring nor free. *We are ourselves in the mode of not being ourselves*. Although we cannot control all of the facets of our existence and the roles we play in our being-for-others, we can manage them by choosing which facets of our existence we allow others to see. Barnes reveals, "[T]here are times when I feel as if 'I' were appealing to resources beyond my everyday self. The appeal is not a prayer addressed to an external power. I do not feel compelled to conclude that I am pounding at the door of the Unconscious. Perhaps on these occasions my consciousness is most urgently at work to refashion its self."[211]

Preliminary Conclusions

Barnes argues that autobiography maps, but does not create, the contingency and freedom of the self; the authentic self is not an object of knowledge.[212] Her autobiography challenges self-representations in which the self is a fixed, enduring object unified by the mind through acts of memory or history. Instead, Barnes presents herself as an ever-changing ego constructed by an alterspecting consciousness. She privileges the Outer self throughout her autobiography, though she recognizes the inherent and ongoing existential conflict between the ego and consciousness, the Inner and Outer self, expressed by Sartre as *être-en-soi* (being-in-oneself) and the *être-pour-soi* (being-for-oneself).[213] "There is no such thing as a 'human nature,' determining how we act and behave. On the contrary, it is our everyday acts and choices that form our identity. Man first of all exists, Sartre argues, and defines himself afterwards."[214] Our being-for-oneself is eclipsed by our being-for-oneself; we understand ourselves only partially, not wholly. Barnes concurs with Sartre: being for-oneself is "being what it is not and not being what it is . . . Being is. Being is in-itself. Being is what it is."[215] I argue that the autobiographical exploration of the self provides occasions for authentic encounters with the self, encounters that lead to self-disclosure and ultimately to self-knowledge.

While autobiographical writing unifies the self so that others may examine who and what we are, writing neither determines nor fixes self-identity. Within philosophical autobiography, three distinct modes of self-reflection—all of which fall within the larger rubric of self-examination—shape self-identity: (1) *Introspection*: looking within the self/life; recollecting experiences, thoughts, and feelings that individuate experience; (2) *Retrospection*: looking back on the self/life; relating experiences on a continuum or in a successive, determining order; and (3) *Alterspection*: looking outside or beyond the self/life and positing or projecting the self as a willing (Nietzsche) or an alienated other (Sartre/Barnes). Though these modes of reflection are not mutually exclusive, few autobiographers adopt all three in their examinations. For example, Augustine, Descartes, and Rousseau appropriate a heavily introspective and retrospective model of self-reflection commonly associated with confession. Nietzsche and Barnes, however, use first-person narration as a mode of philosophical self-exposition, thereby assuming an alterspective mode of reflection. Barnes's conception of the self is more explicit than Augustine's, Descartes', and Rousseau's; she posits and defines the self, whereas they assume or circumscribe it. Her presentation is more transparent, however, than Nietzsche's. For example, she grounds her conception of the self in consciousness, the structure of being, whereas Nietzsche's will to power, the source of our creative acts in the world, bears no direct metaphysical or ontological frame.

Conclusions

Writers approach self-narration from diverging points of view. First-person accounts take shape within the literary space of established genres and cultural milieus. This fact is important, not only because philosophical autobiographies present conflicting views of the first-person, but also because their conflicting views outline a pattern of development within the tradition of philosophy. As such, autobiographical writing adheres closely to the conventions of writing in which it appears, including its use of diction, literary structures, and narrational devices.[216] Thus autobiographies reveal more than an author's view of himself or others or a self in general; autobiographies provide a glimpse into the period in which the author lived or lives, revealing sights unseen and sounds unheard by a reader who is removed from the author's experiences and perspectives.

Thus far I have examined the views of the self embedded within five philosophical autobiographies: Saint Augustine of Hippo's *Confessions*, René Descartes' *Meditations on First Philosophy*, Jean-Jacques Rousseau's *The Confessions*, Friedrich Nietzsche's *Ecce Homo*, and Hazel Barnes's *The Story I Tell Myself*. I have analyzed four specific concepts within each text: God, Time, Memory, and Knowledge. I argue that these concepts reflect the ontological views of the self that each thinker assumes, and they shape the rhetorical dimensions of each autobiographical text. By utilizing them as a framework for analysis, I have attempted to provide continuity to this chapter and to establish a common ground for fruitful comparison. The framework has enabled me to trace the genealogy of the self from ancient to contemporary texts.

Autobiographies enlarge our view of history and human experience. They provide a glimpse into other cultures, revealing insights and experiences to which temporally and spatially absent readers have no other access. They reveal emotions and thoughts that alter our understanding of ourselves. In choosing to understand others, we choose to be affected. We risk a deeply impoverished view of human experience if the perspectives we encounter represent the views of one race, one class, or one gender. Yet self-narration generates a number of unavoidable philosophical problems. I turn my attention to two of these problems in the following chapter, namely, self-deception and self-effacement or concealment. I also offer additional analyses of the philosophical autobiographies examined in this chapter.

Chapter 3

Masking the Self

> For a long time I had been afraid of ending as I had begun, anywhere, in any which way. . . . My vocation changed everything. . . . Chance had made me a man, generosity would make me a book. I could cast my missive, my mind, in letters of bronze; I could replace the rumblings of my life by irreplaceable inscriptions, my flesh by a style, the faint spirals of time by eternity, I could . . . in short, be other, other than myself, other than the others, other than everything.
>
> —Jean-Paul Sartre[1]

Deception and Concealment

Autobiography is a complex form of narration. Its dual function as a genre of writing and a method for self-knowing is mystifying and challenging. It assumes knowledge of one's public standing, an awareness of one's past, a reason or need to individuate oneself from others, and a capacity to understand the significance of one's identity and the nature of one's essence. Charged with pulling together these literary and epistemic elements the autobiographer must construct a narrative that expresses not merely who I am, but who I understand myself to be.[2]

As a mode of philosophical exposition, autobiography presupposes an intensely psychological, philosophical, and rhetorical comportment toward the self. It calls the mind to acknowledge the layers of self-awareness and self-conception that shape our complex relationships with others. The interplay of these multiple dimensions of identity contributes to the richness of autobiographical analysis.

The evocation of wide-ranging emotions contributes to its transformative power. Given the complexity surrounding autobiography, we cannot assume that it is merely a narrative recapitulation of life or a chronology of life history.

Understood properly, autobiographies are narrative portraits or representational maps of one's self and/or life. They reveal who we are *to and for ourselves*, not who we are in every sense of our being. As I have argued throughout this book, every autobiographer is both a writer-self and author-subject tilted in various degrees toward a particular expression of being. Some writers, such as Nietzsche and Barnes, tilt strongly toward the creative dimensions of their literary agency. They manipulate the first-person perspective to create an independent identity and/or to articulate a revolutionary, often negating conception of the self. These writers find ways to transcend their cultural milieus and generate new literary genres. Others follow Augustine and Descartes and focus upon the relation between the self and other entities (e.g., God or the body). They aim to represent the self-other relation in terms of a life history or a philosophical argument. They appropriate self-effacement as a rhetorical device to convey honest revelation. Between these two paradigms, we find writers who manipulate the first-person perspective for the sake of perspicuous self-representation. Rousseau finds a niche here. He limits the scope of self-representation to questions of identity, all the while invoking the language of nature and essence. By masking the self, he is able to formulate a self-representation that conveys the aura of objectivity.

The differences represented by these paradigms shape the orientation of the autobiographer toward his or her subject. Nonetheless, every autobiographer seeks to understand the relation between the nature of the self and his or her individuated identity. If the aim of philosophical autobiography is to produce a representational narrative of the self that is transformative in some way, then the temptation to distort the self becomes increasingly large and problematic. On the one hand, visions of grandeur plague many intellectuals; affective disorders, coupled with hubris, lead to aggrandized representations. Other sources of hyperbole, such as elevated self-status or self-image, reflect particular neuroses created by cultures that measure success by individual achievement on grander and grander scales. Writer bell hooks identifies this phenomenon with the "dominating" culture of America, a culture in which humans must sacrifice each other (and perhaps their integrity) to get ahead: ". . . in our nation individuals lie more and more about all manner of things large and small. This lying often leads to forms of denial wherein individuals are unable to distinguish between fantasy and fact, between wishful dreaming and reality."[3] On the other hand, a writer's weak or defeated ego leads to self-loathing and a diminished representation of his or her achievements. Self-effacement, however well intentioned, sometimes falls prey to the same fate. Some writers objectify themselves in order to give the illusion of honest representation. Others do so to refashion the self or to redefine who or what he or she is. The latter is consistent with the Sartrean claim that sometimes we aim to be other than ourselves, other than everything. We aim to consciously escape or alter our historicity.

The possibility of becoming someone other than oneself is especially problematic from the perspective of the Inner self. From this perspective, experiences we recall through the acts of introspection and retrospection provide for the continuity of a narrative or unity of the self. Misrepresentation of the self—representing oneself in opposition to recollected experience—amounts to either self-deception or intentional reader deception. Because recollected experience provides for narrative continuity and self unity, misrepresentation of the self further fragments the self and may result in a form of disassociation. It also generates increasingly complex rhetorical structures and narrative frameworks. Hence, the act of becoming someone "other than oneself" from the perspective of the Inner self means that one either subconsciously appropriates a false identity or one intentionally deceives others.

The idea of becoming someone other than oneself makes more sense from the perspective of the Outer self. In this account one *becomes* who one is (Nietzsche), or one realizes that one *is* oneself in the mode of not being oneself (Sartre). Either self-reflection (in the form of alterspection) or self-narration creates narrative continuity and self-unity, and the self is fashioned by a matrix of insights, ideas, and literary devices, all of which writers subvert and/or appropriate for the sake of self-transformation. Since the self is constructed either out of consciousness or out of philosophical and literary concepts, then the self will change over time. And since the self will change over time, the writer need not commit herself or himself to any particular self-representation. One becomes who one is by giving birth to the self on paper again and again and again—a discursive exemplification of the Eternal Return.

The ontological and epistemic distance between the Inner self and Outer self raises important questions about the nature of self-representation. First, in what sense is self-representation accurate? That is, to what degree does truth bear upon autobiography? To judge that X's autobiography portrays X either accurately or inaccurately, for example, one would have to treat X as a person with a fixed identity (fixed for at least some quantifiable amount of time, if not indefinitely). This narrated identity would have to be compared not to the person's memory of life, which is presumably the source of his or her identity, but to external sources that coordinate with X's self-narration: documents, personal possessions, and the testimony of acquaintances all aid in this endeavor. If it turns out that the self-representation in question bears little if any relation to the life it intended to represent, we cannot simply deem the narrative "dishonest." Rather, we would have to decide *why and for what purpose* the narrative is inaccurate or incomplete, and what, if any, philosophical value its inaccuracy or incompleteness has. Furthermore, we would need to determine whether the writer is deluded either consciously or subconsciously. Do his or her authorial intentions justify a retelling of facts? Is he or she speaking ironically, and if so, for what end?

My point is that representation is always and necessarily inexact. Just as we do not expect self-portraits to replicate the subject of the painting as a photograph might, we cannot expect autobiography to capture the details of an entire life. What we must ask, then, is not whether the propositional content of self-representation is true or false but whether the self-image presented is fruitful or not, that is, whether it generates self-knowledge and/or contributes to our understanding of the self and its relation to others. The author as a self-representing agent may nuance himself or herself and/or life as he or she deems necessary or desirable, especially if he or she aims to expose the nature of the self. The variation between *one as represented* and *one as encountered in the world* is essential to autobiographical writing; the dialectic of self-knowing originates in the openness between these representations. Does it follow that we can never determine whether a writer (or reader) is deceived? Is deception rendered meaningless by self-representation? Can we as readers maintain a useful interplay between the ontological and rhetorical dimensions of being? Does autobiography help or hinder our ability to recognize ourselves as liminal creatures?

I address these questions throughout the remainder of my analysis. In this chapter, I discuss various conceptions and forms of deception. Deception is a condition that shapes both the writing and reading of self-narration. Though I do not present a full-fledged account of self-deception herein—such an account requires a discrete analysis and is therefore impossible to address fully in this context—I nevertheless acknowledge the importance of self-deception with respect to self-representation. I argue that autobiography fosters the ongoing discussion of the relation between our being and our being-in-the-world, between essence and identity. Now I turn my attention to questions of knowledge and truth and their relation to deception.

Knowledge and Truth in Autobiography

I began this book by noting that autobiographical writing presupposes the capacity to self-reflect. I argued that self-reflection is a cognitive process comprised of three distinct but overlapping self-reflexive acts: *introspection*, *retrospection*, and *alterspection*.[4] Once a person is engaged in self-reflection, she or he not only realizes herself or himself as an existing creature of a certain nature but formulates an awareness of her or his identity in the world. Properly denoted, the realization of essence and the formulation of identity *is* self-knowledge, though these two forms of self-realization do not exhaust the category of self-knowledge entirely.

Epistemic queries drive autobiographical activity. Indeed, the desire to know oneself is fundamental to the search for truth. I argue that self-knowing is richest when initiated by autobiographical writing, because self-narration bifurcates the self into an ontological and a rhetorical self. This bifurcation generates a dialogical interplay between the writer and the author (i.e., between the discovered self and the narrated self). The 'I' becomes both the object and subject of inquiry. Though this interplay complicates the nature and identity of the self, it also makes possible self-knowing.

Epistemic queries surround debates about truth as well. Few scholars today regard themselves as unmitigated advocates of either correspondence or coherence theories of truth (many have embraced pragmatism or structuralism as alternatives). This distinction is nonetheless useful for purposes of autobiographical analysis and interpretation.

A simple account of correspondence and coherence theories, respectively, appears as follows: (1) Truth is the correspondence between a proposition and a set of facts; (2) Truth is the coherence between a set of accepted propositions and a set of facts. If we apply both views to an analysis of autobiography, then the self-narration of X is false unless (a) it corresponds to facts about X, or (b) it coheres with a set of widely admitted or known propositions about X. Both theories presuppose the logical possibility of articulating a true description of X that can therefore adjudicate between true and false self-narrations. The reader's task is to evaluate the autobiographical and biographical data available to determine whether the autobiography is indeed *true*—that is, which facts correspond to or cohere with the autobiography—and thus what, if anything, can be known about X. Hence, both theories of truth presuppose historical accuracy as a criterion for autobiography.

The long-standing assumption embedded in the concept of historical accuracy is that only written narratives verified by an uninvolved neutral party are historically accurate. This party may be one of three types: (1) an unrelated spectator who is observing the events in question, (2) an impartial, third person (e.g., a judge who participates in the proceedings in question but who forms no opinions beyond the scope of his or her duty), and (3) a scholar or an investigator (e.g., Sherlock Holmes, who is adept at analyzing and solving problems and who has a great deal of knowledge about the topic or person in question). Several problems arise within this view of accuracy.

First, both bell hooks and Parker Palmer offer poignant critiques of objectivity throughout their literary and scholarly work. In *Teaching Community*, hooks combines her insights with Palmer's to advance the following strident objection:

> Embedded in the notion of objectivity is the assumption that the more we stand at a distance from something the more we look at it with a neutral view. This is not always the case. . . . Parker Palmer

> writes: 'the ideal of objectivism is to eliminate of subjectivity all biases and preconceptions so that our knowledge can become empirical.' While objectivism can work well in hard sciences and fact-oriented subjects, it cannot serve as a useful basis for teaching and learning in humanities classrooms. In these classrooms much of what students seek to know requires engagement not just with the material but the individual creators whose work we study.[5]

I take her point to apply to autobiography as well. We cannot seek to evaluate the writer-self or his or her relation to the author-subject by appropriating an objective stance. Rather, we must implicate ourselves in the dialogical process of self-narration.

Second, first-person perspectives (including autobiographies) do not meet the criterion of historical accuracy. The function of the first-person is to give an account that is perspectival and personal, to tell a story from and about personal experience. One can of course extend the notion of historical accuracy to include first-person accounts, or one can deny that historical accuracy is a necessary condition of truth in autobiographical writing. In either case, writers and readers of autobiographies who commit themselves to the concept of historical accuracy maintain that there is *a* history to tell, and that the truth about X is determined by X's history and that self-knowledge is commensurate with third-person knowledge. Thus to know thyself is to know thy history. The problem with this thesis is that it forces one to fall back upon a vague understanding of history to justify life choices. The history of a person, on this account, is knowable, meaningful, and self-determining; one can understand one's present situation by looking to one's past. As Nietzsche, Sartre, and countless other scholars and psychoanalysts show, we risk faulty or weak self-conceptions—herd mentality, bad faith, and post-traumatic stress disorder—whenever we rely too heavily upon our past to tell us who we are.

Third, historical accuracy circumvents autobiography, a form of writing and exposition that appears at least partially self-destructive by design. Szabados, for example, argues that a "traditional autobiographical project appears to contain inherently its seeds of self-destruction. Its aim, disengaged self-knowledge, objective stock-taking, and cataloguing of truths about oneself is turned on its head: its goal ends up in self-deceit; its primary intention is frustrated."[6] From Szabados's perspective, the act of disengaging, objectifying, and analyzing oneself is one that destroys oneself. The objectified self is not the same self one identifies with and claims to know.[7]

Fourth, conceiving the relationship between autobiography and truth as historical accuracy ignores the rhetorical dimensions of the text. Consider again the idea of the Outer self: the author-subject who stands opposed to the writer-self. The author present within the autobiography, the figure signified by the 'I' of the text, is not necessarily the writer of the text. The authorial persona suffusing the text exists *because of and in the midst of* the signs that constitute the text: the marks on the page that form the letters, the letters that form words, the words that form sentences, the action described by the sentences, and so on.[8] Since the signifier of the 'I' is the author described within the text and not the writer constructing the text, then the author is a persona one comes to know by reading a text. One must step into a text, refusing to stand outside and ask, "Who are you?" Knowledge of the author, then, is dependent upon an intimate involvement of the reader with the text, because the author exists only within the text. Our understanding of an author, which arises in the process of reading, arises in the form of discursive interpretation and textual analysis rather than in the form of verified facts and propositions.

As a way of foreshadowing my discussion in Chapter 4 and closing the discussion of historical accuracy, let me say something more about interpretation. The understanding of a particular self-representation emerges as a reader explores the relation between the persona presented to him or her and the writer who creates and permeates that persona. Conceived in this way, understanding is the agreement we arrive at through discursive activity—reading, conversing, thinking, and so on. In the context of autobiography, "self-knowledge" signifies the integrity between the self and the subject *that arises through* the dialogical interchange between the writer-self and author-subject. Although autobiography does not exclude notions of accuracy per se, it does not rely upon historical accuracy.

The concept of 'truth' applies to the discursive activities of writing and reading in equally complex ways. The relation between facts and propositions, conceived within analytical philosophy as either correspondence to or the coherence of facts and propositions, bears upon our experiences in the world and the meaning we ascribe to those experiences. Until the status of facts is clear, their relation to truth remains inexplicable. The problem is that we cannot describe, calculate, and restate literary presentations in rigorous, propositional forms. Such truth arises, as Heidegger shows, from an act of concealment and exposure in which propositions alone, not their reference to facts apparent in the world, capture our *dealing with* states of affairs through language. What is not articulated in propositional form alters the state of affairs too, making it impossible for us to base knowledge entirely upon propositions.[9] Truth, then, is always a truth for us. Writers and readers forge a logical and an ontological connection between language and states of affairs. This relationship between states of affairs and language always extends outward from a particular perspective, transforming us even though the states of affairs exist independently of us. We see them, we describe them, and thus we know them in a particular way.

Advancing a Heideggeran notion of circumspective knowledge, Hans-Georg Gadamer describes understanding as a recognition of what we do not know: "[A] full set of experiences, meetings, instructions, and disappointments do not conjoin in the end to mean that one knows everything, but rather that one is aware and has learned a degree of modesty."[10] One can infer from his claim that meaning is the relation between a sign or proposition and what the sign or proposition signifies or expresses. Understanding this relation requires a hermeneutic encounter with these signs mediated by the reader (the human mind) through an act of interpretation. In order to understand the 'I' of a text, one must know the meaning of the signs or propositions within the first-person account. This means that the reader must interpret the signs and propositions that signify the writer-self and author-subject, first deciphering their meaning and establishing the relation between the signs and the persona signified, and second, determining the meaning of authorial utterances.

Though I affirm Gadamer's account of meaning, we would be hasty to dismiss the possibility of a real relation between the self and the subject in autobiography. Although Gadamer contends that meaning (the relation between signs and what is signified) originates in human agency, he does not exclude the possibility that meaning may enter into communities through cultural symbols and icons. Nor does he deny that the relation between the writer and his or her self-representation is only partially symbolic or signifying. To know thyself is to understand the meaning of the signs chosen to represent who one is as well as the nature of the thing choosing the signs. As Szabados contends, "[T]he projects of self-description and self-expression, the project of autobiography, are open-ended like the idea of a work of art."[11] Despite the promise of Gadamer's theory, we still face the difficult problem of adjudicating between self-deceptive or exaggerated descriptions and genuine representations of an author's view of herself or himself.

To begin clearing a hermeneutic ground for such adjudications, I articulate two common conceptions of deception that attach to self-reflexivity: *intentional* and *nonintentional deception*. I then argue that self-deception is phenomenally different from deception thus conceived. I propose an alternative that sheds new light on philosophical autobiography and discuss additional nuances of self-deception and their bearing upon self-representations.

Intentional Deception

The term *intentional deception* carries two distinct meanings: (1) the conscious deception of others (or oneself) by expressing as true a concept or an idea that is known to be false, and (2) the concealment of a concept or an idea that one knows to be true. Fear motivates both types of deception, specifically fear of political persecution, physical harm, or low opinions of others. Yet fear may disguise a deeper intention toward an audience, that is, a writer's aim to change a reader's preconceptions or state of self-awareness in elliptical or esoteric ways. In either case, intentional deception describes a posited mental state of an author-subject.

Descartes exploits intentional deception to disguise his implicit claim that certainty arises from the doubting mind, a belief that is contrary to church doctrine. He begins this appropriation in Meditation One by reporting his intention to doubt those beliefs that he cannot know with certainty. To reject the beliefs he once regarded as true, he intends to deceive himself:

> I think it will be a good plan to turn my will in completely the opposite direction and deceive myself by pretending for a time that these former opinions are utterly false and imaginary. . . . In the meantime, I know that no danger or error will result from my plan, and I cannot possibly go too far in my distrustful attitude. This is because the task in hand does not involve action, but merely the acquisition of knowledge.[12]

As I suggested earlier, Descartes presumes that until we disengage and objectively analyze the self as a thing in itself we remain uncertain of the nature of the self. It follows, then, that we must reject whatever we can doubt until we arrive at *something* (some idea) that can be known with certainty, that is, clearly and distinctly. Descartes ascertains that ideas arrived at through sensory experience are not clear and distinct; they are therefore dubitable. Hallucinations, dreams, or an evil deceiver could produce such effects. However, not even an evil deceiver could falsify the certain knowledge of my existence (If I am deceived, I exist). Does deception mask the *cogito* that displaces the religious foundation of revealed truth? Annette Baier offers us a set of helpful possibilities:

> . . . why the elaborate self-deceptions? What self-conceptions do they serve and protect? The self-conception of one who can be both a pious if unorthodox believer in the church's doctrine and also a scientist? The self-conception of a very clever person who was pretty sure he could outwit any merely human adversaries, so he thought he could afford to "go masked" without fear of inviting uncomfortable unmaskings? Or just someone very interested in deception and self-deception and trying to explore these human capacities in the cleverest and subtlest way he knew how?[13]

Baier concludes that Descartes introduces deception into *Meditations* for didactic reasons: to challenge us to consider the rationality of self-deception, the effect of self-deception, and the criteria for judging self-deception.[14] I share her view, though I also believe that Descartes' use of deception is a ploy for concealing subversive truths, a ploy that allows him to be everywhere and nowhere at the same time, to resist an identity for which he is politically and socially responsible. Self-deception not only allows Descartes to be someone and something other than himself, it invites everyone to be someone and something other than themselves: to be cogitating beings with the same access to truth as the church.

Rousseau, however, employs a form of nonintentional self-deception—"I am forgetful!" he claims—but his rhetorical strategy tells a different tale. Using *The Confessions* like a religious confessional, he conveys to his readers humiliating events and disturbing human encounters. He not only confesses deviant sexual behaviors (flashing young women, for example), but he confesses them as cavalierly as one might confess a disdain for peas. His self-effacing presentation makes no attempt to disguise unseemly actions. Why not? He implies that he was either coerced into committing certain acts, or he was confused about his own desires. He presents himself as a true sufferer of *akrasia*: a weakness of the will in which contradictory desires vie for control. He wants us to believe that he remains an anathema to himself.

But is Rousseau really so self-deceived? He distances himself from his own actions and the consequences thereof by exploiting literary conventions. As I argued in Chapter 2, the focus he places upon himself, the exaggeration of his success, and his frequent use of amnesia as a rhetorical device all point to an elaborate subterfuge that manipulates the reader into regarding Rousseau as a victim of history and social circumstance. Moreover, it seems likely that Rousseau made no distinction between presenting himself as a victim and being a victim: he is what his readers make him, and he writes *The Confessions* solely for them. Though Hartle is right to argue that Rousseau hopes to construct a truthful narrative of his life, he reduces himself to the meek identity of an abused genius or a victimized dissident intellectual. The clarity with which he sees himself seems to pain him. Unlike Descartes, Rousseau recognizes that he cannot be someone else. Nonetheless, he wants us to see someone else. Rousseau strives to deceive us by conflating the writer Rousseau with the author Rousseau.

Both Descartes and Rousseau attribute deception to the author-subject, not the writer-self. If one reads *Meditations* esoterically (or rhetorically), then one must conclude that Descartes (the writer-self) is anything but deceived about the nature of the self or his potentially perilous identity. Indeed, he must see the danger he faces clearly—he must believe that methodological doubt will yield truths as certain as revealed truth and thereby undermine the authority of the church. Hence, to recognize his precarious and potentially dangerous relationship with the church, he, the writer-self, must not be deceived.

Rousseau masks himself for similar reasons. Acutely aware of his reputation, he strives to adjust others' impressions of him by consciously working against his public persona. Only by grasping the external impressions of himself is it possible to formulate alternative impressions. In other words, he must acknowledge who he is for others and for himself in order to reconstruct his identity. As we will see in the following example, Augustine applies deception to the writer-self, which makes it possible for him to proffer a transformed and self-knowing author-subject.

Nonintentional Deception

The second form of deception and the form that I find most interesting is *nonintentional deception*. It connotes the unconscious deception of others (and oneself) by unwittingly holding as true a concept or an idea that is false *but is not known to be false*. Nonintentional deception arises out of ignorance or false belief and therefore characterizes the mental state of the writer-self.

Augustine is a prime example. He speaks of his youth as a time of grand ignorance. Until he reads Cicero, he mistakes sophistry for philosophy. Until he discredits Faustus, he regards "evil" as a dark material substance rather than a privation of the good. Until he meets Ambrose, he reads scripture literally and naively. And so the story goes. Schuster adds that "it was Augustine's opinion that until he accepted God's grace in its full measure he was subject to deception and compulsive behavior and to constrained slavish intellectual activity."[15]

Augustine's deception about the nature of reality, the nature of the self, and the nature of God runs through the first nine books of *The Confessions*. He speaks as a man controlled by animalistic impulses and deceived by false opinions. Here he is not the man of faith and intelligence who history exalts. He lacks knowledge and faith. Until middle age, he remains unaware of his own nature and its relation to God: "I was wholly ignorant of what it is in ourselves which gives us being, and how scripture is correct in saying that we are made 'in God's image.'"[16] Augustine characterizes his preconverted self as blind, unknowing, and mistaken. What, then, does this tell about Augustine's conception of deception?

Deception is a state of ignorance regarding unchanging truth; it occurs when one is mistaken about the nature of real relations in the world. "Augustine thus recognized that all people possess a measure of truth and intelligence through which they can distinguish falsehood from truth and earthly wisdom from divine."[17] In keeping with the Christian claim that truth is revealed rather than discovered or created, Augustine credits God with allowing him to see the truth about himself: "I had my back to the light and my face toward the things which are illuminated. So my face, by which I was enabled to see the things lit up, was not itself illuminated."[18] He proclaims in book 6, "I was being turned around."[19] He argues that God creates us and allows us to exist freely in the world, but God also rewards or punishes us according to whether we obey or disobey his laws. "I saw that when I acted against my wishes, I was passive rather than active; and this condition I judged to be not guilt but punishment."[20] God created people in God's likeness to be honest, loving, forgiving, and so on. Augustine reasons that if we resist this way of being, we resist our own nature and thus remain restless and fragmented. Hence, anyone who is ignorant of his or her own essence and its grounding in God's unchanging nature is blind: "My heart had become gross . . . and I had no clear vision even of my own self."[21] Schuster argues aptly that "through following this personal inner light Augustine was led from confusion, deception, and emotional bondage to the true knowledge and superb harmony of God's wisdom."[22] Unlike Descartes and Rousseau, Augustine implies that we choose to be what we are only out of our ignorance of truth. Deception originates in our deepest sense of being, that is, in our ontological comportment to the world. Though authors may express deception rhetorically, it does not follow that the author-subject is deceived. Indeed, this idea is nonsensical, unless one means by "author-subject deception" a condition ascribed to an author by a writer. In the latter sense, the author-subject conveys and uses deception to assist a reader in overcoming his or her deception, which explains the didactic dimensions of intentional deception.

Preliminary Conclusions

With respect to the role of deception within autobiography, intentional deception applies properly to the author-subject, and nonintentional deception applies to the writer-self. One of the paradoxes of self-deception is that it is impossible for a writer-self to be intentionally self-deceived, for if he or she were deceived, it would be impossible for him or her to know it. Descartes nods toward this paradox by arguing that doubt and deception justify existence.

Though it is useful to demarcate deception in order to analyze autobiographical texts, it is important not to dichotomize deception on either epistemic or ontological grounds. Writers often circumvent truth without malicious intent and ignorance. We need, then, a notion of deception that applies nonparadoxically to the self, one that acknowledges the differences between *self-deception* and *deception* and explains the logical relationship between truth and representation in autobiography.

As we have seen already, the relation between deception and self-deception is complicated by the bifurcation of the self into an author and a writer. For example, deception is commonly understood as an act of falsifying information, concealing facts, and obviating truth. One condition of deception conceived in this way is the existence and use of a network of facts to adjudicate between truth and falsity. Self-representations, however, arise primarily from the storehouse of memory and experience and not from externally sustained information systems to which one can later appeal for verification. One can produce documents to support one's self-conception—documents that support the notion of self qua historical figure—and one can choose to reinforce or subvert those conceptions. But the self qua writer or author is not merely a set of facts or a state of affairs in the world or in a text. The ongoing interchange between identity realization and formation, which invokes the mutual acts of self-realization and formation, gives rise to the self over time. When this process is applied to self-examination vis-à-vis self-narration, the interplay between a subjective and an objective analysis of the self gives rise to the author-subject. Self and self-identity in life and in texts are partly created and partly discovered. Self-deception cannot be considered an act of self-denial, for one is not always and at all times *X*. Given the paradox of deception I described earlier—if we are deceived we cannot know it, therefore, deception cannot apply to the self—how should we define or understand self-deception? My phenomenological account of deception follows.

Self-Deception

Self-deception is a condition that arises from prejudicing or paying selective attention to (or the failure to attend to) certain aspects of oneself in lieu of others. Robert Solomon defines it as an act of simultaneous concealment and revelation.[23] It is an attempt to conceal the self rather than deny the self.[24] Conceived in this sense, self-deception is a form of self-effacement that resides between intentional and nonintentional deception, both of which privilege our relation to ourselves over our relation to others.

Solomon's thesis is that deception understood as either intentional or nonintentional amounts to "self-contained" deception (an internal denial of oneself). Self-contained deception undermines our Inner/Outer way of being in the world, our introspective relationship with ourselves and our social relationships with others. Moreover, self-contained conceptions of deception contribute to the false formulation of self-deception as "knowing and not knowing." Self-deception, which is manifest rhetorically as exaggeration, falsification, and concealment, is not a condition that can be ascribed only to oneself. Rather, self-deception is the obscuring of one's identity for oneself and for others. So while deception and self-deception are distinct, they become enmeshed in the broader phenomenal experience of self-knowing and other-knowing, self-inscribing and self-negating. When we fool ourselves, Solomon explains, "we must either fool or exclude others; and to successfully fool others, we best fool ourselves."[25] His argument continues in the following extended passage:

> Transparency to ourselves can be just as intolerable as transparency to others and for just the same reason. The self, with its flaws and failings, is all too evident. The recognition of one's own motives and the significance of one's own thoughts can be devastating to one's self-image and sense of self. Part of the self is self-presentation and self-disclosure, but an aspect of equal importance is the need to disguise or to hide those facets of the self that are less than flattering, humiliating, or simply irrelevant to the social context or interpersonal project at hand. To a certain extent, this is merely a matter of attention, of editing, of selective self-presentation, but it is not just (or even for the most part) in our own hands. The self is essentially a social construct, and our sense of ourselves depends on other people. . . . One can hide or refuse to disclose oneself to oneself in many ways, notably by ignoring or distracting oneself, but none of these ploys has a ghost of a chance if others cannot be distracted or fooled—or at least put off—as well. . . . And to make it more complicated (as it should be), we do not always know which is which, who is self and who is other.[26]

Solomon's conception shares much affinity for existential notions of deception (inauthenticity or bad faith: forgetting our freedom and responsibility for self-affirmation). For example, Nietzsche argues that self-deception begins historically with Plato when the reflective, Apollinian thinker sees a distinct and an individuated self, not a Dionysian universal ego. Nietzsche aims to transform a misguided history of philosophy by returning to Dionysian irrationality and replacing Plato's search for Forms with the authenticating and self-affirming "will to power."

Yet even if Nietzsche successfully quashes Platonic thinking, the threat of self-deception looms large. Parkes writes, "Nietzsche clearly wants to retain from *The Untimely Meditations* the view that most people are simply self-deceiving in their refusal to face up to the grim facts of life."[27] From a phenomenological perspective, self-deception can emerge whenever we unify character traits, customs, and attitudes to become who we are, to create ourselves. In creating our selves, we may lose sight of the life-affirming possibility of choosing opposing character types or of reconceiving who we are carte blanche. In Nehamas's words, "One may 'give style' to one's character and constrain it by a 'single taste' simply by denying the existence, force, or significance of antithetical styles and tastes and by considering only part of oneself as the whole."[28] We always deceive ourselves by denying the multiplicity of human existence.

We also risk self-deception by suppressing our will to power and passively acknowledging the past without willing all that has happened in the past (i.e., by refusing to affirm the Eternal Return). We might, as Nehamas points out, agree to repeat our life exactly as it has happened and thus to accept the challenge of the Eternal Return, but it remains to be seen whether we will fall blind to all of (or most of) our life, or whether we will intuit life in its complete fullness and richness. "This is a grave difficulty," Nehamas writes, "because Nietzsche allows great freedom in determining what does and what does not in fact constitute part of a life. I might then be exhilarated at the prospect of repeating my life, at being who I am, just because I am attending to a very small part of it and refusing to see myself in my entirety."[29] To *will* a life presupposes that one has faced one's life in its entirety, and this act of self-examination, this process of affirming oneself, may never end.[30] Even Nietzschean creative self-affirmation conceived as living the alterspective life of the *Ubermensch* does not preclude self-deception.

Barnes appropriates a Sartrean conception of self-deception, or *bad faith*. As I argued in Chapter 2, bad faith is the "pretence that one's actions, values, or preferences are determined by something in one's past—heredity, environment, social expectations, objective values, etc."[31] The truth of existence for Sartre is a truth *of* existence, *for* existence, a truth designed to answer the question "Who am I?" and by what conditions do I exist? The search for some objective and universalizable self-representation hinders the process of existential growth, because it tempts us to fall into bad faith and mistake descriptions of ourselves *for* ourselves, thus mistaking how we appear as *who we are*.[32] Bad faith confuses existence with essence, accident with necessity. Authentic creatures, however, realize that they exist not by necessity but by choice. Sartre writes:

> Without the human race, mankind, there is no truth; that is certain. There would remain only an irrational and contingent swarming of individual choices to which no law could be assigned. If some sort of truth exists capable of unifying the individual choices, it is the human race which can furnish this truth for us. But if the race is the truth of the individual, it cannot be a given in the individual without profound contradiction. . . . The for-itself, in order to choose itself as a person, effects the existence of an internal organization which the for-itself surpasses toward itself, and this internal technical organization is in it the national or the human.[33]

To live authentically or in "good faith" is to recognize that we are responsible for the actions, values, and preferences we choose. We begin by acknowledging the limits of our existence as free beings: "I do not choose to be for the Other what I am, but I can try to be for myself what I am for the Other, by choosing myself such as I appear to the Other. . . . Although I have at my disposal an infinity of ways of assuming my being-for-others, *I am not able not to assume it*."[34] An infinite richness of this sort might enrich the Inner/Outer distinction and the search for wholeness. Indeed, it may enable us to discover the essence of the self and use this discovery to create self-identity. Sartre suggests that although we must accept or reject the nature of existence and either fall into self-deception or rise to a state of authentic existence, choosing the way we are for others empowers us to avoid bad faith. He confirms, as Nietzsche does before him, that we are free to choose our own personality and pathways from a host of available characteristics, traits, and modes of being that gives meaning to existence. The aggregation of imposed and created facts about *me*, about my existence, is used in various situations to present myself to others. Nonetheless, these aspects cohere or belong to the self; they *are* who one is, whether we acknowledge them or not:

> As soon as a freedom other than mine arises confronting me, I begin to exist in a new dimension of being. . . . It is I myself who sees a meaning conferred upon me, and I do not have the recourse of accepting the responsibility . . . since it cannot be given to me except in the form of an empty indication.[35]

The relationship between freedom and responsibility runs in two directions. One is what one has *not* chosen to be, and one is not what one has chosen to be. Put more simply, our self-presentations are creations for others; they do not represent who we are. *We are ourselves in the mode of not being ourselves.* Thus we cannot control interpretations of our self-representations. As Kaufmann observes, ". . . readers of Sartre should know, if they have not learned it firsthand from Nietzsche himself, that an act is one event, and the way we interpret it afterward and relate ourselves to it another."[36] Living a self-reflective, artful life means not confusing existence with essence or being with identity. Nonetheless, we must self-consciously manage our existence by choosing which facets of ourselves others see, otherwise we slip into bad faith. Sartre expresses the ease with which we slip into bad faith when he writes about his childhood:

> A bewildered vermin, a waif and stray, without reason or purpose, I escaped into the family play-acting, twisting and turning, running, flying from imposture to imposture. I fled from my unjustifiable body and its dreary confidences.[37]

It follows from Sartre's view that we avoid bad faith by remaining consciously aware of the interplay between the Inner self and the Outer self, between consciousness and the ego. Yet despite our best efforts, we consistently confuse our representations for others for representations *for and of* ourselves. Nietzsche implies that we must assert our will to power consistently and intentionally to avoid self-deception, an implication that Nehamas takes to its logical end by showing that even the willful embracing of an ever-recurring present cannot stave off the seductive influence of the herd.

As I suggested earlier, we cannot avoid self-deception entirely because we are free to create and recreate meaning in the world, a world filled with imposing signs and ideas and values. Self-deception is paradoxically a natural and, to some extent, a necessary outcome of freedom. Because the self is perpetually engaged in the dual process of realization and formation, self-deception is both unintentional and intentional, unconscious and conscious. We are always looking out and looking in, looking back and looking forward, concealing and disclosing both our nature and our identity. We live in the present, but our identity is cast in the past and projected onto the future. How responsible are we, then, for the state of self-deception in which we find ourselves? If self-deception is not wholly unavoidable, to what degree is it harmful to ourselves and others?

Self-Concealment

In "The Vital but Dangerous Art of Ignoring," Annette Baier offers a critical but constructive account of the process that instantiates self-deception. She begins by asserting that self-deception is "the occupational danger of those capable of selective attention."[38] More specifically, it is the act of ignoring the facts about one's consciousness. Sometimes this means we overlook *X* and highlight *Y*; other times we ignore *X* or *Y*.[39] On this view, there is nothing paradoxical about self-deception, because it is not an instance in which deception is applied to oneself. Rather, self-deception is the normal human phenomenon of prejudiced remembrance and reminiscence. Hence, we are always to some degree self-deceived.

Because we necessarily see things from a perspective—disengaged and objectified as in Descartes, or self-relationally circumscribed as in Nietzsche—our perspective shapes not only how we see but what we see forming a historically affected consciousness that cannot but be selective. We choose to highlight certain aspects of our consciousness and disguise others naturally; self-deception is the "*motivated* failure to attend to or recall all of what one knows or once knew."[40] Baier continues:

> Nations attend to some calls on their attention more than to others, write selective histories, and rewrite them as establishments and ideologies change. Also, social mechanisms of many kinds assist individuals in their individual self-deceptive activities, especially when these are coordinated with the maintenance of the preferred collective memory, that needed for a group's current self-esteem. . . . The skills needed to highlight overlooked facts are not so different from those needed to maintain the highlighting of selected facts, so that attention can be diverted from others. Both skills are needed for any interpretation of

> complex data and for revision of past interpretations, for new looks and for reinterpretations.[41]

Both Solomon and Baier imply that our self-conceptions correspond to a large degree to others' conceptions of us. This view is consistent with several recent psychological and sociological views of identity formation. Through the partly subconscious act of self-concealment, we aim to alter opinions (self or public) that deem us undesirable, because we readily internalize these views. Indeed, psychoanalysis reveals that the most painful conceptions of who we really are remain foremost in our consciousness. We aim to reduce suffering by remaking ourselves in one of two ways: either by suppressing conscious views of ourselves so that alternative memories and self-conceptions rise to consciousness, or by altering our memory so that our life narrative changes. A parallel fashioning appears within autobiographical writing. Like the writer-self, our consciousness invests itself in the ongoing process of selecting memories, images, ideas, and representations of the self. The author-subject, like the identity-bearing self, is the product of that selection process, a self represented on paper, in the world.

Beneath the logical accounts of self-contained deception, intentional and nonintentional, lies the phenomenological structure of our relation to others. Expressed as self-concealment, phenomenological accounts of self-deception regard deception as concealment, that is, as the perpetual concealment and revelation of who and what we are both for ourselves and for others. Whereas the logical formulations of self-deception (intentional or nonintentional) falsely dichotomize our phenomenological experiences, self-deception conceived as self-concealment unifies our experiences by implicating the ontological and rhetorical dimensions of experience in the act of concealment and revelation. Similarly, the search for the self invokes a dual process of discovering and creating the self, a process instantiated in autobiography.

Emotion and Deception

In the remaining sections, I examine the interplay between emotion and self-deception and analyze one particularly interesting form of self-concealment common to self-narrations: self-masking. The capacity of emotions to color truth is an important component of self-deception. To understand the epistemic facets of emotional states and their latent ability to transform our thinking and acting in the world, we need to reexamine the cognitive dimension of representational states.

Emotions are representational states that ascribe particular characteristics to formal objects: we "identify emotions by what we feel."[42] Self-deception arises not only from skewed metaphorical "seeing," as Solomon, Baier, and I argue, but also from misperception. Descartes demonstrates that even philosophers are unable to outwit their faulty perceptions. Gadamer recounts a report by Edmund Husserl about his own deceptive perception: "He went to visit the Berlin Panopticum (a house of wax dolls) on Friedrich Street. To his embarrassment, a young lady at the entrance winked at him. Then it dawned on him—'This is a doll!'"[43] Emotions that capture our mistake about certain facts, emotions such as amazement, confusion, and embarrassment, reinforce our sense that truth is more gray than black. We seem to give as much to reality in our interaction with the world as we take from it. Yet we know that we do not construct the world wholesale.

The situation in which we find ourselves as we attempt to see reality *in itself* becomes further complicated by the third-person narratological notions bound up with our notions of objective truth and impersonal knowledge. I mentioned these notions earlier in the context of historical accuracy: the uninvolved observer, the noncommittal arbitrator, and the adept scholar or investigator. Reality does not give itself over to us objectively; consciousness of reality varies from person to person. This raises a number of problematic questions for a view of deception and self-deception. If we highlight certain aspects of reality and ignore others, thereby shaping the reality that we in turn *see*, is self-deception a meaningful act or process? What do our emotions track or signal when our view of reality and of ourselves is challenged?

Emotion and Self-Deception

In "Emotion and Self-Deception," Ronald B. De Sousa argues that we can identify instances of self-deception without appealing to a universal reality and truth. He writes:

> . . . as human beings and manipulators of symbols we are inevitably and very properly the *creators of our own values*. And so it is quite right that for any given desire we should be allowed essentially to define the conditions of its satisfaction. On the other side, we must allow some reality to the possibility of self-deception. And merely to decree that a desire *ostensibly* having a certain object (to go swimming today, for example) can be magically satisfied by something quite different (to *have gone* swimming a week ago) is surely a case of self-deception.[44]

It would be absurd to deny that emotions play a significant role in how we understand reality. They affect how we intuit ourselves, how we perceive other human beings, and how we interpret facts in the world. They also contribute to *akrasia*, a weakness of the will in which contradictory desires compete for control. As De Sousa observes, vanity, envy, ambition, and grief incite us to partake in fantasy, obscuring our vision of who we are.[45] We may intentionally falsify, conceal, or destroy information that we are responsible for providing to others. We may lie. We may in turn feel guilty, though we are not deceived about what we are doing. On the other hand, we may assert what we believe to be true, which turns out to be false. Feelings of guilt in this case would be misplaced. How, then, should we understand the proper relation between fantasy and self-deception, between wish fulfillment and concealment?

Theories of emotion purport to distinguish between deception and mistakes on axiological grounds.[46] For instance, we validate certain emotions and regard them as signs of specific psychological states. Because we regard emotional response as truth signifying, therapists rely upon emotional responses to evaluate psychological states and to determine degrees of rationality. The correlation between rationality and emotion becomes complicated when we attempt to evaluate epistemic claims, especially self-referential epistemic claims. The wide range of appropriate emotional responses to epistemic claims hinders our ability to determine whether one understands the nature of the knowledge claim that he or she utters. Though some emotions are more common and reliable than others, none occur in every instance in which the same epistemic claim is made. Moreover, it appears that our interpretation of appropriateness (and therefore rationality) varies according to our epistemological and metaphysical presuppositions. De Sousa explains this variation by positing sets of paradigms or "dialects" that inform our interpretation of emotions:

> . . . the content of emotions for which two people have the same name will depend on their individual temperaments and the specific details of their learning experiences. When we interpret one another's emotions, therefore, we have a Whorfian problem of translation: our "dialects" determine different experiences. . . . Much the same is true of commonsense judgments of authenticity and appropriateness. We are often content to infer what emotions people *must* be having from our knowledge of the situations in which they find themselves. . . . Allowances are made for variabilities of individual temperament, reactivity, style, upbringing, and so forth; but ultimately the barrier between the neurotic, intrinsically erroneous emotions and the normal one is drawn along *conventional* lines. And this is—up to a point—as it should be: for intuitively the difference between mere transference and authentic emotion is in whether the ostensible object is actually, in its present relation to the subject, fitting for the emotion that it occasions.[47]

Because the content of our emotions is shaped by outside events, we are unable to look solely into ourselves and discover rational psychic states or a fixed psychic awareness of ourselves. Emotions, therefore, manifest like self-deception:

they are not self-contained. They always and necessarily relate to other persons and events. To alter them, we must internalize an external conception of what an emotion is and how it functions with respect to our social and ideological commitments (gender, social position, professional responsibilities, etc.). In other words, we must learn to sublimate emotions and engage the world in "appropriate" and therefore rational ways. These external considerations dramatically shape what we call the self and how we conceive of and alter our own identity.[48]

Reinterpreting or attacking the ideological commitments that buttress our emotive responses requires "consciousness raising." We must bring to light facts about ourselves that can be rejected or accepted as part of one's identity.[49] Self-deception conceived as self-denial ignores the responsibility that one has to realize and create a self-identity from within a sociohistorical framework. However, when reconceived as self-concealment and buttressed by emotions that correlate to rationality, self-deception is a cognitive response to reality that is beyond our making.

The author-subject of autobiography represents our phenomenological urge to be other than ourselves, an urge that we satisfy in the reflective act of alterspection. Of course, this desire to be other than we are presupposes an external reality in which we are free to be other than we are. Some flee from this freedom, as Nietzsche and Barnes argue, and deceive themselves about the nature of existence. Others flee not from the freedom of existence but from the self that appears in consciousness. They therefore conceal the self, in whole or part, through memory or self-narration. Emotions, however, track our response to events in the world as well as our being in the world. As such, they help us determine which facets of ourselves we like and therefore highlight and which we do not like and therefore suppress or remake.

The ongoing process of self-concealment demands that we both realize and create the self. We recreate ourselves by concealing and fulfilling who and what we are to others. In concealing the self that we realize through introspection and retrospection, we disclose new possibilities for our being in the world. Likewise, in ascribing specific characteristics or styles or types to the self that we create through alterspection—by giving "style to one's character"—we fulfill a deep psychic wish to live an artful life.

Self-Masking

One important form of self-concealment is self-masking. Plato's dialogues take on new meaning in light of his confounding admission that he never wrote down his philosophical views.[50] Nietzsche's appropriation of Dionysus, the god of wine and theater, implies that masks can uncover ancient truths. Kierkegaard's use of pseudonyms typifies the power of irony to shape meaning.

Eudora Welty's fictionalized autobiography represents her disdain for the cult of celebrity. In fact, Heilbrun insists that "there can be no question that to have written a truthful autobiography would have defied every one of her [Welty's] instincts for loyalty and privacy."[51] Welty, like Plato, Nietzsche, and Kierkegaard, camouflages herself.

True to its ancient roots, masking is a device for self-disclosure rather than self-denial. "The use of a mask," Parkes dramatically proclaims, "is not necessarily to deceive, even though it conceals the face; and indeed the beauty of masks as disguises lies in their duplex function of presenting and withholding, revealing and concealing, at the same time."[52] Because autobiography simultaneously reveals the author-subject and conceals the writer-self, it elucidates the dual function of self-masking and demonstrates the value of self-masking for philosophical growth.

Plato provides an important illustration in "The Seventh Letter." Composed near the end of his life, the letter aims to distinguish Plato the writer from Plato the philosopher, teacher, and composer of famous dialogues.[53] It reads:

> But this much at any rate I can affirm about any present or future writers who pretend to have knowledge of the matters with which I concern myself, whether they claim to have been taught by me or by a third party or to have discovered the truth for themselves; in my judgment it is not possible that they should have any understanding of the subject. No treatise by me concerning it exists or ever will exist. It is not something that can be put into words like other branches of learning; only after long partnership in a common life devoted to this very thing does truth flash upon the soul, like a flame kindled by a leaping spark, and once it is born there it nourishes itself thereafter.[54]

The letter is perplexing primarily because of its ambiguity. Should we interpret the claim "no treatise by me concerning it [philosophy] exists or ever will exist" to mean that the claims in his dialogues should not be attributed to him? Or that philosophy cannot be stated in propositional form? Or should we conclude that this is an ironical claim designed to obscure Plato's philosophy, so that attentive readers with philosophical *techné* will grasp the true meaning and significance of his claim? Or perhaps the letter means that this letter *and only this letter* contains Plato's thoughts on philosophy?

At the very least, the letter warns Plato's readers to approach his dialogues with caution. Recall that Plato does not appear in any of his dialogues. He enlists a host of characters who engage in philosophical debates. Not only does Plato never appear as a character in the dialogues, we cannot assume that he embeds his view in any particular character. Together his characters mask the writer of the dialogues; they function as a dramatic and deliberately constructed foil. Nonetheless, traditional interpreters of Plato overlook these and other dramatic elements of the dialogues. They extract and dissect, premise by premise, the arguments proffered by Plato's characters from the subtexts and contexts in which they appear. They regard Platonic Socrates as Plato's alter ego and argue that he, therefore, espouses the views that Plato holds to be true. Alas, little textual evidence supports this claim. In fact, Plato appears to pinpoint the weaknesses of Socrates' method by characterizing the negative effect he has on his students. We learn in *Phaedo*, for example, that Plato does not attend Socrates' execution because Plato is sick.[55] In the *Symposium*, Plato characterizes Socrates as an anti-erotic teacher who leaves his students like Alcibiades with feelings of shame. Other criticisms appear throughout the dialogues.

It is significant that Plato wrote dialogues, that he avoids first-person speaking, and that he shrouds philosophy in drama. Leo Strauss is decisive in developing the tradition of Platonic interpretation that accounts for these facts: the dramatic tradition of Platonic interpretation. Strauss depicts Plato as an esoteric writer who "lies in deed or manner or style of expression, but does not lie in speech."[56] Through careful study of the dialogical form, the dramatic moments within the dialogues, and the juxtaposition of various dialogues, Strauss aims to unmask Plato.

Following in a prodigious line of thinkers originally inspired by Leo Strauss, prominent philosophers such as Stanley Rosen, Seth Bernadete, David Roochnik, and Anne-Marie Bowery read Plato with an eye toward the dramatic. They continue to present unorthodox interpretations of the dialogues in response to the many dated and ill-founded views associated with Platonic thought. Bowery in particular interprets the arguments, metaphors, and analogies of Plato's characters in light of, rather than apart from, the drama of the dialogues. She distinguishes between narrated dialogues and enacted dialogues, noting that the narrated dialogues are of two kinds: those narrated by Socrates himself, and those narrated by one of Socrates' disciples. She identifies five narrative features that frame Plato's Socratic dialogues: (1) they are short, (2) they begin *in medias res*, (3) they end abruptly (and thus are inconclusive), (4) they raise one topic for discussion—"What is X?"—and (5) they feature Socrates as the main character.

I share the view that Plato wrote esoterically and dramatically. *Why* he did so is an open question. On the one hand, philosophers such as Descartes, who risk persecution, might choose to disguise their views for political reasons. One could exclude one's own name or character from a text to accomplish this goal, or one could write ironically, stating the opposite of what one believes. Did Plato fear persecution? The execution of his teacher for corrupting the youth and defying the gods of the state forever marked philosophy as a dangerous business. His association with Socrates might lead to a form of guilt by association. But Plato, unlike Socrates, enjoyed the benefit of the academy to protect him from charges of corrupting the youth. He organized formal study rather than engaged in debates on the street. He visibly advocated political and religious life.

On the other hand, one might write esoterically for philosophical reasons. Strauss maintains that only particular readers—true philosophers—can cope with the truth, for the truth is destabilizing and dangerous.[57] It is clear from Plato's use of the dialogue form that he believes we arrive at truth dialectically. Dialectic appears to preserve the process by which we arrive at ideas in our everyday interactions in the world. If by revealing ideas outside of the natural process of logos we thereby threaten a thinker's sense of stability and security, then truth can be dangerous indeed. Did Plato choose the dialogue form because he believed that truth is dangerous? We know he chose to write dialogues that express philosophical concepts in dramatic forms—myths, speeches, distorted time frames—but did he do so to mask his ideas? Some of his myths, the allegory of the cave, for example, express the idea that truth is painful. His initiation of readers into philosophical thinking allows them to see philosophical views slowly and over time.

Yet "The Seventh Letter" speaks directly of truth and the need for readers to comprehend philosophical ideas gradually. If it functions as another Platonic mask, then it is the only one of its kind. Plato was committed to the dialogical form. If dialogue serves the cause of truth, and if truth emerges through dialogical interchanges, then this epistle does not yield truth. Nonetheless, even if "The Seventh Letter" is not an instance of revealed truth, it may still contain a set of true statements about revealed truth.

"The Seventh Letter" suggests that humans acquire truth through the arduous work of creation. We must not only read and interpret texts that express philosophical ideas, but we must engage philosophical ideas as if they are our own and give birth to new ideas. In doing so, one must be willing to wear a mask of our own—to exit the cave as a slave and enter society as a philosopher. We must both discover and create the self.

"The Seventh Letter" frames Plato's dialogues as an epilogue frames a novel: it provides an authorial context for reading and understanding the dialogues. Behind Plato's masks lie powerful truths about the nature of the self and the creative sources of identity. By introducing complexity through the dialogical form, by shrouding the meaning of his work in dramatic encounters between rich characters and masking his ideas and identity, Plato creates a middle ground in which he can be known and understood, a ground that is neither deterministic nor constructivist in nature. His masking merits Parkes's understanding of "authentic" masking" ". . . but there is another kind of masking that could be called, on account of its self-awareness, 'authentic.' Indeed, at its most authentic, this play of masking reaches the level of poetry, where the actor becomes the author."[58]

CONCLUSIONS

As readers of autobiographies, we must adjudicate between intentional self-deception and genuine masking. Nietzsche reminds us that good readers tread lightly upon the texts they read, while "[t]he worst readers are those who behave like plundering troops: they take away a few things they can use, dirty and confound the remainder, and revile the whole."[59] Careful reading of autobiography involves confronting and responding to the 'I' of the text, the identity-bearing ego expressed through the autobiographical work. It also involves raising questions about the relation between the author and the writer, questions that emerge in the interplay of the writer and author as circumscribed by the text itself. It includes raising new questions about the nature of the self who is doing the writing. Finally, it invests us in the process of self-knowing by simultaneously engaging the author (by listening as he or she narrates) and the writer (by visualizing the figure whose ideas are narrated) in tacit dialogue.

Creating a formal hermeneutic process for reading autobiographies allows us to resolve problems invoked by self-deception while acknowledging the distinct voices of the writer-self and the author-subject. For instance, by realizing that neither the first nor the third person has privileged access to the meaning of texts, we avoid treating autobiography as mere historical fact. Moreover, by recognizing that the writer is distinct from the author, we avoid reducing the literary form itself to pure content (to the facts of one's life). The distinction between the author and writer serves two additional and important functions: (1) It allows for the emergence of numerous authors—a plethora of vying interpretations of the author-subject; and (2) It expresses the duality of the self. Thus readers of autobiography share the burden of understanding the self as both bifurcated and whole.

I have argued throughout this chapter that the search for the self culminates in discovery and creation. Autobiographers discover the writer-self through introspection and retrospection, and they unify the self through memory recollection or manipulation. They create the author-subject through alterspection and self-inscription, and they unify the subject through self-narration. Ultimately, the unity of the bifurcated self resides with the readers of autobiography who seek to know the self, a unity made possible by the dialectic of autobiography.

Chapter 4

Transforming the Self

> Writing ought always to advertise a victory—an overcoming of oneself which has to be communicated for the benefit of others; but there are dyspeptic authors who write only when they cannot digest something, indeed when it is still stuck in their teeth: they involuntarily seek to transfer their own annoyance to the reader and in the way to exercise power over him: that is to say, they too desire victory, but over others.
>
> —Friedrich Nietzsche[1]

The Dialectic of Philosophical Autobiography

In the preceding chapters, I described and analyzed the bifurcation of the self within philosophical autobiography. I argued that the act of self-narration—an act of narrative self-mapping in which the autobiographer is simultaneously the object and subject of investigation—bifurcates the self into a writer-self (Inner self) and an author-subject (Outer self). In developing this argument, I examined the interplay between the Inner and Outer dimensions of the self within five philosophical autobiographies: Augustine's *Confessions*, Descartes' *Meditations*, Rousseau's *The Confessions*, Nietzsche's *Ecce Homo*, and Barnes's *The Story I Tell Myself*. I also introduced the concept of the "historical figure," a historically inscribed self who stands apart from the cognitively realized Inner self and the textually inscribed Outer self. Finally, I analyzed self-deception and self-concealment and the difficulties they pose for writers and readers of autobiography. Philosophical autobiography, a genre of writing and a method for self-knowing, provides useful illustrations of each.

In this fourth and final chapter, I evaluate the hermeneutics invoked by autobiography. I note that autobiographical texts presuppose authors and relate authors to writers. The reader discloses the meaning of the author and writer and extrapolates the significance of the author-writer relation. The cultural and historical milieu in which a particular reader and text appear shapes the mediation of the author and writer and the interpretation of texts in significant ways.[2] By instantiating an ontologically fixed but a hermeneutically open process of self-exposition, philosophical autobiography fosters reevaluations of the self. It therefore serves as a corrective to the distorted conceptions of the self that pervade the dialectical history of the self and hamper self-knowledge. I conclude that philosophical autobiography reveals the inherent richness of self-narration and clarifies the interplay between the ontological and rhetorical dimensions of the self.

Two accounts of textual interpretation weigh heavily in my analysis of autobiographical interpretation: Jorge Gracia's view of textual interpretation and Hans-Georg Gadamer's account of hermeneutic acts.[3] I relate their accounts to Nietzsche's use of the author-writer distinction, a distinction intended to jettison Inner conceptions of the self and compel readers to reevaluate their notions of history and autobiography. Nietzsche's revision of the relation between the writer and author breaks down the traditionally conceived I/You relationship so that the author represents both I and you, self and other. Thus Nietzsche brings the reader directly into the text as a member of the "we" to which the "I" and "you" belong. His work establishes a new relation between autobiographers and readers, a relation that Jerome Bruner describes as intersubjective:

> . . . it is probably a mistake to conceive of Self as solo, as locked up inside one person's subjectivity, as hermetically sealed off. Rather, Self seems also to be intersubjective or "distributed" in the same way that one's "knowledge" is distributed . . . to include the friends and colleagues to whom one has access, the notes one has filed, the books one has on one's shelves.[4]

Ecce Homo exemplifies the need for artful interpretations of autobiography—for what Gracia calls "nontextual interpretations." Nietzsche's dramatic masking of the self reinvents the process of self-narration and self-mapping. His self-representation exemplifies the radical shift away from essence and toward identity that we see repeated in contemporary scholarship and cultural artifacts: the genealogy of the self, psychosocial theories of the self, methods of interpretation, autobiography, art, film, and music.

Finally, I examine the differences between male and female autobiography as both a mode of self-exposition and an example of self-narration. Gender is a concrete example of our Inner and Outer being in the world, wherein our essence is human and our identity is either male or female. Hence, gender offers us a way to reassess our notions of "essence" and "identity"; it helps us reconceive the self as a middle self, partly discovered, partly created. I begin with a synoptic account of the challenges that self-bifurcation poses for philosophers.

Self-Bifurcation

The bifurcation of the self complicates the search for the self, in several ways. First, because the narrator assumes the dual status of writer-self (Inner self) and author-subject (Outer self), the 'I' refers to the writer and signifies the author, thus designating both real and symbolic relations between the self and the text. The ambiguous status of the 'I' obscures the philosophical understanding of the self and complicates the work of the reader-interpreter.

Second, the ambiguity of the 'I' in autobiography obscures the relation between one's essence and identity—*what I am* and *who I am*, respectively. This in turn gives rise to several contradictory or conflicting views of the self. These include a denial of essence (Nietzsche), a conflation of essence and identity (Rousseau), and varied unifications of essence and identity (Augustine and memory, Descartes and the cogito, Barnes and consciousness).

Third, the bifurcation of the self generates a dialectical process of self-knowing and implicates the reader in that dialectic. The text and the reader mediate the relation between the writer and the author (and thus the dialectic of self-knowing) in two ways: (1) The text relates the author to the writer, that is, the writer-author is inscribed within and fixed to an ontologically closed but a hermeneutically open text; (2) The reader interprets the relation between the author and writer, that is, the reader engages in hermeneutic acts that disclose the nature of the self generally and the unity of the author-writer specifically. The author transcends his or her inscription within a text, and the writer transcends the boundaries of history, memory, and consciousness within the mind of the reader. The text makes possible wholeness of self by providing an infinitely rich middle ground in which the reader can interpret the identity and essence of the self. The search for the self culminates in artful living.

Self-Narration

Though other creatures experience life successively, only humans derive meaning from the immanent flow of past, present, and future events. Augustine dutifully reminds us that only humans understand life as a whole, for they alone experience time. Humans' capacity to derive meaning from random experiences and create order out of chaos is predicated upon temporality. Stated negatively, humans lack unity outside of the temporal structures that shape their lives and selves; without unity to life and self, experience is meaningless. Kierkegaard recognizes the paradoxical condition of human understanding when he writes that "life can only be understood backwards; but it must be lived forwards."[5] Humans instantiate themselves in time by inscribing themselves in narratives; that is, they connect the shadows of themselves from our birth to the present and unify the self in time. William Mathews observes, ". . . the temporal structure of human processes...is fundamentally narrative . . . processes in life cannot be captured at all in a chronicle of events. What is needed is a narrative proper."[6]

In the Western world, the structure of narration (a beginning, middle or apex, and conclusion) parallels a linear conception of time (past, present, and future). Linear narratives ground the meaning and significance of human experience and ideas by providing unity and coherence to an otherwise random set of events. Both a Humean critique and Nietzschean critique of causality have relevance here; we describe events as though they relate causally and temporally, though we have no evidence that such relations are real. The act of autobiography and the instantiation of self-identity presuppose temporally inscribed events with a distinct beginning and end. The organizations of events around an identified beginning and end may vary, as Nietzsche and Barnes demonstrate, but self-identity presupposes this structure of narration. Ricoeur shows how our experience of reality undermines this narrative arrangement:

> . . . there is nothing in real life that serves as a narrative beginning; memory is lost in the hazes of early childhood; my birth and, with greater reason, the act through which I was conceived, belong more to the history of others—in this case, to my parents—than to me. As for my death, it will finally be recounted only in the stories of those who survive me. I am always moving toward my death, and this prevents me from grasping it as a narrative end.[7]

Yet he also shows that self-identity and unity necessitate a linear series in which life unfolds. Because we co-create our identity in the world, we are, as I have argued, both Inner and Outer, writers and authors, knowers and knowees. This inescapable condition gives rise to several philosophical concerns. Does the act of writing autobiographically distort the self and change who we are and/or what we are? Or do we obscure the relation between the author and writer as we narrate our lives and signify ourselves in written form? Does the imposition of unity onto our lives and selves mislead the reader? The answer to all of these questions is yes and no.

Autobiographers self-consciously create author-subjects who authentically exemplify the discursive relationship between meaning and time. These author-subjects signify the synthetic unity of life experience and self-identity—the organization of life and the self through the organizational patterns of temporally structured minds (ala Augustine and Kant), minds that derive meaning from life experiences, and meaning that attaches to a particular self with a narrative-individuated identity. As Paul Trainor argues, ". . . an autobiography is not a narration of facts but of experience, of how the autobiographical subject responded to find meaning in his life."[8] Even Nietzsche's subversion of time via the Eternal Return connects the meaning of human experience to a circular or recurring notion of time (the past, present, and future folded together into a series of infinite moments). This unfolding experience of time makes it possible for readers to contemplate the relation between meaning and time in their lives. Mathews puts this point more poetically:

> A person crossing a river by means of a series of Steppingstones can look back and in them identify the set of steps which have brought him to his present position. . . . The important thing about the Steppingstones is that the thread of the life seems to move or flow through them. . . . Steppingstones derive their meaning and significance not from the immediate moment, but rather from the movement of the life as a whole.[9]

I will say more about the relation between narration, meaning, and time as I articulate my theory of interpretation. Though my theory draws upon Gracia's and Gadamer's analyses of textual interpretation, it aims to articulate a middle position between their views, a position that sustains and enriches the interplay between the Inner self and the Outer self. I begin with a brief description and comparison of their perspectives. Next, I connect their theories to the overriding framework of this book—the Inner self and the Outer self—and I show how my version of hermeneutics applies to autobiographical interpretation in particular. Finally, I examine the history of the term *gender* as a phenomenological example of the interplay between the Inner self and the Outer self, and I describe the genealogy of the self that underlies the first-person texts of Augustine, Descartes, Rousseau, Nietzsche, and Barnes.

Interpretation and Understanding

In *A Theory of Textuality*, Gracia argues that interpreting textual propositions and expressions involves interpreting the *entities that constitute a text* (ECT hereafter). Hence, a reader must understand the lexical and syntactical meaning of each symbol and semantically significant mark, such as punctuation, and assume an interpretative framework in which to evaluate those terms, propositions, and marks. A host of interpretative frameworks may be available to the reader.

Because interpretations arise within particular hermeneutical frameworks, a range of sometimes incompatible interpretations follows from readings of the same text. Depending upon their framework, readers will understand the semantically significant features of texts differently, which opens up the arena of interpretations and enriches the meaning of texts in significant ways. Nonetheless, interpreting the ECT raises significant problems for both writers and readers.

Suppose that a text originally written in one language is translated into a different language, for example, *The Odyssey* from ancient Greek into modern English.[10] If the lexical meaning of the terms that comprise the text varies from language to language, then the interpretation of the text will vary as well. According to Gracia's theory, which is a variation on a correspondence theory of truth, if the ECT of a text and the lexical meaning attached to the ECT do not correspond to one another, then it follows that the interpretations of texts will not be identical.[11]

Interestingly, Gracia's view of texts (ECT) provides a corollary to the view of the Inner self. He argues that a text (like a writer-self) is an *ontological* entity that may be understood in different ways according to distinct cultural and social systems of meaning (cf. historical figure). Because the text exists in the world, its meaning depends upon the interplay between the text and the public, *not* between the writer and the text, nor between the author and the text. Likewise, the writer-self transcends the text and is not merely a constructed or narratively construed textual identity. The writer-self is an essence that pervades and creates the text and whose identity arises from real relations in the world. I will draw out the parallel between Gracia's view of textuality and the Inner self in a moment.

Now consider Gadamer's view of textual interpretation, which I elaborate on in slightly more detail. Gadamer advances his view of texts and interpretation in *Truth and Method* and *Philosophical Hermeneutics.* In contrast to Gracia, his view provides a corollary to the Outer self. Suppose, for example, that the framework utilized by a reader either clarifies or obscures the semantically significant aspects of the text by shaping what one notices (or does not notice) in the text. This shaping occurs as a result of one's prejudices (prejudgments), habits, and general foreknowledge of the text. Hence, the formation of one's prejudices takes place in relation to the past. The past continues to shape the present when one makes use of terms, ideas, and beliefs that arose in the past and bear upon the present. The reader remains aware of the ways in which history (and, by proxy, culture, politics, social status, gender, etc.) exercises power over consciousness. The reader then becomes aware that his or her own viewpoint, his or her own "horizon," is not privileged and singular but is instead a "fluid and relative moment in the life of effective history, a moment that is indeed productive and disclosive, but one that like all others before it, will be overcome and fused with future horizons."[12]

Gadamer's view of the text as a horizon of meaning parallels the view of the self as an author-subject. Both the text and the author-subject are *rhetorical* entities whose meaning (or identity) is revealed to us through our prejudiced reading (or creation). Just as we understand texts through our prejudices, we understand authors through a writer's prejudices, which conceal the writer and reveal the author. The fusion of a text's horizon with a reader's horizon, like the fusion of an author with a reader, transforms the meaning of texts and self-understanding. As Linge argues:

> This awareness of our own historicity and finitude—our consciousness of effective history—brings with it an openness to new possibilities that is the precondition of genuine understanding. The interpreter must recover and make his own, then, not the personality or the worldview of the author, but the fundamental concern that motivates the text—the question that it seeks to answer and that it poses again and again to its interpreters. . . . Genuine questioning always involves a laying open and holding open of possibilities that suspend the presumed finality of both the text's and the reader's current opinions.[13]

It follows from Gadamer's argument that authors *are not identical with* writers, texts *are not* mere artifacts, and readers *are not* lone investigators. The past and present are intertwined in the horizons of texts, authors, and readers. For example, we cannot describe every text that advances our understanding of history as historically accurate, he argues, because "[n]either the historically limited transmitted text nor the work of art can be regarded as solely dependent on its creator or on its present performer or interpreter."[14] Hence, history is more than a collection of mere facts that can be formulated in propositional language. It is a narrative account of the past that remains open to interpretation and understanding. Likewise, the author is not solely dependent on the writer or the text for identity; he or she is also dependent upon the reader, who mediates the text in which the author appears.

If an autobiographical text represents a fusion of a writer's and an author's horizons, then the interpretation of an autobiography represents a fusion of a text's and a reader's horizons (and, by entailment, the fusion of the writer's, author's, and reader's understanding of the text). Whereas in Gracia's view, texts are ontological entities comprised of specific and meaningful ECT, Gadamer argues that texts are rhetorical entities comprised of indeterminate yet meaningful signs accessed through the lens of a reader's prejudgments. Interpretative conflicts reflect the conflicting horizons of readers and the ongoing dialogue invoked by the reading of the text. In this sense of meaning, Gadamer explains, it is absurd to search for *the one true* interpretation of a text, since neither the author nor the reader determines a text's meaning:

> The real meaning of a text as it addresses the interpreter does not just depend upon the occasional factors which characterize the author and his original public. For it is also always co-determined by the historical situation of the interpreter and thus by the whole of the objective course of history. The meaning of a text surpasses its author not occasionally, but always. Thus understanding is not a reproductive procedure, but rather always a productive one. . . . It suffices to say that one understands differently when one understands at all.[15]

Texts are designed to be deepened and explored, not fixed. Their interpretation, then, must begin with history in mind so that we can identify the features of the text and our life that might form a horizon and thus an understanding of the text. Martha Nussbaum articulates a similar point when she suggests that "it is good, in a more general way, to focus on . . . dilemmas and not to go beyond them, or 'solve' them, because to do so reaffirms and strengthens attachment to the values in question, in such a way that one will be less likely to violate them in other circumstances."[16]

Certainly our linguistic and social contexts are rich enough to bear a multiplicity of interpretations. But how should we interpret autobiographical texts when the act of self-narration bifurcates the self and instantiates an authorial voice within the text? How should we interpret a represented set of events temporally and historically distinct from our lives?

Alasdair MacIntyre offers a third perspective on interpretation that resides between Gracia's and Gadamer's. His view differs from mine insofar as he focuses on the question of identity rather than the relation between identity and essence; he is primarily interested in who I am rather than what I am or the unity of one's essence and identity. He argues that we recognize the possible interpretations of a text or set of events *and* the evidence for those varied interpretations (ECT, historical persona, etc.) simultaneously. Hence, we see what accounts meaningfully for a life representation *as* we realize the extended nature of these possible explanations. Our subsequent understanding of these events either becomes open and variable, or we realize that the event itself is partially indeterminate and infinitely rich. In either case, we see an old event, we experience an old event, in a new way.[17] Because of the posited emotional, psychological, and cognitive distance between myself and the subject or subject matter I am examining, I am able to come to an understanding, perhaps for the first time, about how best to respond to particular possibilities and evidence. This understanding emerges in narratives only.

If we acknowledge that autobiography blurs the distinction between fiction and nonfiction, and if we accept MacIntyre's claim that events in both fictive and factual worlds are interpreted through narratives, then it follows that interpretations of autobiography necessitate the ongoing reconstruction of narratives.[18] As new subtextual information and judgments emerge, new interpretations of texts emerge. The interplay between the Inner self and the Outer self emerges not merely in the act of autobiographical writing but also in the act of interpretation—information and evidence about a writer's life and paradigms and beliefs that shape our understanding of authors bear upon the meaning of autobiographical texts. The interpretation of narratives fosters identity discovery *and* creation; it is a means by which we locate ourselves within a context or setting and see where such lives and/or life roles can lead us.

MacIntyre reminds us that we (and, by extension, our actions) exist within a causally and temporally mediated setting: we are "never more than co-authors of our narratives."[19] Yet he brackets a discussion of essence and its relation to identity and privileges the nuances of identity with respect to narratives. He writes, "[W]e enter human society with one or more imputed character-roles we've been drafted into, and we have to learn what they are in order to understand how others respond to us and how our responses to them are apt to be construed."[20] With respect to autobiographical interpretation, then, we must understand the role we play as readers. A writer's autobiographical account is subject to his or her audience's expectations (both literary and historical). Moreover, a writer's understanding of himself or herself is an irreducible feature of a narrative, a feature that the readers' perspectives and history shape because history is an enacted dramatic narrative in which the characters are also the creators.[21]

This narrative conception of selfhood presupposes two poignant claims: (1) Identity arises from the continuity of a life narrative; to be an individuated self is to be the subject of a history, to be the same person now that you were in the past; and (2) History holds us accountable for the actions and experiences that comprise our life story.[22] Hence, the self is a historically mediated individual whose story grounds his or her identity in the world so that a person is the "same protagonist in a continuing story."[23] Yet the *autobiographing* self is not merely a character with an identity. He or she is both an ontological and a rhetorical being who is bifurcated by self-narration but who is nonetheless a potentially unified individual with an essence and not merely an identity or identities. What account of autobiographical interpretation do these views suggest? How might we employ their views to clarify the interpretation of autobiography?

Gracia on Interpretation

Although Gracia does not address autobiographical texts in particular, his analysis does not exclude the application of his views to first-person writing. In addition, his theory is well suited for an evaluation of autobiographies because of its attention to both the status and function of texts within the larger framework of interpretation. Utilizing his analysis of interpretation for autobiographical analysis is appropriate. My own view borrows from his theory of nontextual interpretation and his claim that interpretations are either adequate or inadequate rather than true or false.

Gracia begins his analysis by acknowledging that writers write for others. They intend for their narrated representations to be read often by a specific, predetermined audience. A reader's awareness of the writer's intended audience/s can aid in the interpretation of texts, because the reader does not always know or understand the contexts in which texts are written and intended to be understood: "[W]ith rare exceptions texts are meant to be read or heard by an audience and they, thus, presuppose a certain context that allows for shortcuts and *lacunae* intended to be filled by the assumptions and views of the audience in question."[24]

The awareness of the audience also shapes the way in which the writer addresses his or her topic and represents himself or herself as an author. Gracia observes that the awareness of an audience's expectations and sensibilities shapes the rhetorical stance of the author. Yet I maintain that autobiography shapes the text in even more dramatic ways. As a mode of self-exposition, autobiography invokes self-reflection. One of the three modes of self-reflection is *alterspection*, a process of looking outside and beyond the self/life and seeing the self as a disconnected, discontinuous "other." Once the writer disassociates himself or herself from the author through the act of alterspection, he or she is free to posit an author who bears little resemblance to the writer himself or herself. The text is what sustains the relation between the writer and author, a relation understood through the act of reader interpretation. Since autobiographies are always and only representational, and representations symbolize but do not imitate the self, then the reader mediates the text and unifies the autobiographical self.

Gracia asserts that the ontology of a text, the meaning of a text, and the identity of the writer-author are determined in part by the culture in which the text is read and the function of the text within that culture. Surely he is right. In his analysis, the meaning of particular texts "depends on the author, the audience, the society in which it is produced, its context, its language, the text itself, and the cultural function it has."[25] He proceeds to argue that the primary function of interpretation is to produce some understanding (in the reader's mind) that is related in some way to the text itself (the ECT and their meaning) and to the reader or audience who reads a text at a particular time. Moreover, he argues that interpretation performs three specific functions: the *Historical Function*, the *Meaning Function*, and the *Implicative Function*:

> . . . the *Historical Function* aims to re-create in the contemporary audience the acts of understanding of the historical author (writer) and the historical audience of the historical text. The aim of the interpreter in this case is to try to have an audience understand a text as its historical author and historical audience understood it. A second specific

> function of interpretations, also concordant with their overall generic function, I shall call the *Meaning Function*. . . . This function is to produce in contemporary audiences acts of understanding that may go beyond the acts of understanding of the historical author and the historical audience . . . revealing aspects of the meaning of the text with which their historical authors and historical audiences were not acquainted. . . . Finally, a third specific function of interpretations, which I shall call *Implicative Function*, is to produce in contemporary audiences acts of understanding whereby those audiences understand the implications of the meaning of texts, regardless of whether the historical authors and the historical audiences were or were not aware of those implications.[26]

If we apply Gracia's theory to autobiography and argue that the purpose of such writing is to convey a particular self-view or self-representation to others, then it appears that the reader's task is to interpret the text historically and thus analyze the meaning of the text in terms of its *Historical Function*.

Some of the early philosophical autobiographies that I examine in this study, particularly Augustine's, aid the audience in reaching philosophical conclusions about the nature of the self and historically verifiable conclusions about authors' lives. Augustine achieves the latter by interjecting and repeating his purpose and aims; he offers an extended confession. He ascribes the meaning of his conversion and other life events to the text itself so that the reader need not go anywhere else for answers about his life. He aims to realize and represent his life accurately. However, this does not exclude the possibility that he and other authors may subconsciously create multiple presentations of themselves and convey multiple understandings of their texts to their audiences. Autobiographies might serve meaning and implicative functions as well. I believe that there are multiple types of the Meaning Function. One of these is the Philosophical Function—the generation of philosophical concepts and/or theories to illustrate philosophical ideas.

For example, the reading of Augustine's *Confessions* from its original production in the fifth century through its continued translation and reading today models the act of narration itself. In seeking to understand Augustine's self-conception and life perception, we read, describe, analyze, and synthesize his narration with our understanding of autobiography. We interpret and evaluate Augustine's account of the self and his life in light of often contrasting perspectives. We move discursively and successively from one point to the next so that the reading of texts parallels the writing of texts. Hence, we reenact the discursive act invoked in creating *Confessions* by instantiating a dialogue that is semiotically related to the text. Gracia writes, "[T]here is no completely predetermined textual meaning. The most there is is a set of vague ideas that an author wishes to convey."[27] Augustine's text may then perform a Meaning Function that is philosophical in nature. But it may also perform a Historical Function wherein the interpreter aims to give a textual interpretation through acts of understanding that transfer the past into the present.

Understanding Texts

Gracia argues that a historical interpretation of a text "seeks to reconstruct the intricate weave of thoughts and ideas and relations that were not recorded in the historical text and are neither part of its meaning nor of the implications of that meaning."[28] By aiming to disclose the context in which a text was written and thereby reveal the facts and features of history surrounding the production of a text, historical interpretations go beyond the scope of the text and the ECT that form it *but not beyond the understanding of the author or original audience*. Hence, historical interpretations reveal more than a text says or denotes but not more than history warrants. Because this form of interpretation focuses explicitly on historical context, it is particularly useful for understanding texts written in ancient and foreign cultures.

We arrive at a historical understanding of a text through what Gracia calls the *Principle of Proportional Understanding*, which says that in order for a contemporary audience to achieve an understanding of a text that is consistent with the author's understanding, the acts of understanding that the text produces in the reader must be equivalent to the acts of understanding that hold between the text taken in the historical context and the historical author and historical audience.[29] This means that the interpreter or reader "creates the text that will produce the kind of thoughts and judgments in the contemporary audience that the historical author and audience had."[30]

If we apply this principle to autobiographical texts, then we realize that for a contemporary audience to understand an author as a historical audience understood that author, the contemporary audience must have in mind the same acts of understanding that the historical audience had in mind (at least approximately). This function is especially important, because readers who are temporally and historically distant from the text's production have difficulty understanding a text fully:

> Now we can see more clearly why interpretation is an integral part of the historical task of understanding texts, for its aim is to bridge the conceptual, cultural, and other contextual gaps that separate the historical text from a later time at which it is being read, heard, or even remembered. It also explains why interpretations need not be consid-

> ered anachronistic simply in virtue of the fact that they add to the historical text, because the function of the additions they contain is precisely to produce such acts of understanding in the contemporary audience that are intentionally the same as those the historical text produced or would have produced in the historical author of the text and the historical audience.[31]

The Historical Function of a text presupposes the ability of a contemporary reader to access and understand the historical and literary context in which the text was produced, as well as the socio-historical situation in which the writer lived. If and only if interpretations satisfy the Historical Function, Gracia states, does a reader achieve a historical understanding of a text. This claim is especially relevant for translators who must interpret denotations and connotations in one language and locate similarly denotative and connotative terms in another language with which to transcribe the original. But in cases where the author and writer are bifurcated—in cases of autobiography—it is unclear what is and/or should be the Historical Function of the text. Is the aim of the Historical Function to denote the writer and connote the author? Rousseau's views of the self and reformulations of history vex the historical interpretation of philosophical autobiography. On what grounds do we interpret an autobiography that attempts to untie itself from a writer's historical context?

Distortions and Paradoxes of Interpretation

Gracia does not presume that the historical interpretation of texts is without problems. In his discussion of the Historical Function he addresses two difficulties that emerge with historical interpretations: the distortion of interpretation and the paradoxical necessity of interpretations. Regarding the distortion of interpretation, Gracia concedes that the acts of understanding produced by interpretations can never be *exactly* the same as the acts of understanding produced by writing a text. Because such acts of understanding are not identical, interpretations of historical texts appear distorted. Again, the problem for translators of texts from one language into another arises.[32] Gracia aims to resolve this problem by clarifying the ontological distinction between texts and their interpretations, showing that interpretations are never presented as the historical text in question. In other words, the purpose of the Historical Function of interpretations is to create *equivalent* or approximate acts of understanding, not of meaning.[33] We take propositions to have specific meanings according to the ECT, but we do not assume that the propositions themselves are necessarily or exactly the same from one language to another, for we know that the ECT are themselves different. I return to the approximation of acts of understanding at the end of this section.

Gracia expresses the paradoxical necessity of interpretations as a dilemma:

> [T]he interpreter either understands a text or does not. If he or she does, then there is no need for an interpretation. But if he or she does not, how can the interpreter know that the interpretation is accurate? Put this way, it would seem that interpretations turn out to be either unnecessary or necessary but impossible.[34]

He attempts to resolve this dilemma by redefining the function of the reader. Under most circumstances, he argues, interpretations that serve a Historical Function presuppose an understanding of the historical text by a reader. However, these circumstances do not make interpretations superfluous. Rather than function as an introspective interpreter, the reader functions as a translator and a literary critic. Moreover, if the purpose of interpretation is to produce an understanding of a text in a contemporary audience and not merely in the mind of one reader, then the reader must convey the meaning of the ECT by discursive description or interpretation.[35] Thus interpretation preserves the integrity of the text and the validity of understanding without relegating meaning to the acts of understanding in the reader's introspectively accessible mind. In short, this means that ". . . just like translators, interpreters prepare the causal framework that makes possible the conveyance of meaning to an audience unfamiliar with the semantic significance of the components of a historical text."[36]

On Gracia's account of interpretation, understanding and interpreting texts are distinctive cognitive acts that arise from the reading of texts. On my account, the ontological and rhetorical bifurcation of the writer and author arises from the writing of autobiographical texts. These two accounts parallel one another in other ways. For Gracia, a text conveys meaning through its ECT, and the interpretation of that text conveys understanding through the reader's acts of interpretation. Consequently, the interpretation of texts, regardless of which function it serves, generates understanding rather than meaning. On my account, a writer constructs his or her authorial self through the narrative acts of self-ascription, thereby bifurcating the essence and identity of the writer and author. However, the process of interpreting authorial selves reveals the implicit, necessary, and unbreakable bridge between the writer and the author—the ontology of the text. As a result, the interpretation of autobiographical texts yields understanding rather than meaning. Just as a reader cannot understand a text through acts of introspection alone, the autobiographer must utilize introspection, retrospection, and alterspection to understand the self fully. Because self-narration creates an authorial persona that is ahistorical, autobiography performs other textual functions, such as Meaning and Implicative functions, and thus requires a different mode of interpretation, which Gracia calls "nontextual interpretations."

Nontextual interpretations invoke contemporary perspectives and analyses in the reading of texts, adding even more significance to the historical understanding of texts. One might, for example, interpret *Confessions* through a feminist or Freudian lens, despite the fact that it was written prior to the development of any feminist ideologies or before the birth of Freudian analysis. Such interpretations do not reveal the author or the audience in the terms they themselves reveal but elevate the text to a new level of understanding.[37]

It follows that there is no determinate intended understanding of texts, though there might be determinate intended meanings. Reading a text is fundamentally a mental act in which ". . . the author and the audience are both subjects who are trying to understand the text."[38] And in some ways, understanding a text is more important to the reader and the audience than conveying the meaning of the text. Gracia contends that ". . . the use of texts is to a great extent tied to these interpretations (Marxist, feminist, historical, literary, and so on), for texts are useful only if they are put to a use beyond the conveyance of meaning."[39] I too argue that autobiography is a useful mode of self-exposition, because it not only describes a writer's life, it also conveys an understanding of the author, a self who remains dialectically related to but ontologically distinct from the writer, and a self that signifies the deeper subconscious dimensions of being. When it is mediated by the prejudgments and ideas of an infinite number of readers, the dialectical encounter between the writer-self and the author-subject transforms our understandings of the self.

Implications

I have defined autobiographies as narrative portraits or representational maps of one's self and/or life. I argue that they reveal who we are *to and for ourselves*, not who we are in every sense of being. I also maintain that every autobiographer is both a writer-self and an author-subject tilted in various degrees toward a particular expression of being. To apply Gracia's analogy, just as the interpretation of a text is not identical to (or correspondent to) the meaning of a text, an autobiographical mapping of an author is not identical to (or correspondent to) the successive events of a writer's life. Rather, autobiography *represents* a writer's life and thus gives us an understanding of that life; but our understanding does not bear a one-to-one relation to the writer's understanding, nor does the text bear a one-to-one relation to the writer's life. It does not follow, however, that all forms of self-mapping serve the same function, or that all interpretations of autobiography are equally useful or productive. As I suggested in Chapter 3, one way to distinguish between productive and nonproductive philosophical autobiographies is by observing how well or how poorly they serve a philosophical function. For example, though Descartes' *Meditations* is not an autobiography per se—it would fail on traditional accounts of "successful" autobiography—it offers a conception of the self (the cogito) that transforms our thinking and writing about the self and validates the process of self-exposition within autobiography. Similarly, Gracia appropriates the concept of 'efficiency' to distinguish between useful and useless interpretations of texts.

Some interpretations are textual in nature, such as translations; others are nontextual, such as feminist readings of Plato's *Symposium*. Insofar as nontextual interpretations add to the understanding of the text by the contemporary audience—and I argue that they do—then they are not only valid but useful. For example, nontextual readings of texts, such as feminist interpretations, intend to reveal something about the author that the author presupposed as true, but the author does not either state or fully explicate the implications of these presuppositions. If textual interpretations aim to convey the meaning of the ECT, including the propositions, then there may be one, definitive interpretation of a text, though we may never achieve it. The value of the notion of a definitive interpretation in this case is regulative and can be useful within the hermeneutical analysis of textual interpretation. However, in nontextual interpretations, we have little reason to search for definitive interpretations, because our aim in producing nontextual interpretations is to understand a text according to some specific methodology or ideology, and thus to engender new and interesting views and uses of texts. In these cases, it is more appropriate to think of interpretations as effective or ineffective or adequate or inadequate, not true or false.[40] I appropriate Gracia's suggestion and argue that we must evaluate philosophical autobiography according to its philosophical function (i.e., by its ability to generate new and productive lines of inquiry into the nature of reality).

To understand philosophical autobiography fully, we must distinguish among the acts involved in the interpretation of exemplary texts, the content of those texts (semantic and ontological), and the significance of textual interpretation. Gracia provides us with several ways of making these distinctions and understanding the nature of autobiographical textuality. He suggests that to understand the dual function of autobiography and the nature of the self it tracks, we must embrace nontextual interpretations and move away from theories of truth toward pragmatic notions of adequacy or productivity. Indeed, he shows us that we have no sound reason to discount interpretations that produce novel understandings of texts.

Consider the vast differences between the conceptions of the self within St. Augustine's *Confessions* and Barnes's *The Story I Tell Myself* and the various purposes these autobiographies serve. The former serves to realize and describe the self to others; the latter serves to construct and ascribe the self for others. By separating textual from nontextual interpretations and by delineating the various functions of autobiography, we can understand the dimensions of philosophical autobiography along with their varied conceptions of the self in new ways. Nontextual interpretations are useful for understanding the adequacy or productivity of their literary and philosophical functions. By showing that interpretation yields understanding rather than meaning and is therefore neither true nor false, Gracia frees the reader to reconsider the relation between the author and the writer and to reconceive the value of self-representation. Though my view deviates from Gracia's in some respects—he does not distinguish the writer from the author and instead refers to a single historical author—we both insist that there is a necessary relation between the reading and the writing of a text that is ever renewed by and instantiated in the dialectical process of interpretation.

Gadamer on Truth in Interpretation

Whereas Gracia concerns himself primarily with the nature of texts, Gadamer focuses his attention upon the nature of understanding. He describes the act of interpretation between texts and readers as a hermeneutic encounter of horizons that reveals the transformative power of interpretation—the revelation of truth as such over and above true and false propositions. For example, in *Truth and Method*, Gadamer describes hermeneutics as a method for opening up the interpretative dimensions of the world and confronting the various forms in which our understanding manifests itself. In *Philosophical Apprenticeships* and *Philosophical Hermeneutics*, he argues that interpretation enables us to understand obscure and unconventional objects (texts, paintings, etc.) whose meaning is alien and whose significance is unknown.[41] By describing hermeneutics as a mode of opening the mind to new experiences and understanding, Gadamer attempts to reorient our thinking about hermeneutics. His view of interpretation weighs heavily in my thinking about self-knowledge.

Traditionally conceived, the purpose of hermeneutics is corrective. Its task is to resolve misunderstandings. Gadamer attempts to secure the openness of inquiry and experience through a new method of philosophical hermeneutics, a method best exemplified by a dialogue in which interlocutors allow themselves to be vulnerable to each other and to the conversation. In this sense, hermeneutics is ontological rather than methodological in nature: "it seeks to throw light on the fundamental conditions that underlie the phenomenon of understanding in all its modes, scientific and nonscientific alike, and that constitute understanding as an event over which the interpreting subject does not ultimately preside."[42] This does not mean that hermeneutics ignores what we already understand, bracketing the familiar horizons of our being-in-the-world in order to address what is alien to us. Rather, the act of interpretation incorporates both the familiar and the alien into a new horizon, bridging the gap between the world we always already exist in and the world that is new and alien. At its best, hermeneutics bridges the personal and/or historical distance between minds and artifacts—between writers and authors, texts and readers, consciousness and creation. It also bridges the gulf between the autobiographing writer-self and the autobiographed author-subject through the mind of a mediating reader.

Translation is another example of a hermeneutic act in which two sets of language horizons are fused, for translation "allows what is foreign and what is one's own to merge in a new form by defending the point of view of the other even if it is opposed to one's own view."[43] The act of translation produces a new text that carries with it the horizon of understanding of the original text, allowing other language speakers to confront other writers and additional perspectives, perspectives they could not confront otherwise. This view is compatible with Gracia's view of the historical function of texts and textual interpretation.

Prejudices and Understanding

Gadamer argues that we become aware of our hermeneutic horizons through our prejudgments or *prejudices*, the ontological condition of experience and understanding:

> It is not so much our judgments as it is our prejudices that constitute our being. This is a provocative formulation, for I am using it to restore to its rightful place a positive concept of prejudice that was driven out of our linguistic usage by the French and the English enlightenment. It can be shown that the concept of prejudice did not originally have the meaning we have attached to it. Prejudices are not necessarily unjustified and erroneous, so that they inevitably distort the truth. In fact, the historicity of our existence entails that prejudices, in the literal sense of the word, constitute the initial directedness of our whole ability to experience. Prejudices are biases of our openness to the world. They are simply conditions whereby we experience something—whereby what we encounter says something to us.[44]

We read and understand texts according to our prejudices, because experiences presuppose our prejudices. Our prejudices disclose the recognition of the other within experience, wherein otherness represents a newly written text, an unfamiliar language, or an unknown person. This means that our experiences and judgments fade away without an ontological grounding in prejudices. Many questions arise from this account of prejudices that bear directly on my study here: Is self-knowledge circumscribed by our prejudices? Do our prejudices make possible self-reflection? Do our prejudices make possible self-knowledge? Does an awareness of the other explain why we write about and thus seek to know ourselves? Does an encounter with the other explain why we choose to narrate our lives? Does the act of narration alienate or estrange us from ourselves?

The Gadamerian gateway into the world of others is language, which contains the "inner infinity" of the dialogue between interlocutors. The object of interpretation, however, may be an infinitely rich text and thus may represent an outer infinity in Gadamer's framework of horizons. It is not surprising, then, that the development of genuine speaking, the use of words to reach another or to say something significant about an alien object, is the universal human task.[45] Indeed, it is the "fundamental dimension of hermeneutics."[46] This claim resonates with the work of Grice and Austin, and even Plato before them. We speak to individuate ourselves and acknowledge or proclaim our rights as individuals. Genuine *writing*, however, makes us knowable to ourselves and to others; it introduces the notion of *traditions* of language use or literary traditions so that written texts disclose the real hermeneutic task: understanding the marks, symbols, signs, and so on that comprise a text.[47] Gadamer proclaims:

> A written tradition is not a fragment of a past world, but has already raised itself beyond this into the sphere of the meaning that it expresses. . . . It is not the document, as a piece of the past, that is the bearer of tradition but the continuity of memory. Through it tradition becomes part of our own world, and thus what it communicates can be stated immediately. . . . That is why our understanding remains curiously unsure and fragmentary when we have no written tradition of a culture but only dumb monuments, and we do not call this information about the past "history." Texts, on the other hand, always express a whole.[48]

How might this view of tradition apply to autobiography? At first glance, Gadamer appears to fall in line with Augustine, Descartes, and Rousseau, who argue that memory (conceived in various ways) unifies the self. But on second glance, he shares an affinity for Nietzsche and Barnes, who claim that the will or consciousness construes and interprets memory through acts of selection, acts that may lead to self-deception, and acts that are comparable to Gadamer's notion of "prejudices." Hence, our prejudices or preselected ideas and images that color our memory shape our self-narration. On a historical scale, prejudices that shape our memory and our self-conceptions also shape the tradition of autobiography, particularly philosophical autobiography, a shaping reflected by the genealogy of the self that suffuses philosophical autobiography.

Working to combine the unifying and concealing elements of memory, Gadamer suggests that understanding a text, especially an autobiographical one, is coincident with the realization of the writer's continuous actions, thoughts, and beliefs. The reader's job is to uncover the writer's (the writer-author) intentions or acts of understanding that communicate the significance of a writer's life. A *true* interpretation is one in which the reader understands the writer as she or he understood herself or himself. Gracia classifies this as "textual interpretation" and argues that it serves only a historical function.[49] On the other hand, the Inner view of the self presupposes that the self is an autonomous agent who disengages herself or himself from her or his own historical, literary, and cultural situation. Therefore, the writer is the ultimate authority of the autobiographed text, even in instances in which she or he is a textually inscribed author.

By contrast, Gadamer denies the possibility of disengaged or unprejudiced understanding. He asks rhetorically, can a knower remove himself or herself from his or her immediate situation in the present by assuming a critical, abstract standpoint, without prejudice, without tradition?[50] His tacit denial initiates a shift in the conception and focus of hermeneutics, a shift that Linge describes in ontological terms:

> An ideal of understanding that asks us to overcome our own present is intelligible only on the assumption that our own historicity is an accidental factor. But if it is an *ontological* rather than a merely accidental and subjective condition, then the knower's own present situation is already constitutively involved in any process of understanding. Thus Gadamer takes the knower's boundness to his present horizons and the temporal gulf separating him from his object to be the productive ground of all understanding rather than the negative factors or impediments to be overcome. Our prejudices do not cut us off from the past, but initially opens it up to us.[51]

Gadamer unwittingly challenges the Cartesian assumptions that have shaped much of the tradition of autobiography by redefining the meaning of history and by analyzing human historicity. He argues that the past does not merely supply the "objects" of interpretation—texts, events, and so on—but establishes the ground upon which interpretations arise: through prejudices and traditions.[52] He reorients our thinking about ourselves by examining the role of historicity in the interpretation of first-person texts.

Gadamer defines understanding as a hermeneutic event in which the reader and the text bring together distinct horizons of meaning. "Understanding itself is not to be thought of so much as an action of subjectivity, but as the entering into an event of transmission in which past and present are constantly mediated. This is what must gain validity in hermeneutical theory, which is much too dominated by the ideal of a procedure, a method."[53] My claim that the reader reunites the ontological and rhetorical dimensions of the self by unifying the author and writer in the act of interpretation is consistent with this view of understanding. The writer, a past historical consciousness and ontological being, creates an author-subject, an ever-new, a present, a rhetorical, and a textual consciousness. The reader mediates the past and present, the writer and the author, by his or her prejudgments about the text that provide a lens through which the meaning of the text is disclosed. Just as the writer-self conceals or masks himself or herself to disclose the author-subject, the reader conceals old analytical methods for the sake of new interpretative methods that disclose new meanings of the text. Interpretations of autobiography should not be considered mere historical scholarship; rather, they must seek out what has been forgotten or covered over by historical analyses:

> . . . our actual experience of the historical consciousness in the last one hundred years has taught us most emphatically that there are serious difficulties involved in its claim to historical objectivity. . . . When we read Mommsen's *History of Rome*, we know who alone could have written it, that is, we can identify the political situation in which this historian organized the voices of the past in a meaningful way. . . . This clearly means, first of all, that the whole reality of historical experience does not find expression in the mastery of historical method. No one disputes the fact that controlling the prejudices of our own present to such an extent that we do not misunderstand the witnesses of the past is a valid aim, but obviously such control does not completely fulfill the task of understanding the past and its transmissions. Indeed, it could very well be that only *insignificant* things in historical scholarship permit us to approximate this ideal of totally extinguishing individuality.[54]

Though history shapes our consciousness in the ways Gadamer suggests, history also transcends our consciousness. We cannot be understood wholly through memory, but because the past continues to bear upon our lives, we have a necessary and an inescapable relationship with the past that creates continuity between the past and the present, thereby bringing the past into the present. Through our consciousness, our past becomes an "inexhaustible source of possibilities of meaning" rather than a transparent source of information.[55]

Historically-effected Consciousness

Gadamer offers a typically Heideggerian description of "historically-effected consciousness " in *Truth and Method*:

> Projecting a historical horizon, then, is only one phase in the process of understanding; it does not become solidified into the self-alienation of a past consciousness, but is overtaken by our own present horizon of understanding. In the process of understanding, a real fusing of horizons occurs—which means that as the historical horizon is projected, it is simultaneously superseded. To bring about this fusion in a regulated way is the task of what we called historically-effected consciousness . . . [and] the central problem of hermeneutics. It is the problem of *application*, which is to be found in all understanding.[56]

Just as the historian is affected by the historicity at work in his or her analyses of historical events or objects, our past experiences shape how we position ourselves toward future experiences, though future experiences remain always open.[57] "History is only present to us in light of our futurity. Here we have all learned from Heidegger, for he exhibited precisely the primacy of futurity for our possible recollection and retention, and for the whole of history."[58]

Hermeneutics discloses and enriches the past by transforming the strangeness of experience into familiar and present ideas of consciousness. Through our historically-effected consciousnesses, we confront the unknown, the negative horizon of experience, with the known, the positive horizon of experience, thereby creating continuity between the past and the future. Subsequent fusions of horizons direct us toward the future and reorient our consciousness away from the past-present dyad of time toward the present-future dyad of time, an orientation that parallels Nietzsche's Eternal Return.

The depth of our understanding of texts depends to some degree upon the time we spend with the alienating dimensions of a text. Gadamer's concept of fusion is a symbol of successful understanding, a dramatic melding of ideas within a dialogue in which two parties or ideas "come under the influence of the truth of the object and are thus bound to one another in a new community. To reach an understanding in a dialogue is not merely a matter of putting oneself forward and successfully asserting one's own point of view but being transformed into a communion in which we do not remain what we were."[59] The act of interpretation can transform the horizons of individuals into a singular, shared moment, experience, and identity. It transforms what we know and how we know.

The disclosing of the ontological and rhetorical dimensions of the self within autobiography requires two distinct hermeneutic acts: (1) dialogical interaction with and mediation of an author and a writer (an interplay of the Inner self and the Outer self), and (2) fusion of the author's-writer's horizon with the reader's historically-effected consciousness (an interplay of the past and the present).[60] These two dialogical acts provide unity to the self and continuity to the text. They also account for the plethora of competing interpretations of texts and conflicting conceptions of the self over time. Theories that tie the meaning of texts and the process of self-knowing to the writer's intentions fail to generate this unity and continuity. Linge illustrates: "[T]he inadequacy of this [intentionalist] theory to deal positively with history is perhaps best seen in its inability to explain the host of competing interpretations of texts with which history is replete, and that in fact constitute the substance of tradition. . . . [I]nterpreters of Plato, Aristotle, or Scripture in different historical eras differed *in what they thought they saw in the text*.[61]

Like Gracia, Gadamer concludes that interpretations are neither true nor false, because commitments to correct or incorrect interpretations ignore the historicity that operates in and constitutes our understanding.[62] Unlike Gracia, Gadamer contends that interpretations do not and cannot perform a Historical Function, that is, one cannot replace one's present historicity with a past historicity, one can only engage the past from one's own present situation:

> The real meaning of a text as it addresses the interpreter does not just depend upon the occasional factors which characterize the author and his original public. For it is also always co-determined by the historical situation of the interpreter and thus by the whole of the objective course of history. . . . The meaning of a text surpasses its author (writer) not occasionally, but always. Thus understanding is not a reproductive procedure, but rather always also a productive one. . . . It suffices to say one understands *differently when one understands at all*.[63]

Understanding a text mimics understanding the self; it is a process of both discovery and creation. For example, as we read a text that is ancient and unknown to us, we open ourselves up to its potential meaning, which draws us into a dialogical encounter with the text and by proxy with ourselves. This back-and-forth game between our horizon of meaning and the text's horizon of meaning reveals the past represented through the present ideas we bring to bear on the text. The meaning of this game is codetermined by the reader in relation to the history that preceded him or her. As such, reading texts enables us to transcend our historical position in part, even though meaning is always mediated by the historicity of life. Gadamer shows the necessarily limited but unfolding understanding of reality constitutive of human existence and implicates both readers and writers in the act of interpretation.

Both writers and readers exemplify the inner and outer dimensions of the self. In conveying the self to others, writers select images both from memory and imagination, and they discover and create the self as *author*. In understanding the self, readers relate the writer to the author (and therefore the past to the present) and mediate the relation between essence and identity through a dialogical encounter within historically-effected consciousness. Writers also exemplify the two-dimensionality of experience by mapping the self in narration, which bifurcates the self into an inner and an outer self, a writer and an author. Readers exemplify this two-dimensionality by utilizing the historical and ontological structures of being to disclose the past in the present. They are, therefore, historically-effected yet future projected. Gadamer suggests that understanding first-person texts requires us to treat autobiographing texts as storehouses of possible meaning, available to us only because of our understanding of the language, the actions, the history of the text, an understanding made possible by the preconditions of understanding and the dialectical nature of the text.

The history of interpretation bears witness to the radical shift from essence to identity that we see exemplified in philosophical autobiography. With the help of thinkers such as Gracia and Gadamer, we have moved away from the idea of one "true" interpretation or ground of textual meaning to the idea of many diverse understandings of texts. Gracia argues that interpretations yield understanding rather than meaning; Gadamer argues that understanding is always conditioned by our prejudices and traditions. Nietzsche's artful transformation of history and self-identity in *Ecce Homo* exemplifies this shift in paradigms.

Nietzsche and the Subversion of the Self

Nietzsche's deconstruction of the self foreshadows his assault on truth: "'Truth' is . . . not something there, that might be found or discovered—but something that must be created and that gives a name to a process, or rather to a will to overcome that has in itself no end—introducing truth as a *process in infinitum*, an active determining—not a becoming conscious of something that is in itself firm and determined."[64] By positing truth as a product of creation and the self as an indeterminate identity whose only essence is a will to power or the potentiality to create order out of chaos, Nietzsche reorients our thinking about the self toward the creative human capacity for truth making. We have a need, he exclaims, a "need for truthfulness, the obligation to show 'by clear and constant signs' who one is."[65] *Ecce Homo* takes up this task and displaces the Inner view of the self with an exaggerated author-subject. Indeed, Nietzsche foreshadows this new Outer self in *The Gay Science* when he asserts that human beings want to become what they are: "new, unique, incomparable [spirits] who give themselves laws, who create themselves."[66]

In keeping with this perspective, the authorial voice that speaks throughout *Ecce Homo* does not claim to speak the truth, nor does it claim to represent Nietzsche's true self. Nietzsche does not write pedagogic or discursive texts modeled on traditional philosophical forms. Rather, he appropriates the creative model of the willful artist and composes aphorisms, poems, and essays of intuitive, streaming thought. His stylistic choices resonate with the figure of Dionysus, the god of wine and theater and the wearer of masks, who represents the structure of reality. Nietzsche's sardonic critique of Western thought and practice undermines the tradition of philosophical thinking about the self. It comes as no surprise that he replaces the disengaged Inner self with an 'I' perspective.

Nietzsche begins his autobiography with a reference to the temporal structure of reality: "[O]n this perfect day . . . the eye of the sun just fell upon my life. I looked back, I looked forward, and never saw so many good things at once. . . . *How could I fail to be grateful to my whole life*? and so I tell my life to *myself*."[67] Here he alludes to the linear conception of time—"looking *back*; looking *forward*"—and he reconceives time as a circle: ". . . grateful to my *whole* life." The temporal structure of reality is not determining and fading; it is ever returning and renewing itself in the affirming thoughts and practices of the artist. Because we are implicated in the circular structure of reality, we too are in the process of creation in the ever-recurring present. Temporality conceived as a series of past-present-future exists as a structure of the rational mind, not a structure of reality; "forward" and "backward," temporal descriptors of narratological notions of causality and "before" and "after" are concepts that have relative meaning according to the position one assumes. Yet the infinite flow of time—the Eternal Return—is the ground of creative possibility. In this sense, we are both discovering and creating creatures. We are conditioned by our past, as Gadamer claims, but we may also reconceive and reascribe meaning to our past in present and future experiences. This process of creative affirmation is infinite. As Martin Heidegger explains, "The gap between the past and present is no 'yawning abyss,' and the link between the present and future is constant inasmuch as *Dasein* is always projecting its possibilities."[68]

Anti-Temporality and Anti-Self

Memory presupposes a linear conception of time. Nietzsche's conception of time as a circle destroys the unity of the self in memory. If, as he argues, the will to power is the unifying force within an infinite process of self-creation, then self-affirmation and self-narration, acts of self-ascription, unify the self. Saying "yes" to the self and to life, ascribing characteristics and style to oneself, and overcoming and consecrating one's past in the present create a self. Understanding oneself means understanding one's twofold relation to the will to power: the dissolution of the self into an infinite will and the individuation of the self within the circular process of creation. Nietzsche proclaims, "This dual series of experiences, this access to apparently separate worlds, is repeated in my nature in every respect: I am a Doppelgänger. I have a 'second' face in addition to my first. And perhaps also a third."[69]

Nietzsche ascribes many author-subjects to his multiplying masks: Dionysus, Zarathustra, the Antichrist, an Immoralist. The 'I' of his texts does not always refer to the historical figure or writer, Friedrich Nietzsche, nor does it signify the same authorial persona. Nietzsche proves that the process of self-construction—the process of ascribing style and character to individuate the ego from the infinite will to power—requires us to privilege some character traits and ignore others. Consequently, the self is always concealed, and self-identity is always changing. We must continuously overcome ourselves in the world. Nehamas draws out the implications of Nietzsche's view to illustrate the positive consequences of an otherwise seemingly destructive view: "The unity of the self, which therefore also constitutes its identity, is not something given but something achieved, not a beginning but a goal."[70]

Self-narration exemplifies the endless process of unifying the self. Here it is important to recall how much Nietzsche relies upon literary models for understanding the world.[71] He urges us to become disciples of artists and then to extend their projects to life: "For with them [artists] this subtle power [of organizing character traits, customs, and so on] usually comes to an end where art ends and life begins; but we want to be the poets of our life."[72] One way to become what one is is to *write* oneself—to self-narrate:

> To "give style" to one's character—a great and rare art! It is practiced by those who survey all the strengths and weaknesses of their nature and then fit them into an artistic plan until every one of them appears as art and reason and even weaknesses delight the eye. . . . Much that is vague and resisted shaping has been saved and exploited for distant views. . . . In the end, when the work is finished, it becomes evident how the constraint of a single taste governed and formed everything large and small. Whether this taste is good or bad is less important than one might suppose, if only it was a single taste![73]

Anti-Autobiography

Does the act of writing philosophical autobiography enable Nietzsche to understand the self and articulate his understanding to others? Does *Ecce Homo* unify him? Yes and no. One reason Nietzsche wrote *Ecce Homo* was to resolve the apparent incongruity of his earlier texts.[74] Yet his autobiography is an anti-autobiography. Manipulating the traditional devices of autobiography, Nietzsche posits many author-subjects and ascribes contradictory claims and traits to them. Though he *as* writer-self remains concealed by the masked subjects he wears, he nonetheless creates a destabilizing interplay between the infinite, unindividuated will to power and an individuated multiplicity of author-subjects. This interplay provides continuity to his work, but his multiple self-presentations give style rather than unity to the author-subjects he projects.

Disclosing the essence of the self simultaneously conceals his identity. Who then is Nietzsche? This question is absurd from a Nietzschean perspective:

> . . . there are by now many different versions of Nietzsche, many of which (like the versions of literary characters) are inconsistent with one another. And this, as I think Nietzsche actually hoped, may make the questions "Who is the real Nietzsche? Which is the correct interpretation of his view?" as easy or as difficult to answer, and perhaps as pointless to pose as "Who is the real Odysseus? Which is the correct version of his story?" . . . In his [Nietzsche's] eyes at least, it is only such a character who can influence history and thought. . . . To make a perfectly unified character out of all that one has done, as Nietzsche wants, may involve us in a vicious effort: we may have to be writing our autobiography as we are living our life, and we would also have to be writing about writing that autobiography . . . and so on, and so on without end. But as Nietzsche had written long before his own end: "Not every end is a goal. A melody's end is not its goal; nevertheless, so long as the melody has not reached its end, it also has not reached its goal."[75]

Throughout *Ecce Homo,* Nietzsche satirizes himself as a philosopher and scholar, hence, the section titles "Why I Write Such Good Books" and "Why I Am So Clever." He does this, in White's view,

> [p]recisely so that we won't take his self-presentation completely seriously. Through exaggeration and hyperbole, Nietzsche offers a self-portrait which calls itself into question at the same time as it focuses our attention upon the traditional devices of autobiography.[76]

When writing in the voice of Zarathustra, he becomes who he is for *that* text, *that* view, *that* philosophy: "For that is what I am through and through: reeling, reeling in, raising up, raising, a raiser, cultivator, and disciplinarian, who once counseled himself, not for nothing: Become who you are!"[77] Not surprisingly, *Ecce Homo* illustrates two forms of self-concealment: the ontological concealment of the writer-self by the author-subject and the rhetorical masking of the author-subject/s by the narration of the writer-self. This interplay between the writer and the author exemplifies the narrative process by which the self becomes both Inner and Outer, enabling us to see our lives as Nietzsche saw his own—as a whole.

Though Augustine, Descartes, and Rousseau conceive the self from a first-person perspective, the use of philosophical autobiography to subvert the self begins with Nietzsche's *Ecce Homo.* He argues that the self is an autobiographing subject who is always and necessarily masked: "However strongly one may develop upwards and appear to leap from one contradiction to another, a close observation will reveal the dovetails where the new building grows out of the old. This is the biographers' task: they must reflect upon their subject on the principle that nature takes no jumps."[78] The reader must reveal the conditions of life that give rise to so many rhetorical masks. In doing so, the reader must assume an interpretative stance toward the self, a stance that enables him or her to reconsider his or her essence and identity. Nietzsche's philosophy necessitates a new audience.

Writing the Author

Autobiographers aim to provide continuity to human experience. We see this reflected in the writer's desire to achieve specific narrative ends—literary, moral, and political. Self-narration may unify our lives from a first-person perspective, but it may also disrupt or disorder our lives as it stabilizes and destabilizes self-identity. Since our literary, moral, and political ends as authors can only be achieved in the act of interpretation, human agency is a condition of autobiography. Self-narration assumes both a means of communication (theory/text/painting/person) and a receiver of the communicated message.

Without readers, there can be no textual meaning, no authorial identity. Yet the meaning of texts also depends upon the reader's sensibilities and identity. Martha Nussbaum explains how a reader's ability to understand authorial experiences and perspectives varies according to his or her experiences and perspectives as well, that is, upon his or her ability to understand other human beings:

> [I]n the reading of a literary text, there is a standard of correctness set by the author's sense of life, as it finds its way into the work. And the text, approached as the creation of human intentions, is some fraction or element of a real human being.[79]

Following Nussbaum's suggestion, I maintain that all literary works, fictional and nonfictional, autobiographical and nonautobiographical, are products of the constructive work of writers whose ideas emerge from lived experience. First-person texts in particular represent the interplay of fact and fiction in two ways: (1) Ordinary human encounters are common literary themes, autobiographical or not. (2) Personal experiences and ideas reflect the sociohistorical context in which writers live. My first point is that fiction and nonfiction, autobiography and nonautobiography, are character and culture dependent. Because the characters within written works interact within a specific context, they do not simply exist as placeholders for human agents; rather, they function *as* human agents (sometimes universally and sometimes existentially). My second point is that there are no independent knowers in any world, fictional or nonfictional, artistic or scientific. Knowers, like agents, live in a particular time and place where certain worldviews are prominent and others are not. These prominent worldviews shape the ideas of writers so that even original or inventive ideas respond to familiar ideas. Both readers and writers are limited by the worlds in which they live. Yet all literary works are aesthetic objects of both seeing and making. Once interpreted, they reveal the insights of the reader and the prejudices of the writer (born out in the author-subject). Therefore, our viewing them *as* intentionally constructed *and* discovered aesthetic objects is essential to understanding them. Nussbaum writes:

> [E]very perspective, in order to do its work, must be determinate and intelligible. But the difference in each perspective . . . is the produced or fictional element contributed by the artistic root of human nature in response to . . . the root of discovery.[80]

I share Nussbaum's conviction that our reactions and emotive responses to texts bear on life and literature in the same dramatic way:

> [L]ife is never simply *presented* by a text; it is always *represented as* something. This "as" can, and must, be seen not only in the paraphrasable content, but also in the style, which itself expresses choices and selections, and sets up, in the reader, certain activities and transactions rather than others.[81]

Choices emerge out of the richness of our own and others' lives. Nussbaum's claim not only casts doubt upon reductive philosophical theories but on reductive views of life and of the self as well. Philosophical autobiography (like all forms of literature) can be a corrective to life. Specifically, it can edify our conceptions of the self.

Nietzsche exemplifies the edifying process of self-creation throughout *Ecce Homo*. Though he regards this process as infinite, this does not mean that one's autobiography is pointless. Rather, this means, as Michel Haar explains, that "Nietzsche's method aims at unmasking, unearthing, but in an indefinite way—i.e., without ever pretending to lift the last veil to reveal any originary identity, any primary foundation."[82] Self-construction is neither arbitrary nor accidental; it is simply inconclusive. Hence, a narrative should not be considered absurd, as Nietzsche attempts to show, just because it lacks a moral that the reader can extract from the narrative and succinctly describe.[83] By contrast, "A narrative is not successful because it allows one to provide such a short answer to the question of its point. A successful narrative does not allow the question to be raised at all. The narrative has already supplied the answer before the question is asked. The narrative itself is the answer."[84] What matters for Nietzsche is that we remain committed to constructing and reconstructing our identities and strive to overcome deterministic views of the self, even if we consistently fall short of this goal. We must orient our actions toward a self that we confront and that confronts us back, a self that we choose yet continually remake. This creative interplay between self-discovery and self-creation culminates in a life of self-knowing. Nussbaum believes that a similar experience of self-knowing can occur in the reading of texts. She writes, "Our actual relation to the books we love is already messy, complex, erotic. We do 'read for life,' bringing to the literary texts we love . . . our pressing questions and perplexities, searching for images of what we might do and be, and holding these up against the images we derive from our knowledge of other conceptions, literary, philosophical, and religious."[85]

Both Nietzsche and Nussbaum show that the dialectical interplay between the Inner self and the Outer self challenges our conceptions of the self and self-identity. As we read first-person texts, we mediate the relation between the author and writer of texts, *and* we mediate the relation between ourselves and others. By fusing our horizons with the alienating other who stands not only outside but against us, we reconcile the Inner and Outer dimensions of our being in the world. We also reshape our notions of the self and our conceptions of identity.

The Gendered Subject

The interplay between the Inner self and the Outer self surfaces in the dialectical history of the terms *gender* and *race*. I focus on gender here because it intersects with philosophical autobiography in four ways. First, gender provides an opening for concrete reflection about the Inner-Outer self, wherein the Inner self is human, the Outer self is male or female. Second, the autobiographical author-subject is always a gendered subject, whereas race remains mysteriously concealed in much discourse. Third, Barnes's philosophical autobiography uses gender to reevaluate the relation between the writer and the author; it therefore exemplifies the intersection between philosophical autobiography and gender. And fourth, gender, like autobiography, functions both as a means for presenting oneself to others and as a lens through which we understand ourselves.

In keeping with the dialectical history of the self, the concept of 'gender' has also shifted away from an Inner perspective—a deterministic perspective—to an Outer perspective—a constructivist perspective. Originally conceived as a set of biophysical structures and innate psychosocial constitutions, gender was thought to be determined by the Internal (or Inner) structures of the physical body. In his Pulitzer Prize-winning novel, *Middlesex*, Jeffrey Eugenides argues that well into the nineteenth century biologists regarded the presence of either gonadal tissue or ovarian tissue in infants as the sole criterion for gender.[86] Today, the term *gender* signifies a much broader and more complex notion of identity, which includes socially constructed behaviors and characteristics that combine with biophysical structures and hormonal levels to delineate maleness and femaleness. Though gender attributes or characteristics are thought to arise from biological differences, they are no longer attributed to innate biological differences.

As we saw in the examples of philosophical autobiography, some individuals and cultures are tilted strongly toward an Inner or innate concept of 'gender' both in their thinking and in their comportment toward the world. Religious communities in particular tend to delineate gender roles by sex rather than by behavior or characteristics. As a child of the American South, one of the nursery rhymes I learned as a young girl ended with the lines ". . . snakes and snails and puppy-dog tails, that's what little boys are made of/sugar and spice and everything nice, that's what little girls are made of." Other social groups are tilted toward the Outer or constructivist concept of 'gender.' They jettison the concept of innate biological difference and choose instead to appropriate male and female characteristics, regardless of their biological structures. Still others strive to neutralize the role of gender in identity formation and in social contexts by assuming androgynous behaviors, looks, and roles in their homes and communities.

Our binary understanding of gender provides for concrete reflection about essence and identity. The female author-subject, for example, has long represented an amorphous *other*. Feminist scholars Carolyn Heilbrun and Judith Butler suggest that for centuries both in America and abroad the concept of 'woman' designated the negation of all things male: *not* strong; *not* rational; *not* moral; and so on. Modern feminists protested male-only customs and practices, such as voting and schooling, to show the absence of women in society. In Mary Wollstonecraft's *A Vindication of the Rights of Woman* (1792), the *other* that defines the concept of 'woman' is not only 'man' but the society that privileges maleness. Indeed, some of the fear that fed the anti-suffragist movement in England in the late 1800s and early 1900s was the idea that women with "male" rights might *become* men (or male-like).

The existential feminism of de Beauvoir, however, exploits the Outer, constructivist view of gender to show that society, *not* biology, determines the meaning of 'woman.' She argues famously in *The Second Sex* that a woman merely assumes an identity constructed for her: she *becomes* a woman. Her freedom is contingent upon her ability to remake herself. In advancing this argument, de Beauvoir creates an intersection between autobiographical writing and gender: woman must *write* herself. As Nancy K. Miller puts it, "To justify an unorthodox life by writing about it is to reinscribe the original violation, to reviolate masculine turf."[87]

Questions regarding the *kind* of author-subject that readers confront in autobiographical writing emerge here, as do the conditions constitutive of the author as 'male' or 'female' (or the writer as 'man' or 'woman'). These conditions include the relation between the body and the self—one's sex and one's subjecthood. They also include the relation between gender and rhetorical stance-authorial voice. Though contemporary feminist theories reflect class, racial, sexual, and cultural differences, they share the belief that 'woman' is a construct; hence, we can no longer tether 'woman' to the 'feminine' *other* or to the sexed body. In *What Can She Know? Feminist Theory and the Construction of Knowledge*, Lorraine Code argues that the sex of the knower is one among a cluster of subjective factors pertaining to the circumstances of cognitive agents that constitute conceptions of knowledge and knowers and give rise to knowledge of others as well as self-knowledge.

Though some autobiographies introduce conceptions of gender that are unique to their self-representations, most assume the conceptions of their culture. The Inner view of gender—the positing of an innate and abiding essence that constitutes a man and woman—emerges out of the sociopolitical regulation of power within culture. Gender, then, is a discursively situated mode of understanding that is shaped by the extant power structures in societies. It reflects the particularly weighted position from which Barnes and others speak, a position we choose freely and express explicitly. In point of fact, Butler argues that because one becomes a woman, 'woman' is a concept in process, a becoming that cannot be said to originate or to end, a notion that does not attach innately or naturally either to a male or female body. Gender is not a closed-off category. Nonetheless, gender conditions the author-subject, which is why I recognize the unique position of Barnes's autobiography in this study. Gender shapes the writer's relation to the author, the way in which the writer chooses to represent himself or herself to the world. It illustrates the delicate interplay between our introspected ideas of ourselves and our alterspected presentations for others. It depicts the phenomenological difference between our experiences of our minds and bodies and the social orientation of our minds and bodies in the world. It suggests that we, both men and women, are also *other*. Gendered beings are always both Inner and Outer selves (part discovered, part created).

Yet the balance between the two selves weighs on the psyche. bell hooks describes the difficulty of managing our inner sense of self and our outer identity as a conflict of wills:

> Sometimes . . . it seems like I am living two separate lives. . . . One way I cope with these two identities is to have different names. As a writer I use bell hooks. . . . Two names will help me to practice detachment—remind me always that I am not my writing always something more. And that it is useful not to be identified with the

> ego. . . . Even striving to be a writer demands more of a public self than I want to be. The contemplative life is so much the life I long for—the space I need to write it.[88]

This interplay gets reflected in the rhetorical stance of the writer as well. Women and men write autobiographies for different reasons. Perhaps because writing was originally a male activity relinquished to women reluctantly, or because men and women map their lives and themselves in different ways, the efforts of women to *write themselves* exaggerate the interplay between the Inner self and the Outer self in significant and useful ways.

Writing Gender

That women and men graph their lives and map themselves in different ways and for different reasons is not a new insight. I introduce this point, however, to connect the discussion of gender to autobiographical writing more generally and to bring my analysis full circle. In Chapter 1, I enumerated five reasons humans write autobiography: (1) to achieve self-knowledge; (2) to unify the self; (3) to communicate the self to others; (4) to give continuity to their lives; (5) to explore the relation between the self and the subject. The question that I concern myself with here is which of these five reasons motivate women autobiographers, both historically and philosophically, and which motivate men autobiographers? What do these motivations suggest about men's and women's views of the self? What are the philosophical and psychological implications of the differences between men's and women's autobiographies?

Carolyn G. Heilbrun, the author of *Writing a Woman's Life*, successfully shows that women autobiographers of the eighteenth and nineteenth centuries wrote to instantiate a self in the world—to create a unifying and meaningful locus of experience. Men, however, who had enjoyed a long and rich tradition of male autobiography, wrote to demonstrate the achievements of their lives.[89] Sadly, Heilbrun notes that during these approximate 200 years, women autobiographers have consistently failed to demonstrate a clear sense of who they are in comparison to their male counterparts. They also have been reluctant to speak about themselves as responsible and self-deserving agents. Instead, they have credited their good fortune as successful writers to God, to men, or to Providence.[90]

This paradigm began to change in the twentieth century. As women began to gain political rights and liberties, they embraced new forms of autobiographical writing and developed distinct rhetorical stances. Heilbrun marks this change by distinguishing between the characteristics of "old" and "new" modes of autobiographical writing. For example, she says of May Sarton, the American poet, novelist, and memoirist, ". . . she had written in the old genre of female autobiography, which tends to find beauty even in pain and to transform rage into spiritual acceptance."[91] Nonetheless, the advances in women's autobiography were slow in coming. Schuster points to the undervaluing of women's work as the primary reason for the sometimes paltry examples of women's autobiography:

> Though in the twentieth century women obtained greater possibilities in this region of intellectual life [writing autobiography], the male still predominated among the philosophical autobiographers. Hagiographies on women and autobiographies by women saints were not uncommon throughout the Middle Ages and even after; however, these saintly lives are not necessarily concerned with philosophy. In *A History of Women in the West*, one is confronted with the many limitations imposed on women in the past: "Roles for which women were destined were silent ones: motherhood and homemaking, tasks relegated to the obscurity of a domesticity that did not count and were not considered worth recounting. Did women so much as have a history?"[92]

One implication of both Heilbrun's study of autobiography and Schuster's argument is that women autobiographers internalize the predominant and regulative concept of gender from which their identities and paradigms for behavior derive. In the eighteenth and nineteenth centuries, women were considered naturally quiet, soft, emotional, and irrational. Men, however, enjoyed the benefits of male privilege and the inferences regarding male gender that followed: strong, rational, sensible, and autonomous. Society regarded women as physically and intellectually inferior to men.

Carolyn Korsmeyer notes that the eighteenth and nineteenth centuries' conception of 'woman' extended to the belief that women are "complete" when they embody and exemplify those virtues that reinforce their delicate and fragile nature, virtues such as "kindness, humility, gentleness, protectiveness, and so on."[93] Women achieved these ideal virtues through the repetitious performance of domestic activities, such as tending house, raising children, and consoling their husbands. These associations fostered a cult of domesticity and created the subliminal message that women should not permit themselves to contemplate the tasks of men. Not surprisingly, the author-subjects of the first women autobiographers are self-effacing, gentle, obsequious, and deferential.

Historically, cultural figures drew gender-based inferences to segregate men's and women's activities, both in location and in kind. This extended to writing as well. Paradigms of "natural" behavior developed along gender lines and influenced the ways in which women and men thought and wrote about themselves. Men and women internalized these paradigms and mirrored gender-appropriate behavior in society. They therefore experienced life through gender; they educated themselves according to its rules; they *wore* gender. The male and female psyche became visible in speech, dress, mannerisms, and behavior. And these differences, however arbitrary and artificial, perpetuated male dominance. As Korsmeyer rightly argues, the organization of distinct male and female tasks "can in no way be construed as a doctrine of 'separate but equal.' . . . Women's sphere and the female virtues are to be considered more accurately as a glorification of a genuinely inferior social status."[94]

Drawing on Robin Lakoff's work in social linguistics,[95] Susan Feldman argues that women not only participate in the roles, expectations, and assumptions of male-dominated traditions, they possess linguistic traits that reflect those traditions.[96] For instance, women's speech patterns reflect various lexical, phonological, and syntactico-pragmatic traits that mirror the social disempowerment of women. Though women have attempted to transcend their experiences of marginalization by appropriating male roles and assuming male identities, Feldman suggests that their voices remain *other*. This otherness carries over into writing as well. As Patricia Spacks argues, "The face a man turns to the world . . . typically embodies his strength, while the only acceptable models for women involve self-deception and yielding."[97]

The gender based differences between men and women autobiographers surface in other features of their work as well. Mary Mason observes the interesting fact that the pattern of autobiographical writing as confession, the pattern established by Augustine and Rousseau, is not modeled in women's autobiographies, for two possible reasons. First, women have difficulty admitting that their life choices, especially when they are successful, were fully their own, and/or that their lives are significant.[98] Second, women tend not to identify with (or perhaps they have been deprived of) written forms that demonstrate personal power and control, either because power and control have been considered masculine, or because women prefer a world without such demonstrable power and control.[99] Thus women who wrote autobiographies during the eighteenth and nineteenth centuries did so in order to organize their experiences and to explore the relationship between writing and understanding, not to unify themselves, to know themselves, or to communicate their self-identity to others.[100] Again, the public conception of the term *woman* opposed the positive qualities attributed to men: women were *not* rational, were *not* strong, were *not* autonomous, and so on. Because of the negative instantiation of 'woman,' women writers lacked the motivating force to create a positive and personal conception of the self. Hence, women lacked a self to be either discovered or created.

Critical theorists and feminists have spent the past century trying to overturn the views of women and men they deem false. Their efforts have been at least partially successful. Contemporary examples of women's autobiography no longer succumb to the flawed views of the self. Women today fully endorse their existence as unique individuals within a unique set of other women. When Julia Kristeva was asked, in a 1996 interview, "What does it mean to you to write at the end of the twentieth century?", she replied, "It means trying to be the most personal I can be by eluding all forms of pressure, whether that's from groups, the media, public opinion, or ideology."[101] Women in the twentieth century gained access to their own personality structures because notions of personhood were extended to them. Kristeva goes on to argue that "writing 'as a woman' . . . should be subordinated to the necessity of writing in one's own name."[102] She, like her male counterparts, is pushing to privilege identity over essence while recognizing the two as proper counterbalançes to one another. In order to maintain the rich interplay between the Inner self and the Outer self, an interplay that we cannot escape, women must create their identities in response to the embedded notions of gender that ground their being in the world.

Contemporary feminists Code and Butler support this move toward the creation of a personal and an autonomous 'I' out of the falsely posited inclusiveness of the term *woman*. In *Gender Trouble*, Butler describes the problems that arise from treating "woman" as a homogeneous category:

> If one "is" a woman, that is surely not all one is; the term fails to be exhaustive, not because a pregendered "person" transcends the specific paraphernalia of its gender, but because gender is not always constituted coherently or consistently in different historical contexts, and because gender intersects with racial, class, ethnic, sexual, and regional modalities of discursively constituted identities.[103]

Code extends Butler's point to writing in general, including autobiographical writing, hoping to refute the attempt by some feminists to find a common woman's voice. She claims that the search for "a common voice" negates the differences that women possess and the subjects that their autobiographies create.[104] Autobiographies "speak a subjectivity that is specifically located, yet open to interpretation, dialogue, and analysis on the basis of the positions it occupies and those it refuses. Nor would it be legitimate to read women's autobiographies as efforts to construct a representative self who could stand for all women."[105]

The interplay between the Inner self and the Outer self surfaces phenomenologically in women's struggle for power and autonomy. On the one hand, women seek unity in solidarity, hoping to gain power and recognition by identifying themselves with a homogenous and marginalized group. On the other, they seek to individuate themselves and find autonomous voices and individual identities. This encounter between the universal and existential condition of women creates a rich middle ground in which the self is refigured. The efforts of women to open up the concept of 'woman' so that it is *neither* Inner *nor* Outer but *both* Inner *and* Outer—general and particular, objective and subjective, referential and signifying, descriptive and ascriptive—undermine weak conceptions of woman based upon bad science and distorted metaphysics. Though the motivational gap between men's and women's autobiography is closing, and women such as Hazel Barnes are writing for reasons that have long been associated with men, I think women's autobiography will remain distinct from men's autobiography primarily because our culture remains committed to gender distinctions, distinctions that shape our experiences in the world.

The interplay between the writer-self and the author-subject illustrates that every writer is both an Inner self and the Outer self tilted toward a particular conception of the self, which shapes his or her identity. Likewise, the interplay between the human self and the gendered subject emerges in the phenomenological experiences of beings-in-the-world. It is mediated both by self-reflection and social reflection (by us and others), and it generates a rich dialectic of the self that mirrors the dialectic of the self in autobiography. Not only is every writer both an Inner self and the Outer self, every *person* is an Inner self and the Outer self. Gender represents the ongoing interplay between essence and identity that defines human existence.

Conclusions

As a genre of writing and a method for self-knowing, philosophical autobiography bifurcates the self into an Inner self and the Outer self, an introspectively discovered and abiding essence (soul, cogito, historical consciousness) over and against a created and changing identity (will or ego). The philosophical autobiographers I analyze in this book assume various postures toward the self. Nietzsche, for example, locates himself within the Outer perspective and calls the self a sociopolitical mistake—an ego that is added to a set of deeds for the purpose of contract creation. By contrast, Augustine reformulates the Platonic notion of an Inner self that forgets itself during the fall into the body. He argues that the chasm between humans and God is created by sin, which separates humans from their original state and blinds them to the depth of their existence, thus preventing them from seeing the essence of their being. "If I had been able to believe," he discloses, "I might have been cured."[106] *Confessions* enables Augustine to recall himself, to meditate, pray, repent, and thereby render himself truthfully to his reader.[107] Descartes complicates the Inner view of the self by assuming a deeply rhetorical stance in *Meditations*. Barnes adds a consciousness-constructing ego to the Outer view of the self. And Rousseau offers a middle perspective between the two.

Like Plato before him, Augustine aims to recover the human and divine elements of existence provided by memory, thereby bridging the past fall of humankind and the present experience of life with a culminating future return to God. Self-reflection in this context is a process of self-discovery characterized by acts of introspection and retrospection—looking inward, looking backward. He argues that through memory, a distention of the mind, the self is unified, and life becomes continuous; thus the self is introspectively realized and retrospectively organized. Augustine is the first philosophical autobiographer to justify self-existence through the formulation of a cogito wherein reflexive awareness of the self verifies existence of the 'I.' The author-subject that pervades Augustine's work offers "a certainty of self-presence."[108]

Despite Augustine's important contribution to the genre of autobiography, his *Confessions* was not recognized as a philosophical exposition of the self until the Enlightenment, when it became widely held that human beings are abiding substances unified through deductive cognition. Descartes disengages himself from God and the world in order to hear and examine cognitive capacities, capacities that make the self transparent to itself and make identity transparent to essence. Because the self is a thinking thing, Descartes reasons that we derive the identity of the inner "thing" and prove the existence of the Outer "being" through thought. He concludes that self-knowledge transcends language and observation. As Hans-Georg Gadamer observes in his own autobiography:

> Descartes' rejection of historical and traditional prejudices as the starting points of knowledge forced him to fall back upon the isolated self in his quest for a certain foothold in knowledge. He [Descartes] held unprejudiced "self"-knowledge to be certain because of its autonomous location outside the flux of contemporary opinion and the handed-down literary tradition upon which opinion is based.[109]

Descartes' reformulation of the Augustinian cogito—I am doubting, therefore I am thinking, therefore I exist—exemplifies the modern penchant for disengaged self-reflection:

> . . . the modern ideal of disengagement requires a reflexive stance. We have to turn inward and become aware of our own activity and of the processes which form us. We have to take charge of constructing our own representation of the world, which otherwise goes on without order. . . . Disengagement demands that we stop simply living in the body or within our tradition or habits and, by making them objects for us, subject them to radical scrutiny and remaking.[110]

Descartes' abstraction of the cogito leads to a bifurcation of the mind and the body, a bifurcation that is later unified in the abiding physiological structures and substance of the brain, not in the phenomenological experiences of existence. From a Cartesian perspective, self-reflection is a process of discovery or introspection *only*.

Rousseau attempts to temper Cartesian rationalism with emotion by presenting humans as creatures of reason and feeling. He directs his reflections back to the world to justify his actions. He thus hopes to represent himself as a figure of the "inner citadel."[111] By conflating the Inner self and the Outer self into one historical figure, Rousseau redefines the self as a composite of intellect and emotion and unified in history through the due influence of the past over the present. He relies on history to provide continuity and unity to the self, a self that is incidentally embedded in time. Yet Rousseau maintains that the self's identity is determined by the social forces in which the self is situated, because time is historicized. He also believes that our identities can be altered through writing, our narratives challenged, and our selves bracketed, allowing the author of texts to merge with the writer of texts, and blurring the rhetorical and ontological dimensions of the self. Dilthey concludes that ". . . whatever he [Rousseau] had done and suffered and whatever was corrupt within him, he felt, and this was, after all, the ideal of his age, that he was a noble, generous soul who felt for humanity. This he wanted to show the world; he wanted to justify his spiritual existence by showing it exactly as it was."[112] The invocation of the historical figure in *The Confessions* initiates the shift from the Inner to the Outer self. Self-reflection for Rousseau is an act of creation disguised as an act of discovery.

Nietzsche shatters the concept of the self as an Inner essence when he announces the death of God. He shrouds the self in literary rather than metaphysical terms, denying the essentialist metaphysics of his philosophical forefathers. He argues that those who deny the transitory nature of existence, the herd, are unable to look into the chaos of life and will the self. They choose instead to posit fixed but false ideals: life-denying ideals. *Ecce Homo* aims to turn the self on its head. By arguing that the self is merely a host of perspectives erupting from a posited point of origin—the will to power—Nietzsche suggests that the self is created rather than discovered. In doing so, he raises doubts about theories of the self that universalize experience and moralize being. Subsequent views of the self such as Barnes's lose their essentialist edge and gain a perspectivist flair. In fact, many of the constructivist views that displace the Inner self reveal the linguistic characteristics of the late Wittgenstein and early Derrida. Scholars began to embrace the view that the understanding of human life and of the social world is an unending, discursive task. Martin Heidegger and Hans-Georg Gadamer recast the self in hermeneutic terms.

Barnes extends the literary and hermeneutic analyses of the self to psychological and sociological conceptions of the 'I' as an ego in the world and not merely a persona in a text. In her hands, the self becomes a mask-wearing subject whose existence conceals the fluid and ego-dissolving nature of consciousness. She argues that self-representation maps but does not create the contingency and freedom of the self, for the self is not a fixed, enduring object unified by the mind through memory or history. Rather, it is an ever-changing ego constructed by an alterspecting consciousness.

Following Nietzsche's and Barnes's lead, contemporary theorists view the self as a construct that individuals co-create and co-interpret. We see this transition within the genre of philosophical autobiography as well. Once regarded as a subdivision of biography, philosophical autobiography circumscribes a meaningful process of self-reflection that proceeds from the absolute notion of God through the unifying elements of memory and time to a confrontation with the bifurcated self.[113] The transition from disengaged conceptions of the self to historically and socially affected notions of subjectivity parallels the literary transition from ancient forms of hagiography to postmodern styles of autobiography. From a philosophical perspective, the movement from the Inner self to the Outer self represents a movement from the universal to the particular.

Rather than live out our autobiographical accounts, we live up to them. We strive to unify our selves and provide continuity to our experiences through self-reflection and self-narration. To reconcile our inner sense of being and our outward identity in the world, we must reevaluate the relation between self-discovery and self-creation, between the Inner self and the Outer self. Philosophical autobiography preserves this relation and thus creates the conditions for self-knowing by embedding memory and/or consciousness within the process of self-reflective narration. The phenomenological structure of the self and the process of finding, masking, and making the self that arises from it connects and counterbalances the past and the present. The dialectical confrontation with the bifurcated self recontextualizes experience and generates new forms of self-reflection.

Acts of interpretation preserve the interplay between the past and future, an interplay that is realized in the present through the fusion of textual horizons and the infinity of new understandings. The hermeneutic encounter between the reader and the autobiographical text transforms the self into an introspective, a retrospective, and an alterspective being-in-the-world. Hence, philosophical autobiography discloses the discovered self (the writer-self circumscribed and unified by time, memory, and history) *and* the created self (the radically free and self-constructing author-subject inscribed in language).

This narrative interplay within philosophical autobiography illustrates the phenomenological interplay of the self in the world. Because gender denotes the Inner and Outer natures of our being in concrete and explicit ways, it offers us a way of reevaluating essence and identity, a way of recognizing and exaggerating the Inner and Outer dimensions of our existence. For example, gender discloses our human essence and our male or female identity. Though we each represent a gendered category, we defy those categories by projecting our own distinctive identities in the world. Sometimes we conceal ourselves by wearing masks that hide our fragmenting selves. Sometimes we fool ourselves into thinking that we are nothing other than our masks. Yet we remain more: more than our masks, more than our bodies, more than our gender, more than our narratives. And we remain *other*. Our pasts circumscribe us, our memories track us, our minds absorb us, and our identities fix us. We nonetheless detach from these representations, altering ourselves and our identities. Functioning as a corrective to the fragmenting nature of life, philosophical autobiography locates the self in the rich and mysterious middle ground between essence and identity, between the psyche and the ego, between order and chaos.

The search for the self leads neither to the Inner self nor the Outer self but to the middle self between the two. The dialectical history of the self that suffuses philosophical autobiography exemplifies the infinite interplay between the Inner self and the Outer self. Philosophical autobiographers utilize the introspective, retrospective, and alterspective modes of self-reflection as a means of self-examination. Looking inward, backward, and outward, they show that self-narration does not culminate in self-knowledge; rather, it initiates an ongoing process of self-knowing. By embracing the Inner and Outer dimensions of our being—by both discovering and creating ourselves—we implicate ourselves in the process of self-knowing and artful living. We satisfy the Delphic dictum, "Know thyself," in the richest possible sense.

Notes

INTRODUCTION

1. Plato, *The Symposium*, trans. Alexander Nehamas and Paul Woodruff (Indianapolis, IN, and Cambridge, MA: Hackett, 1989), 175d.

2. Ibid., 209d, 223d.

3. By writing, we avoid the fate of *The Symposium's* Alciabiades, a student of Socrates', who returns to his old ways once he leaves his teacher's side.

4. There are others ways to define and classify "philosophical autobiography." Schlomit C. Schuster, for example, defines it as "a narrative self-questioning of the self, its social context, and existence at large." See *The Philosopher's Autobiography: A Qualitative Study* (Westport, CT: Praeger, 2003), 16.

I define philosophical autobiography more descriptively as self-reflection in first-person narration. Within the larger rubric of "self-reflection," I include three distinct modes of reflection: introspection (looking within the self/life; seeing the self from within); retrospection (looking back on the self/life; seeing the self from without); and alterspection (looking outside and beyond the self/life; seeing the self as a disconnected, discontinuous Other).

5. Alexander Nehamas, *The Art of Living* (Berkeley: University of California Press, 1998), 5.

6. Ibid., 2–3.

7. For similar analyses of self-presentation within written texts, see Michel Foucault, "What Is an Author?," in *The Foucault Reader*, ed. Paul Rabinow (New York: Pantheon Books, 1984), 101–20, and Paul Ricoeur, *Oneself As Another*, trans. Kathleen Blamey (Chicago: University of Chicago Press, 1992).

8. Carl G. Vaught, *The Quest for Wholeness* (Albany: State University of New York Press, 1992), 3.

9. Karen Hanson, *The Self Imagined: Philosophical Reflections on the Social Character of Psyche* (New York: Routledge & Kegan Paul, 1986), 152.

10. See Shlomite C. Schuster, *The Philosopher's Autobiography*, 205.

11. I had the privilege of sitting in on Carl Vaught's Augustine course in the fall of 2003. It was in this context that he made this statement about Augustine's *Confessions*.

12. This particular articulation of Descartes' modus operandi summarizes Carl Vaught's view of Cartesian philosophy. Stanley Rosen and Anne-Marie Bowery have articulated similar views in different places.

13. Autobiographers of the Post-classical and Renaissance periods assume that philosophical views of the self determine (and should be reflected in) literary descriptions of the subject, whereas autobiographers of the Modern period, such as Nietzsche and Barnes, challenge the widely held view that self-identity arises from the unity of one's experiences organized over time.

14. We see this process exhibited, for example, in popular role-playing Internet games such as XMEN and JUBILEE, games wherein participants create characters and enact story lines they co-create with other online participants.

15. Sean Murphy, "Art: The Movement," in *New Cultural Icons*, ed. Sean Murphy (July 2002): 19.

16. Gerald Marzorati, "Phat Folk," *New York Times Magazine*, July 14, 2002, 30.

17. Sean Murphy, "Literature: The Movement," in *New Cultural Icons*, ed. Sean Murphy (July 2002): 23.

18. Though it is an ontological phenomenon, self-deception is paralleled on the rhetorical level.

19. Nehamas, *The Art of Living*, 24–25.

20. Friedrich Nietzsche, *Ecce Homo*, trans. and ed. Walter Kaufmann (New York: Random House, 1967), 315, emphasis in original.

21. Ibid., 335.

22. Plato, *Phaedrus*, in *The Collected Dialogues of Plato*, trans. R. Hackforth (Princeton, NJ: Princeton University Press, 1989), 230a.

Chapter 1

1. Nietzsche, *Ecce Homo*, 217. Nietzsche's expressed desire to expose his "true" self is, of course, ironic, but his intention to be heard as the man who authored a set of sometimes incongruous texts and aphorisms is honest. His analysis of his life's work through an autobiographical form strengthens his conviction that his texts alone unify his personality, his person, and his perspective.

2. Our first task in considering autobiography as a method of philosophical exposition is to state, examine, and either accept or reject competing presuppositions of the self.

3. I elaborate on Grice's and Austin's theory of speech act in Chapter 2.

4. A genealogical examination of the 'I' would include the following: the Cartesian cogito or thinking thing whose essence entails its own existence; Thomas Hobbes's

and John Locke's social contract theories wherein individuals surrender their rights to a sovereign person or body (either permanently or temporarily) in exchange for protection; John Stuart Mill's argument for individual liberty over and against the surreptitious tyranny of the majority; and Nietzsche's and Foucault's arguments regarding the hegemony of the masses, which must be mitigated by individual freedom and expression.

5. Søren Kierkegaard, *Fear and Trembling*, trans. Alastair Hannay (New York: Penguin, 1985), 88–91, 95.

6. Ludwig Wittgenstein, *Philosophical Investigations*, trans. G. E. M. Anscombe (New York: Macmillan, 1958), 223.

7. We can define fragmentation in various ways. For this study, I define fragmentation as a bifurcation of the self into an ontological writer-self and a rhetorical author-subject.

8. Quoted in Schuster, *The Philosopher's Autobiography*, 13.

9. Ricoeur makes a similar but stronger point in *Oneself As Another*: "I hold here as paradigmatic of the philosophies of the subject that the subject is formulated in the first-person—ego cogito—whether the 'I' is defined as an empirical or transcendental ego, whether the 'I' is posited absolutely (that is, with no reference to an Other) or relatively (ecology requiring the intrinsic complement of inter-subjectivity). In all these instances, the subject is 'I.'" See Ricoeur, *Oneself As Another*, 4.

10. Heidegger embraces Nietzsche's concrete belief that man must mask himself. He then abstracts the insight, transforming it into his own distinctive claim: Truth must conceal itself. He transfigures Nietzsche's fierce Dionysian artist into *Dasein*, an abstract embodiment of authentic living. Also, one cannot help but notice the religious allusions contained in *Ecce Homo*. The title is taken from the New Testament, book of John 19:5, where Pilate presents Christ to the masses and asks them to "Behold the Man." The self-ascribed personae reflect a Trinitarian Godhead: Dionysus (the holy spirit), Zarathustra (Jesus, the son), and the Antichrist (God, the father).

11. Friedrich Nietzsche, *On the Genealogy of Morals*, trans. Walter Kaufmann (New York: Random House, 1967), 201.

12. Susan Orlean, *The Orchid Thief* (New York: Ballantine, 1998), 287, 290.

13. Paul Ricoeur expresses the grammatical capacity of the subject in *Oneself As Another*. He confesses that the first intention of his work is to show that the first-person singular has primacy over the positing of a subject insofar as propositions such as "I am, I think" depend on the grammar of natural languages that allows distinctions between the self and the I—the reflective consciousness—to emerge. His aim is to re-introduce the question of selfhood, the "who" of philosophical theses, that lies within the tradition of philosophical investigations in the West by analyzing the grammatical, temporal, and dialectical dimensions of the subject. See *Oneself As Another*, 1–4.

14. Stanley Rosen, *The Limits of Analysis* (New Haven, CT: Yale University Press, 1980), 193.

15. Even without a traditionally conceived ontological self, Nietzsche struggles with his own version of bifurcated existence: self qua construct and self qua author. In

this book, I aim to strike a middle ground between essentialist and constructivist accounts of the self. For now I offer a few observations about the history of philosophical autobiography and its contribution to the philosophical study of the self.

16. See Kaufmann's introduction to *Ecce Homo*, 201.

17. Martin Heidegger elucidates the ontological structure of our being-in-the-world. Specifically, he reveals the relation between our thrownness, a condition of our being-in-the-world, and our facticity, the constraints on the possibilities of being as entailed in our thrownness. See Heidegger, *Being and Time*, trans. John Macquarrie and Edward Robinson (New York: Harper & Row, 1972), 190–93, 221–22.

18. Stanley Rosen, "Suspicion, Deception, and Concealment," Arion X (1991): 112–27, 123.

19. According to Alasdair MacIntyre ("Epistemological Crises, Dramatic Narrative, and the Philosophy of Science," *The Monist* 60 (1977): 452–72, 453), we not only present ourselves in undeceiving and intelligible ways, we also present ourselves in unambiguous and unironical ways. However, one need only glance at Nietzsche's work to see that ambiguity and irony are tools of writing that he mastered. I do think, however, that Nietzsche's attempt to present himself in multiple and sometimes contradictory ways was not designed to deceive his readers; rather, it was a method for proving that "Nietzsche" does not exist (i.e., that there is no substantial, metaphysical, identical, "true" self behind the masks that he wears). Perhaps we can have it both ways. MacIntyre further argues, "Sharing a culture means sharing schemata which are constitutive of and normal for intelligible actions performed by me and as a means for the interpretation of action of others."

20. Schuster, *The Philosopher's Autobiography*, 4. Derrida's claim is found in "Mnemosyne," *Memories for Paul de Man* (New York: Columbia University Press, 1984).

21. Schuster, *The Philosopher's Autobiography*, 6.

22. Plato, *The Symposium*, 1989), 201b–212c.

23. Michel Foucault argues that the Greek epic was created to extend the immortality of the hero. Moreover, he claims that our own culture has "metamorphosed this idea of narrative, or writing, as something designed to ward off death." See "What Is an Author?," 101–20, 102.

24. According to Donald Phillip Verene ("The Limits of Argument: Argument and Autobiography," *Philosophy and Rhetoric* 26 [1993]: 1–8): "Autobiography is a completely modern term . . . which comes into modern European Language at the very end of the eighteenth century and the beginning of the nineteenth. It is coined from the Greek *autos* (self), *bios* (life), and *graphe* (writing) to describe a kind of literature of the self, the writing of one's own life, a self-biography" (5).

25. Ricoeur, *Oneself As Another*, 310–11. Ricoeur follows Heidegger's analysis of *Dasein* as a being situated according to the thematic modes of being-in-the-world.

26. Ricoeur explains the relationship between the self and the I in this way: "To say *self* is not to say *I*. The *I* is posited—or is deposed. The *self* is implied reflexively in the operations, the analysis of which precedes the return toward this self." See *Oneself As Another*, 18.

27. Ibid., 3.

28. See Georg Misch's two-volume analysis of the history of autobiography, particularly volume 1, *A History of Autobiography in Antiquity,* ed. Karl Mannheim (London: Routledge & Kegan Paul, 1950), 1–17. Early in his work, Misch addresses the "special" manner in which we are self-conscious, 'I'-saying beings. He also implies that our capacity to say 'I' is coincident with our capacity to write 'I,' to write about ourselves, though he fails to make the connection explicit. His analysis turns upon self-presentations through the 'I' rather than the logical, psychological, or social connections between speaking and writing.

29. Even in instances where the you is an invisible you, that is, where the writing and speaking are impersonal insofar as no particular perspective is presented and no personal pronouns are used, the views expressed carry authorial force and parade as the speaker's own views and perspectives.

30. More will be said of this in later chapters alongside discussions of interpretation. For now I want to suggest that the performative nature of writing, which is related to the public presentation of speaking, allows the writer to appeal to a number of creative elements to unfold a story or life event.

31. Misch, *A History of Autobiography in Antiquity,* vol. 1, 5.

32. Ibid., 7.

33. Julia Kristeva, *Julia Kristeva Interviews,* ed. Ross Mitchell Guberman (New York: Columbia University Press, 1996), 16.

34. Hetty Clews argues for the uniqueness of the authorial figure in autobiographical works in *The Only Teller: Readings in the Monologue Novel* (Victoria, British Columbia: Sono Nis Press, 1985), 192.

35. Kristeva, *Julia Kristeva Interviews,* 230.

36. Foucault, "What Is an Author?," 101.

37. Ibid., 119.

38. Ibid., 102.

39. Jorge Gracia, *A Theory of Textuality* (Albany: State University of New York Press, 1995), 4.

40. Lorraine Code, *What Can She Know? Feminist Theory and the Construction of Knowledge* (Ithaca, NY: Cornell University Press, 1991), 310.

41. See Misch, *A History of Autobiography in Antiquity,* vol. 1, 3-4.

42. H. A. Hodges, *Wilhelm Dilthey* (New York: Oxford University Press, 1944), 29.

43. For Dilthey, conversations, letters, diaries, and other personal expressions and engagements constitute the empirical side of a human life. By examining these objects that remain after the life has ceased, we can understand that life from a more intimate point of view, from the subjective point of view. See Wilhelm Dilthey, *Patterns and Meaning in History,* trans. B. G. Teubner and ed. H. P. Rickman (London: George Allen & Unwin, 1961), 103, 41.

44. Ibid., 41.

45. Dilthey, *Patterns and Meaning in History*, 85.

46. Jerome Bruner, "Self-Making and World-Making," *Journal of Aesthetic Education* 25:1 (Spring 1991): 67–78. See esp. 76–78. See also Mary Warnock, *Imagination and Time* (Cambridge, MA: Blackwell, 1994), 128.

47. Goldstein's position is most clearly described by Deborah Knight in "Selves, Interpreters, Narrators," *Philosophy and Literature* 18 (October 1994): 274–86, 278–79.

48. Ibid., 282.

49. On the first account, our subjective experiences and beliefs may not coincide with facts about us. This realization permanently severs our mind, the locus of our "I," and its judgments about the world from the factuality of our being in the world. This view does not allow for our existence in the world to be an uncontrollable, determining factor of our identity. On the second account, my existence as a being-in-the-world is jeopardized by the act of storytelling—unless others continue to tell stories about me, I disappear. Unless all of the stories about me are known by myself and others, I cannot exist *as myself*. This view severs the individual's identity from his or her own singular awareness of self-identity. However strong our desire to say that we are the subjects of our histories, we must, as Deborah Knight insists, "disabuse ourselves of the idea that there is one correct story which could ideally be achieved by synthesizing all the storied versions" (ibid.).

50. The only autobiography that rivals its philosophical intensity and literary beauty is Nietzsche's *Ecce Homo*. Unlike Augustine's text, Nietzsche's is markedly anti-Christian and unconventional. His aphoristic style is more akin to the writings of the pre-Socratics than his contemporaries.

51. Saint Augustine, *Confessions*, trans. R. S. Pine-Coffin (New York: Penguin, 1961), 169. See book 8, part 7.

52. Genevieve Lloyd, "The Self As Fiction: Philosophy and Autobiography," *Philosophy and Literature* 10 (October 1986): 168–85, 173.

53. Richard J. White, "Autobiography against Itself," *Philosophy Today* 35:3–4 (Fall 1991): 292.

54. Quoted from bell hooks, *Teaching Community* (New York: Routledge, 2003), 180.

55. I am indebted to Amy Antonika for this point. Her insightful reading has aided me in distinguishing between Glazer's and Vaught's teleological perspectives in a number of places.

56. White, "Autobiography against Itself," 291–303, 293.

57. Martin Warner, "Philosophical Autobiography: St. Augustine and John Stuart Mill," *Philosophy and Literature: Royal Institute of Philosophy Lecture Series 16*, ed. A. Phillips Griffiths (Cambridge: Cambridge University Press, 1984), 189–210, 208.

58. Jean-Jacques Rousseau, *The Confessions*, trans. J. M. Cohen (New York: Penguin, 1953), 17.

59. Dilthey, *Patterns and Meaning in History*, 88.

60. Rousseau, *The Confessions*, 262.

61. Clews, *The Only Teller*, 192.

62. Nehamas, *The Art of Living*, 187.

63. Ibid., 17.

64. For now it is sufficient to think of a narrative as an *account* of a sequence of events. A more sophisticated and precise definition will be introduced later.

65. Code, *What Can She Know?*, 35.

66. Mieke Bal, "First-Person, Second Person, Same Person: Narrative As Epistemology," *New Literary History* 24 (1993): 293–320.

67. Gracia, *A Theory of Textuality*, 123–27.

68. Warner, "Philosophical Autobiography," 208.

69. Hazel Barnes, *The Story I Tell Myself* (Chicago: University of Chicago Press, 1997), 2.

70. White, "Autobiography against Itself," 298.

71. Rosen, *The Limits of Analysis*, 190.

72. Nietzsche, *Ecce Homo*, 206, translator's introduction.

73. Ibid., 217, preface, section 1.

Chapter 2

1. Rousseau, *The Confessions*, 65.

2. It appears that we have entered an age of self-representation. Documentaries and personal interviews dominate the big (and small) screen. Memoirs comprise a substantial percentage of published monographs. Portraiture and self-portraiture lead the art market in sales and profits percentages. Pop stars and entertainers swap bands and group performances for solo careers and individual shows that garner status and recognition. Sporting events advertise big-name players with individual styles and distinctive forms of athletic expression. Mass media creates a mythic world in which happiness translates to independence (financial, social, legal, and physical). Youth, wealth, beauty, and status determine self-worth. Certainly this image of success imbues the American psyche with new, self-regarding sensibilities.

3. Cf. with the closest-continuer theory, e.g., Robert Nozick, "Personal Identity through Time," in *Personal Identity*, ed. Raymond Martin and John Barresi (Oxford: Blackwell, 2003), 92–114. Philosophers utilize various methods for creating continuity for life narratives and unity of self, including memory, self-reflection, and self-narration. For example, memory connects who I am now with who I was in the past, thus providing continuity in my life. Besides Augustine, Rousseau, and, to some degree, Descartes, Freud holds

a variation of the view that identity derives from our recollected pasts (particularly wherein repressed memories might explain present fears and neuroses). Socrates, Kierkegaard, and Schuster argue, however, that self-reflection creates continuity in one's life and unity to one's self (Augustine and Descartes share an affinity for this view as well, since they argue that thinking justifies existence). By reflecting on past experiences in either a philosophic or therapeutic context, we connect our past and present without allowing the past to determine or overshadow our present. Finally, Nietzsche, Sartre, Barnes, and Richard Wollheim suggest that self-narration creates continuity in life and unity of self by allowing one to reconcile one's past to one's present and future, thereby collating dimensions of life (past and present) within a cohesive but an infinitely rich narrative.

4. I reject both of these accounts and argue instead that personal identity is both ascriptive and descriptive: we are freely ascribing rhetorical subjects and ontologically constrained selves.

5. Béla Szabados, "Autobiography after Wittgenstein," *Journal of Aesthetics and Art Criticism* 50:1 (Winter 1992): 2.

6. Ibid., 3.

7. Charles Taylor, *Sources of the Self* (Cambridge, MA: Harvard University Press, 1989), 184.

8. It is helpful here to recall the distinction introduced in Chapter 1 between the author and writer: the author is the persona or ego who the writer creates for his or her reader; the writer is the individual, the metaphysical being, who produces the artifact we call a text. In this chapter, I introduce a third notion of subjecthood, namely, the "historical figure," the characterization of a writer by others, a persona that is created outside of autobiographical texts.

9. The author falls into this category as well, though authorship will not be discussed in more detail here. I do maintain that the persona of the text is sometimes authorial and sometimes character laden, though the author and subject are not mutually exclusive (as in autobiography). The writer is the person, the ontological being, who is the ground of the persona of the text, and the historical figure is a constructed figure believed to be the same as the writer whose existence is designed by sources and information other than the writer's own work—other biographies, records, documents, and so on.

10. Henry Chadwick, *Augustine* (Oxford: Oxford University Press, 1986), 67.

11. Ibid.; see also Peter Brown, *Augustine of Hippo* (Los Angeles: University of California Press, 1967); Carl Vaught, *The Journey toward God in Augustine's Confessions: Books I–VI* (Albany: State University of New York Press, 2003); *Access to God in Augustine's Confessions* (Albany: State University of New York Press, 2005); *Encounters with God in Augustine's Confessions* (Albany: State University of New York Press, 2004).

12. Augustine, *Confessions*, trans. Henry Chadwick (Oxford: Oxford University Press, 1998), ix, introduction.

13. Ibid.

14. Chadwick, *Augustine*, 66–67.

15. *Confessions*, 1.6.9. Further references to this work will be given by book/chapter/paragraph to allow readers to find these references in any translation.

16. Ibid, 2.1.1.

17. Chadwick, *Augustine*, 70.

18. *Confessions*, 7.18.24–7.19.25.

19. In a different sense, Augustine's conception of God is consistent with a Platonic representation of the divine. Susan Kinz aptly notes that Augustine's God, like a Platonic one, is a god that is "both present in the world as the creator of all things in their hierarchical order and beyond the world as a power greater than being itself." I thank Tom Hanks for sharing this insight with me.

20. Quotation taken from Chadwick, *Augustine*, 70. For a similar analysis of Augustine's argument, see Dilthey, *Patterns and Meaning in History*, 87.

21. E. L. Allen, *Guidebook to Western Thought* (London: English University Press, 1957), 63.

22. Quoted from Schuster, *The Philosopher's Autobiography*, 85. See also Etienne Gilson, *The Christian Philosophy of St. Augustine*, trans. L. E. M. Lynch (New York: Random House, 1960), 18.

23. Chadwick, *Augustine*, 71–72.

24. Ibid., 130.

25. Schuster, *The Philosopher's Autobiography*, 78, 83.

26. Augustine, *Confessions*, 1.5.6. R. S. Pine-Coffin's translation is more poetic. He translates this passage as follows: "My soul is like a house, small for you [God] to enter, but I pray you to enlarge it. It is in ruins, but I ask you to remake it. It contains much that you will not be pleased to see: this I know and hide."

27. Augustine, *Confessions*, 11.25.32.

28. Ibid.

29. Ibid., 1.2.2.

30. Ibid., 12.21.30.

31. Ibid., 11.27.36.

32. Ibid., 11.28.37.

33. Ibid., 11.27.36.

34. Emmet T. Flood, "The Narrative Structure of Augustine's Confessions: Time's Quest for Eternity," *International Philosophical Quarterly* 28 (June 1988): 141–62, 153.

35. Ibid.

36. Ibid., 155.

37. Danne Polk, "Temporal Impermanence and the Disparity of Time and Eternity," *Augustinian Studies* 22 (1991): 63–82, 74.

38. For further elaboration of this position, see Taylor, *Sources of the Self*, 130–33.

39. Lloyd, "The Self As Fiction," 168-85, 170.

40. Schuster, *The Philosopher's Autobiography*, 94.

41. Augustine, *Confessions*, 244: "The storms of incoherent events tear to pieces my thoughts . . . until that day they are purified and molten by the fire of your love, I flow together to merge into you."

42. Lloyd, "The Self As Fiction," 183.

43. Schuster, *The Philosopher's Autobiography*, 83.

44. As quoted by John J. Britt, *Rhetorical Mosaic for a Kaleidoscope of Sound: Poetry As a Road to Understanding the Prose Voice* (New York: Peter Lang, 1994), 68.

45. Chadwick, *Augustine*, 71.

46. The complete title is *Meditations on First Philosophy in which the Existence of God and the Distinction of the Soul from the Body Are Demonstrated.* A rather audacious title, it seems, explained perhaps by René Descartes' rhetorical intention to posit himself as an orthodox thinker to the clergy he addresses directly. [trans. Donald A. Cress (Indianapolis: Hackett, 1993)].

47. Ibid., 27.

48. J. O. Urmson and Jonathan Rée, eds., *The Concise Encyclopedia of Western Philosophy & Philosophers* (London: Unwin Hyman, 1989), 235.

49. Descartes, *Meditations*, 13.

50. Ibid.

51. Ibid., 14.

52. Ibid.

53. Ibid., 13, emphasis added.

54. Ibid., 13–14.

55. Ibid., 18.

56. Ibid., 16.

57. Ibid., 17. Descartes remarks, "Yesterday's meditation has thrown me into such doubts that I can no longer ignore them. . . . It is as if I had suddenly fallen into a deep whirlpool; I am so tossed about that I can neither touch bottom with my foot, nor swim up to the top."

58. Descartes realized, of course, that Galileo had been sentenced to life imprisonment, which was commuted to house arrest, because of the implications of his scientific views, that is, because he argued that the sun, not the earth, is the center of the universe, thus countering the cosmological views of the Church (which were supported by biblical references). Perhaps he feared that he would be forced to admit that the existence of God could not be established by his method. See trans. Cress's introduction to Descartes, *Meditations*, viii.

59. Descartes, *Meditations*, 6, emphasis added.

60. Ibid., 1.

61. Ibid., 7.

62. Ibid., 8.

63. Ibid., 18.

64. Ibid.

65. Ibid., 18–19, emphasis added.

66. Ibid., 20.

67. Ibid., 30, emphasis added.

68. Bernard Williams, "*Descartes*," in *The Concise Encyclopedia of Western Philosophy & Philosophers*, ed. J. O. Urmson and Jonathan Rée (London: Urwin Hyman, 1989), 75.

69. Descartes, *Meditations*, 30.

70. Ibid., 35, 51–52.

71. Williams, "Descartes," 75.

72. Ricoeur, *Oneself As Another*, 6.

73. Descartes, *Meditations*, 53.

74. Ibid., 29.

75. Williams, "Descartes," 75.

76. Descartes, *Meditations*, 45.

77. Ibid., 46.

78. Ibid., 35.

79. Stanley Rosen draws much attention to this shift in the concept of the soul in his early work, *The Limits of Analysis.*

80. Descartes, *Meditations*, 18.

81. Ibid.

82. Ibid.

83. Taylor, *Sources of the Self*, 175.

84. Ibid.

85. Descartes, *Meditations*, 2–3.

86. Ricoeur, *Oneself As Another*, 5.

87. Descartes, *Meditations*, 17. The relationship between doubt and deception will be explicated in Chapter 3.

88. Ibid., 14.

89. Ibid., 18.

90. Code, *What Can She Know?*, 50–53.

91. Heidegger, *Being and Time*, 128–29.

92. I am grateful to Carl Vaught for clarifying this important outcome of Kant's work.

93. Heidegger, *Being and Time*, 4–8.

94. Descartes, *Meditations*, 23.

95. Ricoeur, *Oneself As Another*, 7, emphasis in original.

96. Rousseau, *The Confessions*, 155.

97. Rousseau was, of course, eventually banned from city after city because of his anti-democratic views.

98. Rousseau, *The Confessions*, 113.

99. Ibid., 9.

100. J. M. Cohen argues that "Rousseau set out to win his reader's sympathy for himself, and to gain posthumous partisans who would compensate him for the misunderstanding of which he felt he had been a victim throughout the long misery of his life. His method was to draw the pattern of his feelings while at the same time narrating the events of his earlier years. For what was important to him was not so much to tell of his history and achievements, as to prove himself a man who, with all his imperfections, was nevertheless fundamentally honest and good" (Rousseau, *The Confessions*, 7). For further analysis, see Cohen's entire introduction to *The Confessions*, 7–14.

101. Schuster, *The Philosopher's Autobiography*, 112.

102. Ibid.

103. Ibid.

104. Rousseau, *The Confessions*, 415.

105. See Jean-Jacques Rousseau, *The Social Contract*, trans. Maurice Cranston (New York: Penguin, 1968), 181; Thomas P. Neill, *Makers of the Modern Mind* (Milwaukee, WI: Bruce, 1949), 164, 184.

106. Rousseau, *The Confessions*, 20.

107. Ibid., 152.

108. Ibid., 386. Rousseau also confesses his obsession with women earlier in book 5, stating, "My passions have made me live, and my passions have killed me. What passions it may be asked . . . [i]n the first place, women. When I possessed one my senses were quiet, but my heart never. At the height of my pleasure the need for love devoured me" (210).

109. Rousseau's constructivist leanings are most explicit in his discussions of the author, which I examine later in this section.

110. Rousseau, *The Confessions*, 169.

111. Ibid., 28, 373.

112. Ibid., 373.

113. Schuster, *The Philosopher's Autobiography*, 144; Huck Gutman, "Rousseau's Confessions: A Technology of the Self," in *Technologies of the Self*, ed. L. H. Martin, H. Gutman, and P. Hutton (Amherst: University of Massachusetts Press, 1988), 99–121.

114. Schuster, *The Philosopher's Autobiography*, 144.

115. Ibid.

116. Rousseau, *The Confessions*, 544.

117. Rousseau describes his relationship with "Mamma," Madame de Warens, in this way: "For it was not, as I have said, a love relationship, but a more real possession, depending not on the senses, on sex, age, or personal beauty, but on everything by which one is oneself, and which one cannot lose except by ceasing to be" (*The Confessions*, 213).

118. Rousseau, *The Confessions*, 362.

119. Ibid., 157.

120. Ibid., 579.

121. Dithey, *Patterns and Meaning in History*, 88.

122. Rousseau, *The Confessions*, 338, emphasis added.

123. Ibid., 574, emphasis added.

124. Rousseau declares of himself on p. 333 of *The Confessions*, "Never for a moment in his life could Jean-Jacques have been a man without feelings or compassion, an unnatural father. I may have been mistaken, but I could never be callous." However, on p. 516, he argues the opposite case, stating, "Long separation from a child one does not yet know weakens and finally destroys paternal and maternal feeling; and one will never lose a child one has put out to nurse as much as one suckled under one's own eyes."

125. Szabados, "Autobiography after Wittgenstein," 4–5.

126. Rousseau, *The Confessions*, 335: "I have promised to write my confessions, but not to make my apologies; so I will stop here. My duty is to tell the truth; my readers' to be just; and that is all that I shall ever ask of them."

127. Schuster, *The Philosopher's Autobiography*, 126.

128. Ibid., 378.

129. Ibid., 379.

130. Rousseau, *The Confessions*, 546.

131. Schuster, *The Philosopher's Autobiography*, 118–19.

132. Rousseau, *The Confessions*, 158.

133. Nietzsche, *Ecce Homo*, 218.

134. Ibid., 217.

135. Nietzsche, *On the Genealogy of Morals*, 84.

136. Friedrich Nietzsche, *The Gay Science*, trans. Walter Kaufmann (New York: Random House, 1974), 298.

137. Friedrich Nietzsche, *The Birth of Tragedy*, trans. Walter Kaufmann (New York: Random House, 1967). Dionysian versus Apollinian impulses: chaotic, meaningless, potentiality; fixed meaning.

138. Nietzsche, *On the Genealogy of Morals*, 84.

139. Ibid., 85.

140. Ibid., 299.

141. Ibid., 37.

142. Ibid., 174.

143. Ibid., 299–300.

144. Nietzsche, *Thus Spoke Zarathustra*, 125.

145. George J. Stack, "Emerson, Nietzsche, and Naturalistic Ethics," *The Humanist* (November–December 1990): 21–25, 46. See especially p. 25.

146. Ivan Soll, "Nietzsche on Cruelty, Asceticism, and the Failure of Hedonism," in *Nietzsche, Genealogy, and Morality*, ed. Richard Schacht (Los Angeles: University of California Press, 1994), 168–92. Soll discusses what he calls Nietzsche's "psychology of power" and its relation to the drive for power and strength on pp. 168–73.

147. Nietzsche, *On the Genealogy of Morals*, 79.

148. Nietzsche, *Ecce Homo*, 219.

149. Ibid., editor's introduction, 206.

150. Ibid., 202.

151. Nietzsche, *On the Genealogy of Morals*, 67.

152. Ibid., 97.

153. Urmson and Rée "Nietzsche," in *The Concise Encyclopedia of Western Philosophy & Philosophers*, 225.

154. Schuster reports that William Spengemann identifies three genres of autobiography: historical, philosophical, and poetical. I would add "confessional" to this list, which seems to be different in both form and content from these three. Also, "historical" might be subsumed under all three (could not one give a confessional, philosophical, or poetical reading to history?)? I identify Augustine and Rousseau as "confessional" autobiographies, Descartes as philosophical, and Nietzsche and Barnes as poetical. See Schuster, *The Philosopher's Autobiography*, 3–4.

155. Nietzsche, *Ecce Homo*, editor's introduction, 206.

156. John T. Wilcox, *Truth and Value in Nietzsche: A Study of His Metaethics and Epistemology* (Ann Arbor: University of Michigan Press, 1974), 51–52.

157. See Alexander Nehamas, "How One Becomes What One Is," in *Nietzsche, Life As Literature* (Cambridge, MA: Harvard University Press, 1985), 183–84.

158. Ibid., 181–82.

159. Friedrich Nietzsche, *Thus Spoke Zarathustra*, trans. Walter Kaufmann (New York: Penguin, 1966), 158.

160. Nietzsche, *The Gay Science*, 341.

161. For various critical interpretations of the Eternal Return, see Andrew Nicol's "Nietzsche's Eternal Return" at http://www.philosophyclassics.com/essays.

162. Friedrich Nietzsche, *The Will to Power*. trans. Walter Kauffman and R. J. Hollingdale, (New York: Vintage Press, 1968), 35.

163. Ibid., 546.

164. Nietzsche, *On the Genealogy of Morals*, 58, emphasis in original.

165. Ibid., 61.

166. Ibid., 118.

167. Friedrich Nietzsche, *Beyond Good and Evil*, trans. Marianne Cowan (South Bend, IN: Gateway, 1955), 229–30, emphasis in original.

168. Nehamas, *Nietzsche, Life As Literature*, 182.

169. Ibid., 177. Nehamas notes that the notion of "subject as multiplicity" emerges over and over in Nietzsche's *The Will to Power*, trans. Walter Kaufmann and R. J. Hollingdale (New York: Vintage Press, 1968).

170. Nietzsche, *Ecce Homo*, 247.

171. Ibid., 119.

172. Nimrod Aloni, *Beyond Nihilism: Nietzsche's Healing and Edifying Philosophy* (New York: University Press of America, 1991), 32.

173. John Atwell, "Nietzsche's Perspectivism," *The Southern Journal of Philosophy* (1981): 157–70. See especially 162.

174. Nietzsche, *Ecce Homo*, editor's introduction, 207. In the *Antichrist*, Nietzsche argues that the Jesus of the Gospels and the historic Jesus are not the same.

175. Aloni, *Beyond Nihilism*, 32.

176. Nietzsche, *Ecce Homo*, editor's introduction, 208.

177. Richard Rorty, *Contingency, Irony, and Solidarity* (New York: Cambridge University Press, 1989), 99.

178. Edith Kern, *Existential Thought and Fictional Technique: Kierkegaard, Sartre, and Beckett* (New Haven, CT: Yale University Press, 1970), viii.

179. Barnes, *The Story I Tell Myself*, 293.

180. Cited in Schuster, *The Philosopher's Autobiography*, 44, and taken from Barnes, "Who Is the Subject of Autobiography?," *Sartre Studies International* 4:2 (1998): 25.

181. Though the meaning of the concepts varies, her conception of the relation between "consciousness" and "ego" parallels my understanding of the relation between

the Inner self and the Outer self. I will say more about his parallel in Chapter 3, where I discuss the *être-en-soi* (being-in-oneself) and the *être-pour-soi* (being-for-oneself).

182. Barnes, *The Story I Tell Myself*, xviii.

183. Schuster, *The Philosopher's Autobiography*, 45.

184. Ibid., 46.

185. Ibid.

186. Schuster makes this important point about Sartre, though I connect it to Barnes. See Schuster, *The Philosopher's Autobiography*, 155.

187. Ibid., 154.

188. Ibid., 155.

189. Ibid.

190. Ibid., 46.

191. Barnes, *The Story I Tell Myself*, 47.

192. Ibid., introduction, xiv.

193. Ibid., 147. Barnes, of course, relies upon Sartre's layering of consciousness: pre-consciousness and consciousness. The pre-consciousness engages the undifferentiated structure of being, giving rise to consciousness that particularizes one's engagement in the world by presenting and concealing various parts of being.

194. J. O. Urmson and Jonathan Rée, eds., *The Concise Encyclopedia of Western Philosophy & Philosophers* (New York: Routledge, 2000), 287.

195. Ibid., 15.

196. Schuster, *The Philosopher's Autobiography*, 150; last part quotation from Robert Champigny, "Sartre on Sartre," in *The Philosophy of Jean-Paul Sartre*, ed. P. A. Schillp (La Salle, IL: Open Court Press, 1981), 88.

197. Ibid., 211.

198. Ibid., 304.

199. White, "Autobiography against Itself," 300.

200. Barnes, *The Story I Tell Myself*, 311.

201. Robert Martin defines "bad faith" and "good faith" in the following way: "Bad faith is the pretense that one's actions, values, or preferences are determined by something in one's past. . . . Good faith, its opposite, is the accepting that one is the author of, and responsible for, actions, values, and preferences." See Martin, *The Philosopher's Dictionary*, 3rd ed. (Toronto: Broadview Press, 2002), 38.

202. Ibid., 104.

203. Jean-Paul Sartre, *Being and Nothingness: An Essay on Phenomenological Ontology*, trans. Hazel E. Barnes (New York: Philosophical Library, 1956), 665.

204. Ibid., 292–93.

205. Kearney, *The Concise Encyclopedia of Western Philosophy & Philosophers*, 288.

206. Schuster, *The Philosopher's Autobiography*, 150.

207. Ibid., 295.

208. Ibid., 304.

209. Ibid., 677.

210. Ibid., 671.

211. Barnes, *The Story I Tell Myself*, 318.

212. Lloyd, "The Self As Fiction," 168–85, 184.

213. I regard the Inner self as nonconstructed, just as Sartre regards "being-for-oneself" as consciousness (though Sartre's conception of consciousness does not line up exactly with ancient and medieval conceptions of the 'soul' or 'mind'). Also, I treat the Outer self as a constructed object with specifically conceived and contextualized roles and responsibilities, just as Sartre regards the world, the body, and the ego as constructed aspects of consciousness. Nonetheless, Sartre remains more of a constructivist than I. I will say more about the similarities and differences between our views in Chapter 3.

214. Kearney, *The Concise Encyclopedia of Western Philosophy & Philosophers*, 287.

215. Sartre, *Being and Nothingness*, 28–29.

216. Insofar as the features of writing, such as plot structure, diction, and narration, are shared by works of all kinds—documentaries, novels, short stories, and so on, the criteria for establishing fiction and fact cannot be made on the basis of the literary techniques involved. The content of the work, if it can be viewed apart from the form in which it is presented, must be used to adjudicate truth and falsity. However, in many instances, the truth and falsity of narrative accounts are determined primarily on the basis of other sources—records, historical documents, archaeological sites, and so on, rather than on the basis of the narrative itself.

Chapter 3

1. Jean-Paul Sartre, *The Words*, trans. Bernard Frechtman (New York: George Braziller, 1964), 193–94.

2. Readers may, of course, see the author differently than he or she sees himself or herself. There are few hermeneutic limitations to how an author, not merely a text, can be understood.

3. hooks, *Teaching Community*, 29.

4. See Introduction to this work, note 4.

5. hooks, *Teaching Community*, 129.

6. Szabados, "Autobiography after Wittgenstein," 7.

7. Though I concede Szabados's point, I do not find the objectification of the self to be necessarily unproductive. For example, Descartes objectifies the self for the sake of a new conception of the self. Nietzsche deconstructs the self to overthrow what he regards as a false consciousness. The bifurcation of the self is a necessary product of self-narration and one that yields self-knowledge.

8. Gracia refers to such signs as ECT, entities that constitute a text. See Gracia, *A Theory of Textuality*, 4–5. He writes that a text "... may be taken to be composed of several signs such as the words of which it is composed, the punctuation ... and so on. But in another sense the text is constituted, at least in part, by the lines, points, ink marks, and such, which constitute the signs that compose the text. ... For the sake of simplicity, I shall refer to the entities that are used as signs as entities that constitute the signs and I shall refer to the signs as being constituted by these entities" (ibid., 5).

9. Gadamer explains Heidegger's notion of truth in *Philosophical Apprenticeships*, trans. Robert R. Sullivan (Cambridge, MA: MIT Press, 1987), 188.

10. Ibid., 189.

11. Szabados, "Autobiography after Wittgenstein," 10.

12. Quoted by Annette C. Baier, "The Vital but Dangerous Art of Ignoring," in *Self and Deception: A Cross-Cultural Philosophical Enquiry*, ed. Roger T. Ames and Wimal Dissanayake (Albany: State University of New York Press, 1996), 53–72, 59.

13. Ibid., 69–70.

14. Ibid., 70.

15. Schuster, *The Philosopher's Autobiography*, 106.

16. *Confessions*, trans. Henry Chadwick (New York: Oxford University Press, 1998), 44.

17. Schuster, *The Philosopher's Autobiography*, 106.

18. *Confessions*, 4.30.1, pg. 70 of Chadwick translation.

19. Ibid., 94.

20. Ibid., 114.

21. Ibid., 112.

22. Schuster, *The Philosopher's Autobiography, 106.*

23. Robert C. Solomon, "Self, Deception, and Self-Deception in Philosophy," in *Self and Deception: A Cross-Cultural Philosophical Enquiry*, ed. Roger T. Ames and Wimal Dissanayake (Albany: State University of New York Press, 1996), 91–121, 102–103.

24. Nietzsche explores the limits of this metaphor in *Human, All Too Human*, trans. R. J. Hollingdale (Cambridge: Cambridge University Press, 1986), vol. 2, part 2, 301–95.

25. Solomon, "Self, Deception, and Self-Deception in Philosophy," 103.

26. Ibid.

27. Graham Parkes, "Facing the Self with Masks: Perspectives on the Personal from Nietzsche and the Japanese," in *Self and Deception: A Cross-Cultural Philosophical Enquiry*, ed. Roger T. Ames and Wimal Dissanayake (Albany: State University of New York Press, 1996), 300.

28. Alexander Nehamas, *Nietzsche: Life As Literature* (Cambridge, MA: Harvard University Press, 1985), 185–86.

29. Ibid., 163.

30. Ibid.

31. Martin, *The Philosopher's Dictionary*, 38.

32. Roquentin, the protagonist of Sartre's *Nausea*, gives up his project of coming to *know* M. de Rollebin, the historical figure, through the process of researching, writing, and unifying the events of M. de Rollebin's life into a biography. See Sartre, *Nausea*, trans. Lloyd Alexander (New York: New Directions, 1964), 94.

33. Sartre, *Being and Nothingness*, 665.

34. Ibid., 677.

35. Ibid., 671.

36. Kaufmann, intro. to Nietzsche, *On the Genealogy of Morals*, 206.

37. Sartre, *The Words*, 93.

38. Baier, "The Vital but Dangerous Art of Ignoring," 54.

39. Ibid., 55.

40. Ibid.

41. Ibid., 55–56.

42. Ronald B. De Sousa, "Emotion and Self-Deception," in *Perspectives on Self-Deception*, ed. Brian P. McLaughlin and Amélie Oksenberg Rorty (Berkeley: University of California Press, 1988), 324–41, 329.

43. Gadamer, *Philosophical Apprenticeships*, 35.

44. De Sousa, "Emotion and Self-Deception," 326, emphasis in original.

45. Ibid., 327.

46. De Sousa describes the appropriateness of an emotion to its object as "axiological rationality" (ibid., 327). He maintains that our intuitions reflect different conceptions of rationality, three of which he elaborates on in this article: strategic rationality, cognitive rationality, and axiological rationality. Strategic rationality is the assessment of a representational state in light of the probable value of its consequences, and cognitive rationality is the assessment of a representational state in terms of its adequacy to some objective state of the world of which it purports to be true (ibid., 326–27).

47. Ibid., 331-32, emphasis in original.

48. Ibid., 336.

49. Ibid.

50. Plato, "The Seventh Letter," in *Phaedrus and Letters VII and VIII*, trans. Walter Hamilton and ed. Betty Radice (New York: Penguin Press, 1973), 344c–345a.

51. Carolyn G. Heilbrun, *Writing a Woman's Life* (New York: W. W. Norton & Company, 1988), 14.

52. Parkes, "Facing the Self with Masks," 288–313.

53. Plato, "The Seventh Letter," 344d.

54. Ibid.

55. Plato, *Phaedo*, trans. F. J. Church (New York: Macmillan, 1951), 59b.

56. Shadia B. Drury, *The Political Ideas of Leo Strauss* (New York: St. Martin's Press, 1988), preface, xi. Drury is an anti-Straussian, but her discussion of Strauss's views is lucid and insightful. She represents his work fairly, though she views his overall project with much skepticism.

57. Ibid., 5–6.

58. Parkes, "Facing the Self with Masks," 300.

59. Nietzsche, *The Gay Science*, 245.

Chapter 4

1. Nietzsche, *Human, All Too Human*, 248.

2. See Gracia, *A Theory of Textuality*, 181–214. Gracia suggests behavioral criteria for testing and identifying textual understanding. While I find his thesis compelling, I focus upon the process of textual understanding rather than on the signification of understanding.

3. See Gracia's *A Theory of Textuality: The Logic and Epistemology*, and Hans-Georg Gadamer's *Truth and Method*, trans. Joel Weinsheimer and Donald G. Marshall (New York: Continuum Press, 1989) and *Philosophical Hermeneutics*, trans. and ed. David E. Linge (Berkeley: University of California Press, 1976).

4. Bruner, "Self-Making and World-Making," 76.

5. Søren Kierkegaard, *The Essential Kierkegaard*, trans. and ed. Howard and Edna Hong (Princeton, NJ: Princeton University Press, 2000), 78.

6. William Mathews, "Interpreting Lives: Some Hermeneutical Problems in Autobiography and Biography," *Irish Philosophical Journal* 3 (Spring 1986): 32.

7. Ricoeur, *Oneself As Another*, 160.

8. Paul Trainor, "Autobiography As Philosophical Argument: Socrates, Descartes, and Collingwood," *Thought* 63 (December 1988): 378–96, 392.

9. Mathews, "Interpreting Lives," 27–41, 30–31.

10. Gracia traces the etymology of "interpretation" from the Latin *interpretatio*, a form of *interpres* meaning "to spread abroad." He explains that the Latin term developed

three meanings: (1) to give the meaning of whatever was being interpreted; (2) to bring out what was hidden and unclear, to make plain what was irregular, and to provide an account of something; and (3) to translate a text into a different language (Gracia, *A Theory of Textuality*, 147).

11. This problem, along with the obvious difference between the ECT of the text in the different languages, leads Gracia to conclude that *Hamlet* in English and *Hamlet* in German are not the same text, though they are the same work or interpreted text. He argues, "Consider *Don Quixote*, for example. If we follow my suggestion, we have in the first place a text; namely, the group of entities, used as signs, that are selected, arranged, and intended by Cervantes to convey a certain meaning to the audience he had in mind in the context of his time. The text is, as mentioned earlier, an artifact constructed for the purpose of conveying meaning. . . . This text can be translated into other languages, that is, different artifacts can be used to produce the same understanding. But in the case of translation we do not any longer have the same text, although we still have the same work. The work, I propose, is the meaning of the group of signs and, therefore, independent of it insofar as other groups of signs can be used to convey it" (Gracia, *A Theory of Textuality*, 65).

12. Gadamer, *Philosophical Hermeneutics*, editor's introduction, xix.

13. Ibid., xxi.

14. Ibid., xxv.

15. Gadamer, *Truth and Method*, translated here by Linge from the German *Wahrheit and Methode*: Grundzuge einer philosophischen Hermeneutik (Tubingen: Mohr, 1960), 280.

16. Martha C. Nussbaum, *Love's Knowledge: Essays on Philosophy and Literature* (New York: Oxford University Press, 1990), 66.

17. See MacIntyre, "Epistemological Crises, Dramatic Narrative, and the Philosophy of Science," 457.

18. Ibid.

19. Ibid.

20. Ibid., 216.

21. Ibid., 214.

22. Ibid., 217.

23. Susan Feldman, "Objectivity, Pluralism, and Relativism: A Critique of MacIntyre's Theory of Virtue," *The Southern Journal of Philosophy* 24 (1986): 307–20.

24. Gracia, *A Theory of Textuality*, 151.

25. Ibid., 134.

26. Ibid., 153–54.

27. Ibid., 113.

28. Ibid., 165.

29. Ibid., 156.

30. Ibid., 157.

31. Ibid.

32. Ibid.

33. Ibid., 158.

34. Ibid.

35. Ibid.

36. Ibid., 159.

37. Ibid., 166–67.

38. Ibid., 158.

39. Ibid., 168.

40. Ibid., 178–79.

41. See Gadamer, *Philosophical Hermeneutics*, editor's introduction, xii. Linge describes the rise of hermeneutics in very precise terms, explaining the shift between viewing hermeneutics as a method and later as an ontological mode of being via understanding.

42. Ibid., xi.

43. Gadamer, *Philosophical Hermeneutics,* 82–94, 94.

44. Ibid., 3–17, 9.

45. Ibid. Gadamer describes this hermeneutic act in *Truth and Method* as well: "All understanding is interpretation, and all interpretation takes place in the medium of a language that allows the object to come into words and yet is at the same time the interpreter's own language" (389).

46. Gadamer, *Philosophical Hermeneutics*, 17.

47. Ibid., 390–91. Gadamer, like Gracia, distinguishes between deciphering the marks that comprise a text and the meaning of a text's propositions as a whole. Unlike Gracia, Gadamer views all instances of understanding as instances of interpretation. Gracia maintains a distinction between acts of understanding (mental acts produced by interpretation) and interpretation (deciphering signs and symbols). See Gadamer, *Truth and Method*, 391.

48. Gadamer, *Truth and Method*, 391.

49. Gadamer, *Philosophical Hermeneutics*, xiv.

50. Ibid.

51. Ibid.

52. Ibid., xv.

53. Gadamer, *Truth and Method*, 285.

54. Gadamer, *Philosophical Hermeneutics*, 6, emphasis in original.

55. Ibid., editor's introduction, xix.

56. Gadamer, *Truth and Method*, 307.

57. Gadamer, *Philosophical Hermeneutics*, 44–58, 48.

58. Ibid., 9. Gadamer adopts Heidegger's notion of "futurity" here as the character of projection that aligns itself with Dasein's temporality and is in turn manifested through Dasein's "thrownness," the limits and possibilities of Dasein.

59. Gadamer, *Truth and Method*, 379.

60. Gadamer, *Philosophical Hermeneutics*, xxiv.

61. Ibid., emphasis in original.

62. Ibid., xxv.

63. Gadamer, *Truth and Method*, 280. In *Truth and Method* Gadamer argues that "part of real understanding . . . is that we regain the concepts of a historical past in such a way that they also include our own comprehension of them" (374).

64. Nietzsche, *The Will to Power*, 552.

65. See Nehamas, "How One Becomes What One Is," 173–74.

66. Nietzsche, *The Gay Science*, 335. According to Nehamas, "*Thus Spoke Zarathustra* is constructed around the idea of creating one's own self, or what comes to the same thing, the *Übermensch*. Zarathustra and his disciples as well are constantly described as 'creators.' Nietzsche is paying Goethe, one of his few true heroes, his highest compliment when he writes of him that 'he created himself'" (Nehamas, *Nietzsche: Life As Literature*, 174).

67. Neitzsche, *The Gay Science*, 221, author's introduction.

68. Heidegger, *Being and Time*, 182.

69. Nietzsche, *Ecce Homo*, 225.

70. Nietzsche, *Nietzsche: Life As Literature*, 182.

71. See Nehamas, *Nietzsche: Life As Literature*, 194, for more on this point.

72. Nietzsche, *The Gay Science*, 299.

73. Ibid., 185.

74. Nehamas, *Nietzsche: Life As Literature*, 195.

75. Ibid., 198–99, and back to 198.

76. White, "Autobiography against Itself," 298.

77. Nietzsche, *Thus Spoke Zarathustra*, 239.

78. Nietzsche, *Human, All Too Human*, 198, also cited by Nehamas.

79. Nussbaum, *Love's Knowledge*, 70.

80. Stanley Rosen, "The Whole Story," *Myths and Fictions*, ed. Shlomo Biderman and Ben-Ami Scharfstein (Leiden: E. J. Brill Press, 1993), 17–40, 29.

81. Nussbaum, *Love's Knowledge*, 5.

82. Michel Haar, "Nietzsche and Metaphysical Language," in *The New Nietzsche*, trans. Cyril and Liliane Welch, ed. and intro. David Allison (Cambridge, MA: MIT Press, 1994), 5–36, 7.

83. Nehamas, *Nietzsche: Life As Literature*, 163.

84. Ibid., 163–64.

85. Nussbaum, *Love's Knowledge*, 29.

86. Jeffrey Eugendies, *Middlesex* (New York: Picador, 2002), 410.

87. Heilbrun, *Writing a Woman's Life*, 11.

88. hooks, *Wounds of Passion* (New York: Henry Holt and Company, 1997), 158.

89. Heilbrun, *Writing a Woman's Life*, 118.

90. Ibid., 18–50.

91. Ibid., 12.

92. Schuster, *The Philosopher's Autobiography*, 39.

93. Carolyn Korsmeyer, "Reason and Morals in the Early Feminist Movement: Mary Wollstonecraft," in *Women and Philosophy: Towards a Theory of Liberation*, ed. Carol C. Gould and Marx W. Wartofsky (New York: G. P. Putnam's Sons, 1976), 97–111, 98.

94. Ibid.

95. Feldman appears to be most influenced by the arguments presented by Robin Lakoff in *Language and Woman's Place* (New York: Harper & Row, 1975).

96. Feldman presents her own view of traditions alongside her attack on Alasdair MacIntyre's work. See "Objectivity, Pluralism, and Relativism, 307–20.

97. Ibid., 22.

98. Ibid.

99. Ibid., 17.

100. I enumerated the five reasons why people write autobiographies. They are: (1) to achieve self-knowledge; (2) to unify the self; (3) to communicate the self to others; (4) to give continuity to their lives; and (5) to explore the relation between the self and the subject. Given the evidence presented above, women autobiographers of the eighteenth and nineteenth centuries, and perhaps a bit later, did not engage in autobiographical writing for the same reasons as men of those centuries.

101. Kristeva, *Julia Kristeva Interviews*, 123.

102. Ibid., 122.

103. Judith Butler, *Gender Trouble* (New York: Routledge, Chapman & Hall, 1990), 3.

104. Code, *What Can She Know?*, 259–60.

105. Ibid., 310.

106. Augustine, *Confessions*, 116.

107. Dilthey remarks that both Augustine's and Rousseau's autobiographies (along with Goethe's) are "the most direct expressions of reflection of life." See Dilthey, *Patterns and Meaning in History*, 87.

108. Ibid., 133.

109. Gadamer, *Philosophical Apprenticeships*, vii.

110. Ibid., 175.

111. Cf. Szabados, "Autobiography after Wittgenstein," 3.

112. Dilthey, *Patterns and Meaning in History*, 88.

113. Again, Dilthey regards autobiography as an authentic source of self-knowledge because it expresses one's view of oneself *as* a figure present in the historical consciousness of humankind.

Bibliography

Allen, E. L. *Guidebook to Western Thought.* London: English University Press, 1957.

Aloni, Nimrod. *Beyond Nihilism: Nietzsche's Healing and Edifying Philosophy.* New York: University Press of America, 1991.

Atwell, John. "Nietzsche's Perspectivism." *The Southern Journal of Philosophy* (1981): 157–70.

Augustine, Saint. *Confessions.* Trans. Henry Chadwick. Oxford: Oxford University Press, 1991.

———. *Confessions.* Trans. S. Pine-Coffin. New York: Penguin, 1961.

Baier, Annette C. "The Vital but Dangerous Art of Ignoring." In *Self and Deception: A Cross-Cultural Philosophical Enquiry,* ed. Roger T. Ames and Wimal Dissanayake, 53–72. Albany: State University of New York Press, 1996.

Bal, Mieke. "First-person, Second Person, Same Person: Narrative As Epistemology." *New Literary History* 24 (1993): 293–320.

Barnes, Hazel. *The Story I Tell Myself.* Chicago: University of Chicago Press, 1997.

Britt, John J. *Rhetorical Mosaic for a Kaleidoscope of Sound: Poetry As a Road to Understanding the Prose Voice.* New York: Peter Lang, 1994.

Brown, Peter. *Augustine of Hippo.* Los Angeles: University of California Press, 1967.

Bruner, Jerome. "Self-Making and World-Making." *Journal of Aesthetic Education* 25:1 (Spring 1991): 67–78.

Bruss, Elizabeth. *Autobiographical Acts: The Changing Situation of a Literary Genre.* Baltimore, MD: Johns Hopkins University Press, 1976.

Butler, Judith. *Gender Trouble.* New York: Routledge, Chapman & Hall, 1990.

Casey, Edward S. "Man, Self, and Truth." *The Monist* 55 (1971): 218–54.

Cavell, Stanley. *A Pitch of Philosophy: Autobiographical Exercises.* Cambridge, MA: Harvard University Press, 1994.

Chadwick, Henry. *Augustine.* Oxford: Oxford University Press, 1986.

Chamberlin, Daniel Frank. *Narrative Perspective in Fiction: A Phenomenological Mediation of Reader, Text, and World.* Toronto: University of Toronto Press, 1990.

Clarke, W. Norris. "Medalist's Address: The Philosophical Importance of Doing One's Autobiography." *Proceedings of the American Catholic Association* 15 (1980): 17–25.

Clews, Hetty. *The Only Teller: Readings in the Monologue Novel.* Victoria, British Columbia: Sono Nis Press, 1985.

Code, Lorraine. *Rhetorical Spaces: Essays on Gendered Spaces.* New York: Routledge, 1995.

———. *What Can She Know? Feminist Theory and the Construction of Knowledge.* Ithaca, NY: Cornell University Press, 1991.

Davidson, Donald. "First-Person Authority." *Dialectica* 38 (1984): 101–11.

Dennett, Daniel C. "The Interpretation of Texts, People, and Other Artifacts." *Philosophy and Phenomenological Research* 50 (1990): 177–94.

———. "Why Everyone Is a Novelist." *Times Literary Supplement* (September 1988): 16–22.

Derrida, Jacques. "Mnemosyne." *Memories for Paul de Man.* New York: Columbia University Press, 1984.

Descartes, René. *Meditations on First Philosophy.* 3rd ed. Trans. Donald A. Cress. Indianapolis, IN: Hackett, 1993.

De Sousa, Ronald B. "Emotion and Self-Deception." In *Perspectives on Self-Deception*, ed. Brian P. McLaughlin and Amélie Oksenberg Rorty, 324–41. Berkeley: University of California Press, 1988.

Dilthey, Wilhelm. *Patterns and Meaning in History*. Trans. B. G. Teubner and ed. H. P. Rickman. London: George Allen & Unwin, 1961.

———. *Wilhelm Dilthey: Selected Writings*. Trans. and ed. H. P. Rickman. Cambridge: Cambridge University Press, 1976.

Drury, Shadia B. *The Political Ideas of Leo Strauss*. New York: St. Martin's Press, 1988.

Eugendies, Jeffrey. *Middlesex*. New York: Picador, 2002.

Feldman, Susan. "Objectivity, Pluralism, and Relativism: A Critique of MacIntyre's Theory of Virtue." *The Southern Journal of Philosophy* 24 (1986): 307–20.

Flood, Emmet T. "The Narrative Structure of Augustine's Confessions: Time's Quest for Eternity." *International Philosophical Quarterly* 28 (June 1988): 141–62.

Foucault, Michel. "What Is an Author?" In *The Foucault Reader*, ed. Paul Rabinow, 101–20. New York: Pantheon Books, 1984.

Gadamer, Hans-Georg. *Philosophical Apprenticeships*. Trans. Robert R. Sullivan. Cambridge, MA: MIT Press, 1987.

———. *Philosophical Hermeneutics.* Trans. and ed. David E. Linge. Berkeley: University of California Press, 1976.

———. *Truth and Method.* Trans. Joel Weinsheimer and Donald G. Marshall. New York: Continuum Press, 1989.

Gilson, Etienne. *The Christian Philosophy of St. Augustine.* Trans. L. E. M. Lynch. New York: Random House, 1960.

Gracia, Jorge J. E. *A Theory of Textuality.* Albany: State University of New York Press, 1995.

———. *Texts: Ontological Status, Identity, Author, Audience.* Albany: State University of New York Press, 1996.

Graybeal, Jean. "Nietzsche's Riddle." *Philosophy Today* 32 (Fall 1988): 232–43.

Gutman, Huck. "Rousseau's Confessions: A Technology of the Self." In *Technologies of the Self,* ed. L. H. Martin, H. Gutman, and P. Hutton. Amherst: University of Massachusetts Press, 1988.

Haar, Michel. "Nietzsche and Metaphysical Language." In *The New Nietzcshe,* trans. Cyril and Liliane Welch and ed. David Allison, 5–36. Cambridge, MA: MIT Press, 1994.

Hanson, Karen. *The Self Imagined: Philosophical Reflections on the Social Character of Psyche.* New York: Routledge & Kegan Paul, 1986.

Heidegger, Martin. *Being and Time.* Trans. John Macquarrie and Edward Robinson. New York: Harper & Row, 1972.

Heilbrun, Carolyn G. *Writing a Woman's Life.* New York: W.W. Norton & Company, 1988.

Herman, David. "Autobiography, Allegory, and the Construction of Self." *British Journal of Aesthetics* 35:4 (October 1995): 351–60.

Hodges, H. A. *Wilhelm Dilthey.* New York: Oxford University Press, 1944.

hooks, bell. *Teaching Community: A Pedagogy of Hope.* New York: Routledge, 2003.

———. *Wounds of Passion.* New York: Henry Holt and Company, 1997.

Hull, Robert. "Epistemology and the Autodevaluation of Morality: Towards an Atheoretical Nietzsche." *Southwest Philosophy Review* 8 (1992): 119–25.

Kern, Edith. *Existential Thought and Fictional Technique: Kierkegaard, Sartre, and Beckett.* New Haven, CT: Yale University Press, 1970.

Kierkegaard, Søren. *Fear and Trembling.* Trans. Alastair Hannay. New York: Penguin, 1985.

———. *The Point of View for My Work As an Author.* Trans. Walter Lowrie. New York: Oxford University Press, 1939.

———. *Repetition.* Trans. Howard and Edna Hong. Princeton, NJ: Princeton University Press, 1983.

Kinz, Susan. "Augustine's Erotic Ascent." *Contemporary Philosophy* 15 (1993): 11–15.

Knight, Deborah. "Selves, Interpreters, Narrators." *Philosophy and Literature* 18 (October 1994): 274–86.

Korsmeyer, Carolyn. "Reason and Morals in the Early Feminist Movement: Mary Wollstonecraft." In *Women and Philosophy: Towards a Theory of Liberation,* ed. Carol C. Gould and Marx W. Wartofsky, 97–111. New York: G. P. Putnam's Sons, 1976.

Kristeva, Julia. *Julia Kristeva Interviews.* Ed. Ross Mitchell Guberman. New York: Columbia University Press, 1996.

Lakoff, Robin. *Language and Woman's Place*. New York: Harper & Row, 1975.

Lloyd, Genevieve. *Being in Time*. New York: Routledge Press, 1993.

———. "The Self as Fiction: Philosophy and Autobiography." *Philosophy and Literature* 10 (October 1986): 168–85.

Luckás, Georg. *The Luckás Reader*. Ed. Arpad Kadarkay. Oxford: Blackwell, 1995.

Lyas, Colin. "The Relevance of the Author's Sincerity." *Philosophy and Fiction*. Ed. Peter Lamarque. Aberdeen, U.K.: Aberdeen University Press, 1983.

MacIntyre, Alasdair. *After Virtue*. 2d. ed. Notre Dame, IN: University of Notre Dame Press, 1984.

———. "Epistemological Crises, Dramatic Narrative, and the Philosophy of Science." *The Monist* 60 (1977): 452–72.

Martin, Robert. *The Philosopher's Dictionary*. 3rd ed. Toronto: Broadview Press, 2002.

Mateas, Michael, and Phoebe Sengers. *Narrative Intelligence*. Ed. Michael Mateas and Phoebe Sengers. Philadelphia, PA: John Benjamins, 2003.

Mathews, William. "Interpreting Lives: Some Hermeneutical Problems in Autobiography and Biography." *Irish Philosophical Journal* 3 (Spring 1986): 27–41.

Misch, Georg. *A History of Autobiography in Antiquity*. Vols. 1 and 2. Ed. Karl Mannheim. London: Routledge & Kegan Paul, 1950.

Nehamas, Alexander. *The Art of Living*. Berkeley: University of California Press, 1998.

———. *How One Becomes Nietzsche: Life As Literature*. Cambridge, MA: Harvard University Press, 1985.

Neill, Thomas P. *Makers of the Modern Mind*. Milwaukee, WI: Bruce, 1949.

Nietzsche, Friedrich. Beyond Good and Evil. Trans. Marianne Cowan. South Bend, IN: Gateway, 1955.

———. *The Birth of Tragedy*. Trans. Walter Kaufmann. New York: Random House, 1967.

———. *Ecce Homo*. Trans. and ed. Walter Kaufmann. New York: Random House, 1967.

———. *The Gay Science*. Trans. Walter Kaufmann. New York: Random House, 1974.

———. *Human, All Too Human*. Trans. R. J. Hollingdale. Cambridge: Cambridge University Press, 1986.

———. *On the Genealogy of Morals*. Trans. Walter Kaufmann. New York: Random House, 1967.

———. *Thus Spoke Zarathustra*. Trans. Walter Kaufmann. New York: Penguin, 1966.

———. *Twilight of the Idols*. Trans. R. J. Hollingdale. New York: Penguin, 1968.

———. *The Will to Power*. Trans. Walter Kaufmann and R. J. Hollingdale. New York: Vintage Press, 1968.

Nozick, Robert. "Personal Identity through Time." In *Personal Identity*, ed. Raymond Martin and John Barresi. Oxford: Blackwell, 2003.

Nussbaum, Martha C. *Love's Knowledge: Essays on Philosophy and Literature*. New York: Oxford University Press, 1990.

Parkes, Graham. "Facing the Self with Masks: Perspectives on the Personal from Nietzsche and the Japanese." *Self and Deception, A Cross-Cultural Philosophical Enquiry*. ed. Roger T. Ames and Wimal Dissanayake, 288-313. Albany: State University of New York Press, 1996.

Pascal, Roy. *Design and Truth in Autobiography*. (Cambridge, MA: Harvard University Press, 1960.

Plato. *The Collected Dialogues of Plato*. Trans. R. Hackforth. Princeton, NJ: Princeton University Press, 1989.

———. *Phaedo*. Trans. by F. J. Church. New York: Macmillan, 1951.

———. *Phaedrus and Letters VII and VIII*. Trans. Walter Hamilton and ed. Betty Radice. New York: Penguin Press, 1973.

———. *The Symposium*. Trans. Alexander Nehamas and Paul Woodruff. Indianapolis, IN, and Cambridge, MA: Hackett, 1989.

Polk, Danne. "Temporal Impermanence and the Disparity of Time and Eternity." *Augustinian Studies* 22 (1991): 63–82.

Rée, Johnathon. *Philosophical Tales*. New York: Methuen & Co., 1987.

Rickman, H. P. *Dilthey Today: A Critical Appraisal of the Contemporary Relevance of His Work*. New York: Greenwood Press, 1988.

Ricoeur, Paul. *Oneself As Another*. Trans. Kathleen Blamey. Chicago: University of Chicago Press, 1992.

Rorty, Richard. *Contingency, Irony, and Solidarity*. New York: Cambridge University Press, 1989.

Rosen, Stanley. *The Limits of Analysis*. New Haven, CT: Yale University Press, 1980.

———. "The Metaphysics of Ordinary Experience." *Harvard Review* (Spring 1995): 41–57.

———. "Squaring the Hermeneutical Circle." *Review of Metaphysics* 44 (June 1991): 707–28.

———. "Suspicion, Deception, and Concealment." *Arion* X (1991): 112–27.

Rosenau, Hartmut. "Self-Reflection and Autobiography—Kierkegaard's Writings about Himself." *History of European Ideas* 20:1–3 (1995): 183–88.

Rousseau, Jean-Jacques. *The Confessions*. Trans. J. M. Cohen. New York: Penguin, 1953.

———. *The Social Contract*. Trans. Maurice Cranston. New York: Penguin, 1968.

Ryle, Gilbert. *The Concept of Mind*. New York: Hutchinson Press, 1949.

Sartre, Jean-Paul. *Being and Nothingness: An Essay on Phenomenological Ontology*. Trans. Hazel E. Barnes. New York: Philosophical Library, 1956.

———. *Nausea*. Trans. Lloyd Alexander. New York: New Directions, 1964.

———. *The Words*. Trans. Bernard Frechtman. New York: George Braziller, 1964.

Schuster, Shlomit. *The Philosopher's Autobiography: A Qualitative Study*. Westport, CT: Praeger, 2003.

Soll, Ivan. "Nietzsche on Cruelty, Asceticism, and the Failure of Hedonism." In *Nietzsche, Genealogy, and Morality*, ed. Richard Schacht, 168–92. Los Angeles: University of California Press, 1994.

Solomon, Robert C. "Self, Deception, and Self-Deception in Philosophy." In *Self and Deception: A Cross-Cultural Philosophical Enquiry*, ed. Roger T. Ames and Wimal Dissanayake, 91–122. Albany: State University of New York Press, 1996.

Stack, George J. "Emerson, Nietzsche, and Naturalistic Ethics." *The Humanist* (November–December 1990): 21–25.

Szabados, Béla. "Autobiography after Wittgenstein." *Journal of Aesthetics and Art Criticism* 50:1 (Winter 1992): 1–12.

Szavaj, Janos. *The Autobiography. Budapest: Akademiai Kiado*, 1984.

Taylor, Charles. *Sources of the Self*. Cambridge, MA: Harvard University Press, 1989.

Trainor, Paul. "Autobiography As Philosophical Argument: Socrates, Descartes, and Collingwood." *Thought* 63 (December 1988): 378–96.

Urmson, J. O., and Jonathan Rée, eds. *The Concise Encyclopedia of Western Philosophy and Philosophers*. New York: Routledge, 2000.

Vaught, Carl. *Access to God in Augustine's Confessions*. Albany: State University of New York Press, 2005.

———. *The Journey toward God in Augustine's Confessions: Books I–VI*. Albany: State University of New York Press, 2003.

———. *The Quest for Wholeness*. Albany: State University of New York Press, 1992.

———. *Encounters with God in Augustine's Confessions*. Albany: State University of New York Press, 2004.

Verene, Donald Phillip. "The Limits of Argument: Argument and Autobiography." *Philosophy and Rhetoric* 26 (1993): 1–8.

Warner, Martin. "Philosophical Autobiography: St. Augustine and John Stuart Mill." In *Philosophy and Literature: Royal Institute of Philosophy Lecture Series* 16, ed. A. Phillips Griffiths, 189–210. Cambridge: Cambridge University Press, 1984.

Warnock, Mary. *Imagination and Time*. Cambridge, MA: Blackwell, 1994.

White, Richard J. "Autobiography against Itself." *Philosophy Today* 35:3–4 (Fall 1991): 291–303.

Wilcox, John T. *Truth and Value in Nietzsche: A Study of His Metaethics and Epistemology*. Ann Arbor: University of Michigan Press, 1974.

Wittgenstein, Ludwig. *Philosophical Investigations*. Trans. G. E. M. Anscombe. New York: Macmillan, 1958.

Wollstonecraft, Mary. *A Vindication of the Rights of Woman*. Ed. Charles W. Hagelman Jr. New York: Norton Press, 1967.

Yancy, George. *The Philosophical i: Personal Reflections on Life in Philosophy*. Ed. George Yancy. Lanham, MD: Rowman & Littlefield, 2002.

Index